Extending Docker

Master the art of making Docker more extensible,
composable, and modular by leveraging plugins
and other supporting tools

Russ McKendrick

BIRMINGHAM - MUMBAI

Extending Docker

First published: June 2016

Production reference: 1100616

Published by Packt Publishing Ltd.
Livery Place
35 Livery Street
Birmingham B3 2PB, UK.

ISBN 978-1-78646-314-2

www.packtpub.com

Credits

Author
Russ McKendrick

Reviewer
Francisco Souza

Commissioning Editor
Pratik Shah

Acquisition Editor
Rahul Nair

Content Development Editor
Mayur Pawanikar

Technical Editor
Danish Shaikh

Copy Editor
Vibha Shukla

Project Coordinator
Nidhi Joshi

Proofreader
Safis Editing

Indexer
Mariammal Chettiyar

Production Coordinator
Arvindkumar Gupta

Cover Work
Arvindkumar Gupta

About the Author

Russ McKendrick is an experienced solution architect who has been working in IT and related industries for the better part of 23 years. During his career, he has had varied responsibilities in a number of industries, ranging from looking after an entire IT infrastructure to providing first-line, second-line, and senior support in client-facing and internal teams for corporate organizations.

Russ works almost exclusively with Linux, using open source systems and tools across dedicated hardware, virtual machines to public and private clouds at Node4 Limited, where he heads up the Open Source solutions team.

About the Reviewer

Francisco Souza is a software engineer working in the video area at *The New York Times*. He is also one of the creators of Tsuru, an open source cloud platform, which is built on top of Docker and other open source solutions, including CloudStack and the Go programming language.

www.PacktPub.com

eBooks, discount offers, and more

Did you know that Packt offers eBook versions of every book published, with PDF and ePub files available? You can upgrade to the eBook version at www.PacktPub.com and as a print book customer, you are entitled to a discount on the eBook copy. Get in touch with us at customercare@packtpub.com for more details.

At www.PacktPub.com, you can also read a collection of free technical articles, sign up for a range of free newsletters and receive exclusive discounts and offers on Packt books and eBooks.

https://www2.packtpub.com/books/subscription/packtlib

Do you need instant solutions to your IT questions? PacktLib is Packt's online digital book library. Here, you can search, access, and read Packt's entire library of books.

Why subscribe?

- Fully searchable across every book published by Packt
- Copy and paste, print, and bookmark content
- On demand and accessible via a web browser

Table of Contents

Preface

In the past few years, Docker has emerged as one of the most exciting new pieces of technology. Numerous companies, both enterprise and start-ups, have embraced the tool.

Several first-party and third-party tools have been developed to extend the core Docker functionality. This book will guide you through the process of installing, configuring, and using these tools, as well as help you understand which is the best tool for the job.

What this book covers

Chapter 1, Introduction to Extending Docker, discusses Docker and some of the problems that it solves. We will also discuss some of the ways in which the core Docker engine can be extended to gain additional functionality.

Chapter 2, Introducing First-party Tools, covers the tools provided by Docker to work alongside the core Docker Engine. These are Docker Toolbox, Docker Compose, Docker Machine, and Docker Swarm.

Chapter 3, Volume Plugins, introduces Docker plugins. We will start by looking at the default volume plugin that ships with Docker and look at three third-party plugins.

Chapter 4, Network Plugins, explains how to extend our container's networking across multiple Docker hosts, both locally and in public clouds.

Chapter 5, Building Your Own Plugin, introduces how to best approach writing your own Docker storage or network plugin.

Chapter 6, Extending Your Infrastructure, covers how to use several established DevOps tools to deploy and manage both your Docker hosts and containers.

Chapter 7, *Looking at Schedulers*, discusses how you can deploy Kubernetes, Amazon ECS, and Rancher, following the previous chapters.

Chapter 8, *Security, Challenges, and Conclusions*, helps to explain the security implications of where you deploy your Docker images from, as well as looking at the various tools that we have covered in the previous chapters and the situations they are best deployed in.

What you need for this book

You will need either an OS X or Windows laptop or desktop PC that is capable of running VirtualBox (`https://www.virtualbox.org/`) and has access to both Amazon Web Service and DigitalOcean accounts with permissions to launch resources.

Who this book is for

This book is aimed at both developers and system administrators who feel constrained by their basic Docker installation and want to take their configuration to the next step by extending the functionality of the core Docker engine to meet the business' and their own ever-changing needs.

Conventions

In this book, you will find a number of text styles that distinguish between different kinds of information. Here are some examples of these styles and an explanation of their meaning.

Code words in text, database table names, folder names, filenames, file extensions, pathnames, dummy URLs, user input, and Twitter handles are shown as follows: "Once installed, you should be able to check whether everything worked as expected by running the Docker `hello-world` container."

A block of code is set as follows:

```
### Dockerfile
FROM php:5.6-apache
MAINTAINER Russ McKendrick <russ@mckendrick.io>
ADD index.php /var/www/html/index.php
```

When we wish to draw your attention to a particular part of a code block, the relevant lines or items are set in bold:

```
version: '2'
services:
  wordpress:
    container_name: "my-wordpress-app"
    image: wordpress
    ports:
      - "80:80"
    environment:
      - "WORDPRESS_DB_HOST=mysql.weave.local:3306"
      - "WORDPRESS_DB_PASSWORD=password"
      - "constraint:node==chapter04-01"
```

Any command-line input or output is written as follows:

```
curl -sSL https://get.docker.com/ | sh
```

New terms and **important words** are shown in bold. Words that you see on the screen, for example, in menus or dialog boxes, appear in the text like this: "To move to the next step of the installation, click on **Continue**."

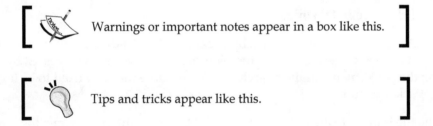

Warnings or important notes appear in a box like this.

Tips and tricks appear like this.

Reader feedback

Feedback from our readers is always welcome. Let us know what you think about this book — what you liked or disliked. Reader feedback is important for us as it helps us develop titles that you will really get the most out of.

To send us general feedback, simply e-mail feedback@packtpub.com, and mention the book's title in the subject of your message.

If there is a topic that you have expertise in and you are interested in either writing or contributing to a book, see our author guide at www.packtpub.com/authors.

Customer support

Now that you are the proud owner of a Packt book, we have a number of things to help you to get the most from your purchase.

Downloading the example code

You can download the example code files for this book from your account at `http://www.packtpub.com`. If you purchased this book elsewhere, you can visit `http://www.packtpub.com/support` and register to have the files e-mailed directly to you.

You can download the code files by following these steps:

1. Log in or register to our website using your e-mail address and password.
2. Hover the mouse pointer on the **SUPPORT** tab at the top.
3. Click on **Code Downloads & Errata**.
4. Enter the name of the book in the **Search** box.
5. Select the book for which you're looking to download the code files.
6. Choose from the drop-down menu where you purchased this book from.
7. Click on **Code Download**.

You can also download the code files by clicking on the **Code Files** button on the book's webpage at the Packt Publishing website. This page can be accessed by entering the book's name in the **Search** box. Please note that you need to be logged in to your Packt account.

Once the file is downloaded, please make sure that you unzip or extract the folder using the latest version of:

*   WinRAR / 7-Zip for Windows
*   Zipeg / iZip / UnRarX for Mac
*   7-Zip / PeaZip for Linux

The code bundle for the book is also hosted on GitHub at `https://github.com/PacktPublishing/ExtendingDocker`. We also have other code bundles from our rich catalog of books and videos available at `https://github.com/PacktPublishing/`. Check them out!

Errata

Although we have taken every care to ensure the accuracy of our content, mistakes do happen. If you find a mistake in one of our books—maybe a mistake in the text or the code—we would be grateful if you could report this to us. By doing so, you can save other readers from frustration and help us improve subsequent versions of this book. If you find any errata, please report them by visiting http://www.packtpub. com/submit-errata, selecting your book, clicking on the **Errata Submission Form** link, and entering the details of your errata. Once your errata are verified, your submission will be accepted and the errata will be uploaded to our website or added to any list of existing errata under the Errata section of that title.

To view the previously submitted errata, go to https://www.packtpub.com/books/ content/support and enter the name of the book in the search field. The required information will appear under the **Errata** section.

Piracy

Piracy of copyrighted material on the Internet is an ongoing problem across all media. At Packt, we take the protection of our copyright and licenses very seriously. If you come across any illegal copies of our works in any form on the Internet, please provide us with the location address or website name immediately so that we can pursue a remedy.

Please contact us at copyright@packtpub.com with a link to the suspected pirated material.

We appreciate your help in protecting our authors and our ability to bring you valuable content.

Questions

If you have a problem with any aspect of this book, you can contact us at questions@packtpub.com, and we will do our best to address the problem.

1
Introduction to Extending Docker

In this chapter, we will discuss the following topics:

- Why Docker has been so widely accepted by the entire industry
- What does a typical container's life cycle look like?
- What plugins and third-party tools will be covered in the upcoming chapters?
- What will you need for the remainder of the chapters?

The rise of Docker

Not very often does a technology come along that is adopted so widely across an entire industry. Since its first public release in March 2013, Docker has not only gained the support of both end users, like you and I, but also industry leaders such as Amazon, Microsoft, and Google.

Docker is currently using the following sentence on their website to describe why you would want to use it:

> *"Docker provides an integrated technology suite that enables development and IT operations teams to build, ship, and run distributed applications anywhere."*

There is a meme, based on the disaster girl photo, which sums up why such a seemingly simple explanation is actually quite important:

So as simple as Docker's description sounds, it's actually a been utopia for most developers and IT operations teams for a number of years to have tool that can ensure that an application can consistently work across the following three main stages of an application's life cycle:

1. Development
2. Staging and Preproduction
3. Production

To illustrate why this used to be a problem before Docker arrived at the scene, let's look at how the services were traditionally configured and deployed. People tended to typically use a mixture of dedicated machines and virtual machines. So let's look at these in more detail.

While this is possible using configuration management tools, such as Puppet, or orchestration tools, such as Ansible, to maintain consistency between server environments, it is difficult to enforce these across both servers and a developer's workstation.

Dedicated machines

Traditionally, these are a single piece of hardware that have been configured to run your application, while the applications have direct access to the hardware, you are constrained by the binaries and libraries you can install on a dedicated machine, as they have to be shared across the entire machine.

To illustrate one potential problem Docker has fixed, let's say you had a single dedicated server that was running your PHP application. When you initially deployed the dedicated machine, all three of the applications, which make up your e-commerce website, worked with PHP 5.6, so there was no problem with compatibility.

Your development team has been slowly working through the three PHP applications. You have deployed it on your host to make them work with PHP 7, as this will give them a good boost in performance. However, there is a single bug that they have not been able to resolve with App2, which means that it will not run under PHP 7 without crashing when a user adds an item to their shopping cart.

If you have a single host running your three applications, you will not be able to upgrade from PHP 5.6 to PHP 7 until your development team has resolved the bug with App2, unless you do one of the following:

- Deploy a new host running PHP 7 and migrate App1 and App3 to it; this could be both time consuming and expensive
- Deploy a new host running PHP 5.6 and migrate App2 to it; again this could be both time consuming and expensive
- Wait until the bug has been fixed; the performance improvements that the upgrade from PHP 5.6 to PHP 7 bring to the application could increase the sales and there is no ETA for the fix

If you go for the first two options, you also need to ensure that the new dedicated machine either matches the developer's PHP 7 environment or that a new dedicated machine is configured in exactly the same way as your existing environment; after all, you don't want to introduce further problems by having a poorly configured machine.

Virtual machines

One solution to the scenario detailed earlier would be to slice up your dedicated machine's resources and make them available to the application by installing a hypervisor such as the following:

- **KVM**: http://www.linux-kvm.org/

- **XenSource**: http://www.xenproject.org/

- **VMware vSphere**: http://www.vmware.com/uk/products/vsphere-hypervisor/

Once installed, you can then install your binaries and libraries on each of the different virtual hosts and also install your applications on each one.

Going back to the scenario given in the dedicated machine section, you will be able to upgrade to PHP 7 on the virtual machines with App1 and App2 installed, while leaving App2 untouched and functional while the development work on the fix.

Great, so what is the catch? From the developer's view, there is none as they have their applications running with the PHP versions, which work best for them; however, from an IT operations point of view:

- **More CPU, RAM, and disk space**: Each of the virtual machines will require additional resources as the overhead of running three guest OS, as well as the three applications have to be taken into account

- **More management**: IT operations now need to patch, monitor, and maintain four machines, the dedicated host machine along with three virtual machines, where as before they only had a single dedicated host.

As earlier, you also need to ensure that the configuration of the three virtual machines that are hosting your applications match the configuration that the developers have been using during the development process; again, you do not want to introduce additional problems due to configuration and process drift between departments.

Dedicated versus virtual machines

The following diagram shows the how a typical dedicated and virtual machine host would be configured:

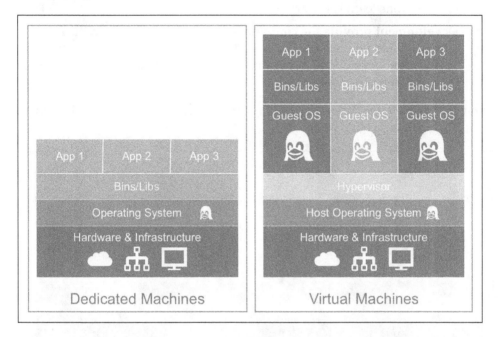

As you can see, the biggest differences between the two are quite clear. You are making a trade-off between resource utilization and being able to run your applications using different binaries/libraries.

Containers

Now we have covered the way in which our applications have been traditionally deployed. Let's look at what Docker adds to the mix.

Back to our scenario of the three applications running on a single host machine. Installing Docker on the host and then deploying each of the applications as a container on this host gives you the benefits of the virtual machine, while vastly reducing the footprint, that is, removing the need for the hypervisor and guest operating system completely, and replacing them with a SlimLine interface directly into the host machines kernel.

The advantages this gives both the IT operations and development teams are as follows:

- **Low overhead**: As mentioned already, the resource and management for the IT operations team is lower
- **Development provide the containers**: Rather than relying on the IT operations team to configure each of the three applications environments to machine the development environment, they can simply pass their containers to be put into production

As you can see from the following diagram, the layers between the application and host operating system have been reduced:

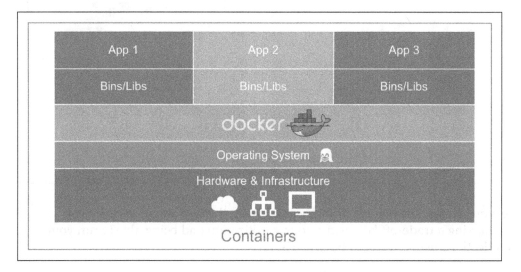

All of this means that the need to use the disaster girl meme at the beginning of this chapter should be now redundant as the development team are shipping the application to the operations in a container with all the configuration, binaries, and libraries intact, which means that if it works in development, it will work in production.

This may seem too good to be true, and to be honest, there is a "but". For most web applications or applications that are pre-compiled static binaries, you shouldn't have a problem.

However, as Docker shares resources with the underlying host machine, such as the Kernel version, if your application needs to be compiled or have a reliance on certain libraries that are only compatible with the shared resources, then you will have to deploy your containers on a like-for-like operating system, and in some cases, hardware.

Docker has tried to address this issue with the acquisition of a company called Unikernel Systems in January 2016. At the time of writing this book, not a lot is known about how Docker is planning to integrate this technology into their core product, if at all. You can find out more about this technology at `https://blog.docker.com/2016/01/unikernel/`.

Everyone should be using Docker?

So, is it really that simple, should everyone stop using virtual machines and use containers instead?

In July 2014, Wes Felter, Alexandre Ferreira, Ram Rajamony, and Juan Rubio published an IBM research report titled An Updated Performance Comparison of Virtual Machines and Linux Containers and concluded:

> *"Both VMs and containers are mature technology that have benefited from a decade of incremental hardware and software optimizations. In general, Docker equals or exceeds KVM performance in every case we tested. Our results show that both KVM and Docker introduce negligible overhead for CPU and memory performance (except in extreme cases). For I/O intensive workloads, both forms of virtualization should be used carefully."*

It then goes on to say the following:

> *"Although containers themselves have almost no overhead, Docker is not without performance gotchas. Docker volumes have noticeably better performance than files stored in AUFS. Docker's NAT also introduces overhead for workloads with high packet rates. These features represent a tradeoff between ease of management and performance and should be considered on a case-by-case basis."*

The full 12-page report, which is an interesting comparison to the traditional technologies we have discussed and containers, can be downloaded from the following URL:

`http://domino.research.ibm.com/library/cyberdig.nsf/papers/0929052195DD819C85257D2300681E7B/$File/rc25482.pdf`

Less than a year after the IBM research report was published, Docker introduced plugins for its ecosystem. One of the best descriptions I came across was from a Docker software engineer, Jessica Frazelle, who described the release as having batteries included, but replaceable, meaning that the core functionality can be easily replaced with third-party tools that can then be used to address the conclusions of the IBM research report.

At the time of writing this book, Docker currently supports volume and network driver plugins. Additional plugin types to expose more of the Docker core to third parties will be added in the future.

Life cycle of a container

Before we look at the various plugins and ways to extend Docker, we should look at what a typical life cycle of a container looks like.

Using the example from the previous section, let's launch the official PHP 5.6 container and then replace it with the official PHP 7.0 one.

Installing Docker

Before we can launch our containers, we need to get Docker up and running; luckily, this is a simple process.

In the following chapter, we will be getting into bootstrapping our Docker environments using Docker Machine; however, for now, let's perform a quick installation of Docker on a cloud server.

The following instructions will work on Ubuntu 14.04 LTS or CentOS 7 instances hosted on any of the public clouds, such as the following:

- **Digital Ocean**: https://www.digitalocean.com/
- **Amazon Web Services**: https://aws.amazon.com/
- **Microsoft Azure**: https://azure.microsoft.com/
- **VMware vCloud Air**: http://vcloud.vmware.com/

You can also try a local virtual machine running locally using the following:

- **Vagrant**: https://www.vagrantup.com/
- **Virtualbox**: https://www.virtualbox.org/
- **VMware Fusion**: http://www.vmware.com/uk/products/fusion/
- **VMware Workstation**: http://www.vmware.com/uk/products/workstation/

I am going to be using a CentOS 7 server hosted in Digital Ocean as it is convenient to quickly launch a machine and then terminate it.

Once you have your server up and running, you can install Docker from the official Yum or APT repositories by running the following command:

```
curl -sSL https://get.docker.com/ | sh
```

If, like me, you are running a CentOS 7 server, you will need to ensure that the service is running. To do this, type the following command:

```
systemctl start docker
```

Once installed, you should be able to check whether everything worked as expected by running the Docker `hello-world` container by entering the following command:

```
docker run hello-world
```

Once you have Docker installed and confirmed that it runs as expected, you can download the latest builds of the official PHP 5.6 and PHP 7.0 images by running the following command:

```
docker pull php:5.6-apache && docker pull php:7.0-apache
```

For more information on the official PHP images, refer to the Docker Hub page at `https://hub.docker.com/_/php/`.

Now that we have the images downloaded, it's time to deploy our application as we are keeping it really simple; all we going to be deploying is a `phpinfo page`, this will confirm the version of PHP we are running along with details on the rest of the containers environment:

```
mkdir app1 && cd app1
echo "<?php phpinfo(); ?>" > index.php
```

Now the index.php file is in place. Let's start the PHP 5.6 container by running the following command:

```
docker run --name app1 -d -p 80:80 -it -v "$PWD":/var/www/html php:5.6-apache
```

This will have launch an `app1` container. If you enter the IP address of your server instance or a domain which resolves to, you should see a page that shows that you are running PHP 5.6:

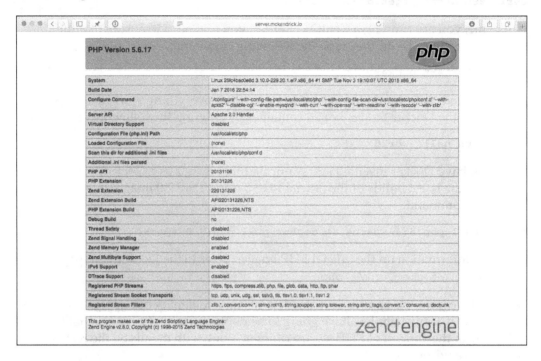

Now that you have PHP 5.6 up and running, let's upgrade it to PHP 7. Traditionally, this would mean installing a new set of packages using either third-party YUM or APT repositories; speaking from experience, this process can be a little hit and miss, depending on the compatibility with the packages for the previous versions of PHP that you have installed.

Luckily in our case, we are using Docker, so all we have to do is terminate our PHP 5.6 container and replace with one running PHP 7. At any time during this process, you can check the containers that are running using the following command:

```
docker ps
```

This will print a list of the running containers to the screen (as seen in the screenshot at the end of this section). To stop and remove the PHP 5.6 container, run the following command:

```
docker rm -f app1
```

Once the container has terminated, run the following command to launch a PHP 7
container:

```
docker run --name app1 -d -p 80:80 -it -v "$PWD":/var/www/html php:7.0-
apache
```

If you return to the `phpinfo` page in your browser, you will see that it is now
running PHP 7:

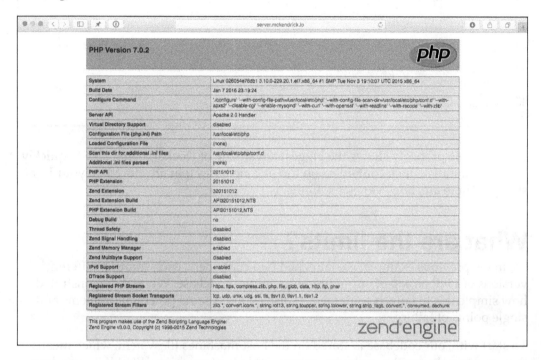

To terminate the PHP 7 container, run the `docker rm` command again:

```
docker rm -f app1
```

A full copy of the preceding terminal session can be found in the following screenshot:

```
root@server:~/app1 — ssh server — 181×26
[root@server ~]# docker pull php:5.6-apache && docker pull php:7.0-apache
5.6-apache: Pulling from library/php

Digest: sha256:9a160d036f8c60f25a66570e950db7ad45b1c3d836f96ce0ad3319b5fdbe3c50
Status: Image is up to date for php:5.6-apache
7.0-apache: Pulling from library/php

Digest: sha256:c5157937eb7848eeaf2378838215151f55e99684b98861ecfe0c2371a1a503f3
Status: Image is up to date for php:7.0-apache
[root@server ~]# mkdir app1 && cd app1
[root@server app1]# echo "<?php phpinfo(); ?>" > index.php
[root@server app1]# docker run --name app1 -d -p 80:80 -it --name app1 -v "$PWD":/var/www/html php:5.6-apache
ec6397f30fc25e057fd1a556b59911328048b0d1ce32d242057fa17cd2573338
[root@server app1]# docker ps
CONTAINER ID        IMAGE              COMMAND               CREATED           STATUS            PORTS                  NAMES
ec6397f30fc2        php:5.6-apache     "apache2-foreground"  4 seconds ago     Up 3 seconds      0.0.0.0:80->80/tcp     app1
[root@server app1]# docker rm -f app1
app1
[root@server app1]# docker run --name app1 -d -p 80:80 -it --name app1 -v "$PWD":/var/www/html php:7.0-apache
13a1b6447f2bbe18f0c6c55f61eba061d27e1e18e6292f65c9950041c893bb0f
[root@server app1]# docker ps
CONTAINER ID        IMAGE              COMMAND               CREATED           STATUS            PORTS                  NAMES
13a1b6447f2b        php:7.0-apache     "apache2-foreground"  11 seconds ago    Up 10 seconds     0.0.0.0:80->80/tcp     app1
[root@server app1]# docker rm -f app1
app1
[root@server app1]# 
```

This example probably shows the biggest advantage of Docker, being able to quickly and consistently launch containers on top of code bases that are stored on your local storage. There are, however, some limits.

What are the limits?

So, in the previous example, we launched two containers, each running different versions of PHP on top of our (extremely simple) codebase. While it demonstrated how simple it is to launch containers, it also exposed some potential problems and single points of failure.

To start with, our codebase is stored on the host machines filesystem, which means that we can only run the container on our single-host machine. What if it goes down for any reason?

There are a few ways we could get around this with a vanilla Docker installation. The first is use the official PHP container as a base to build our own custom image so that we can ship our code along with PHP. To do this, add `Dockerfile` to the `app1` directory that contains the following content:

```
### Dockerfile
FROM php:5.6-apache
MAINTAINER Russ McKendrick <russ@mckendrick.io>
ADD index.php /var/www/html/index.php
```

We can also build our custom image using the following command:

```
docker build -t app1:php-5.6 .
```

When you run the build command, you will see the following output:

```
● ● ●                          root@server:~/app1 — ssh server — 111×24
[root@server ~]# cd ~/app1/
[root@server app1]# docker build -t app1:php-5.6 .
Sending build context to Docker daemon 3.072 kB
Step 1 : FROM php:5.6-apache
 ---> e83c39465589
Step 2 : MAINTAINER Russ McKendrick <russ@mckendrick.io>
 ---> Running in dee77e251df8
 ---> fecb38909ed8
Removing intermediate container dee77e251df8
Step 3 : ADD index.php /var/www/html/index.php
 ---> 0576a9430ce5
Removing intermediate container 3f64b2f23252
Successfully built 0576a9430ce5
[root@server app1]# docker images
REPOSITORY          TAG               IMAGE ID          CREATED             VIRTUAL SIZE
app1                php-5.6           0576a9430ce5      55 seconds ago      480.4 MB
php                 7.0-apache        2f16964f48ba      4 days ago          521 MB
php                 5.6-apache        e83c39465589      4 days ago          480.4 MB
hello-world         latest            0a6ba66e537a      3 months ago        960 B
[root@server app1]#
```

Once you have your image built, you could push it as a private image to the Docker Hub or your own self-hosted private registry; another option is to export the custom image as a `.tar` file and then copy it to each of the instances that need to run your custom PHP container.

To do this, you will run the Docker save command:

docker save app1:php-5.6 > ~/app1-php-56.tar

This will make a copy of our custom image, as you can see from the following terminal output, the image should be around a `482M` tar file:

```
● ● ●                          root@server:~/app1 — ssh server — 111×6
[root@server app1]# docker save app1:php-5.6 > ~/app1-php-56.tar
[root@server app1]# ls -lhat ~/app1-php-56.tar
-rw-r--r-- 1 root root 482M Jan 12 20:56 /root/app1-php-56.tar
[root@server app1]#
```

Now that we have a copy of the image as a tar file, we can copy it to our other host machines. Once you have copied the tar file, you will need to run the Docker load command to import it onto our second host:

docker load < ~/app1-php-56.tar

Then we can launch a container that has our code baked in by running the following command:

```
docker run --name app1 -d -p 80:80 -it app1:php-5.6
```

The following terminal output gives you an idea of what you should see when importing and running our custom container:

```
[root@server ~]# docker images
REPOSITORY          TAG            IMAGE ID          CREATED            VIRTUAL SIZE
hello-world         latest         0a6ba66e537a      3 months ago       960 B
[root@server ~]# docker load < ~/app1-php-56.tar
[root@server ~]# docker images
REPOSITORY          TAG            IMAGE ID          CREATED            VIRTUAL SIZE
app1                php-5.6        f32da3d8c333      17 minutes ago     480.4 MB
hello-world         latest         0a6ba66e537a      3 months ago       960 B
[root@server ~]# docker run --name app1 -d -p 80:80 -it app1:php-5.6
dbbb9da1ed67834fa83cab290a3f1b073dd2a011541d1314fb836b83454f9f3d
[root@server ~]# docker ps
CONTAINER ID      IMAGE           COMMAND               CREATED          STATUS          PORTS                 NAMES
dbbb9da1ed67      app1:php-5.6    "apache2-foreground"  3 seconds ago    Up 2 seconds    0.0.0.0:80->80/tcp    app1
[root@server ~]# 
```

So far so good? Well, yes and no.

It's great that we can add our codebase to a custom image out of the box, then ship the image via either of the following ways:

- The official Docker Hub
- Our own private registry
- Exporting the image as a tar file and copying it across our other hosts

However, what about containers that are processing data that is changing all the time, such as a database? What are our options for a database?

Consider that we are running the official MySQL container from `https://hub.docker.com/_/mysql/`, we could mount the folder where our databases are stored (that is, `/var/lib/mysql/`) from the host machine, but that could cause us permissions issues with the files once they are mounted within the container.

To get around this, we could create a data volume that contains a copy of our `/var/lib/mysql/` directory, this means that we are keeping our databases separate from our container so that we can stop, start, and even replace the MySQL container without destroying our data.

This approach, however, binds us to running our MySQL container on a single host, which is a big single point of failure.

If we have the resources available, we could make sure that the host where we are hosting our MySQL container has multiple redundancies, such as a number of hard drives in RAID configuration that allows us to weather more than one drive failure. We can have multiple **power supply units (PSU)** being fed by different power feeds, so if we have any problems with the power from one of our feeds, the host machine stays online.

We can also have the same with the networking on the host machine, NICs plugged into different switches being fed by different power feeds and network providers.

While this does leave us with a lot of redundancy, we are still left with a single host machine, which is now getting quite expensive as all of this redundancy with multiple drives, networking, and power feeds are additional costs on top of what we are already paying for our host machine.

So, what's the solution?

This is where extending Docker comes in, while Docker, out of the box, does not support the moving of volumes between host servers, we can plug in a filesystem extension that allows us to migrate volumes between hosts or mount a volume from a shared filesystem, such as NFS.

If we have this in place for our MySQL container, should there be a problem with the host machine, there will be no problem for us as the data volume can be mounted on another host.

Once we have the volume mounted, it can carry on where it left off, as we have our data on a volume that is being replicated to the new host or is accessible via a filesystem share from some redundant storage, such as a SAN.

The same can also be said for networking. As mentioned in the summary of the IBM research report, Docker NAT-based networking could be a bottleneck when it comes to performance, as well as designing your container infrastructure. If it is a problem, then you can add a networking extension and offload your containers network to a **software-defined network (SDN)** rather than have the core of Docker manage the networking using NAT and bridged interfaces within iptables on the host machine.

Once you introduce this level of functionality to the core of Docker, it can get difficult to manage your containers. In an ideal world, you shouldn't have to worry about which host your container is running on or if your container/host machine stops responding for any reason, then your containers will not automatically pop up on another host somewhere within your container network and carry on where it left off.

In the following chapters of this book, we will be looking at how to achieve some of the concepts that we have discussed in this chapter, and we will look at tools written by Docker, designed to run alongside the core Docker engine. While these tools may not be as functional as some of the tools we will be looking at in the later chapters, they serve as a good introduction to some of the core concepts that we will be covering when it comes to creating clusters of Docker hosts and then orchestrating your containers.

Once we have looked at these tools, we will look at volume and networking plugins. We will cover a few of the more well-known plugins that add functionality to the Docker core that allows us to have a more redundant platform.

Once we have been hands-on with pre-written plugins, we will look at the best way to approach writing your own plugin.

In the final chapters of the book, we will start to look at third-party tools that allow you to configure, deploy, and manage the whole life cycle of your containers.

Summary

In this chapter, we have looked at Docker and some of the problems it solves. We have also discussed some of the ways in which the core Docker engine can be extended and the problems that you can solve with the additional functionality that you gain by extending Docker.

In the next chapter, we will look at four different tools provided by Docker to make deploying, managing, and configuring Docker host instances and containers as simple and seamless as possible.

2
Introducing First-party Tools

Docker provides several tools that extend the functionality outside of the core Docker engine. In this chapter, you will walk-through installing, configuring, and running the following tools:

- Docker Toolbox
- Docker Machine
- Docker Swarm
- Docker Compose

These tools, while not as functional as some of the more advanced ones that we will be working with in the upcoming chapters, will serve as a good introduction to both adding additional functionality to core Docker engine as well as concepts for deploying and orchestrating your containers, which we will be doing more of towards the end of the book.

Docker Toolbox

Before we start to look at how to use the three other tools, we should look at installing them on our local machine. In the previous chapter, we downloaded a script supplied by Docker and piped it through bash to quickly configure the official Docker YUM or APT repository (depending on the operating system you are running) on an already provisioned server, the command we executed was as follows:

```
curl -sSL https://get.docker.com/ | sh
```

This is useful if you already have a Linux-based server up and running on one of the many cloud services or locally on virtual machine; however, what if you want to install Docker on a non-Linux operating system such as Mac OSX or Windows?

Always check the source. It is best practice to check the source of the bash script that you are going to be downloading and installing; in our case, you can check this by going to `https://get.docker.com/` in your browser.

Before we look at the tools that Docker provides to do just that, we should answer the question why?

Why install Docker locally?

So, why would we want to install Docker Toolbox, Compose, Machine, and Swarm on a non-Linux machine? Well, to start with, you need to remember that Docker, at its core, is an API to Linux Kernel-based technologies, such as run (`https://github.com/opencontainers/runc`) and LXC (`https://linuxcontainers.org`), so while you will not be able to launch containers on your Mac OS X or Windows machine, you will be able to interact with a Docker installation on a Linux machine.

Being able to interact with Docker from your local machine means that you launch and interact with containers across multiple hosts that can be hosted externally on a public cloud/hosting service or locally on a virtual machine.

Luckily, Docker has you covered for installing Docker and the three other services that we are going to be looking at in this chapter on your local machine.

Installing Docker Toolbox

Docker provides a global installer for all of their tools called Docker Toolbox, it makes installing the following software as painless as possible:

- Docker Client
- Docker Machine
- Docker Compose
- Docker Kitematic
- VM VirtualBox

To get started, you will need to be running a machine that either has Mac OS X 10.8+ or has Windows 7+ installed. In my case, I am running Mac OS X 10.11 (El Capitan); there is very little difference between the Mac OS X and Windows installers:

1. First of all, to get started, you will need to download the installer from the Docker website. You can find links to download an executable for your chosen operating system at `https://www.docker.com/docker-toolbox/`.

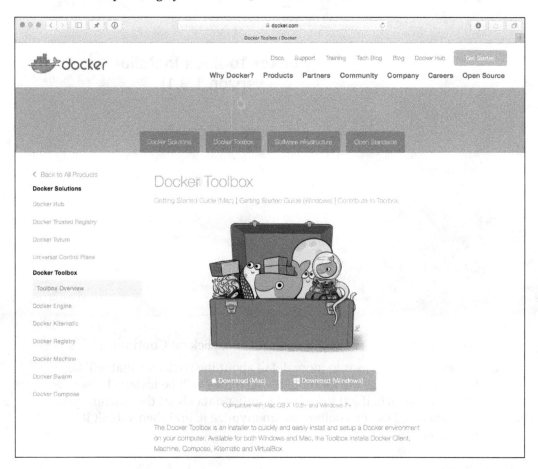

2. Once you have downloaded the installer, you can launch it by double-clicking on it. You will then be presented by a series of screens and install options.

The first screen is a welcome page that confirms the version of the toolbox you are running. If you downloaded from the page in the preceding screenshot, then you will always have the latest version:

3. To move to the next step of the installation, click on **Continue**.

4. The next screen goes into more detail about the packages that will be installed, as well as the location at which they will be installed. There is also a box, which, if left ticked, will gather data about the machine you are installing Docker Toolbox on, anonymize it, and then submit it back to Docker.

This information is useful in giving Docker an idea about the types of machine their software is being installed on, and also it will report back any errors that you may encounter when running the installer:

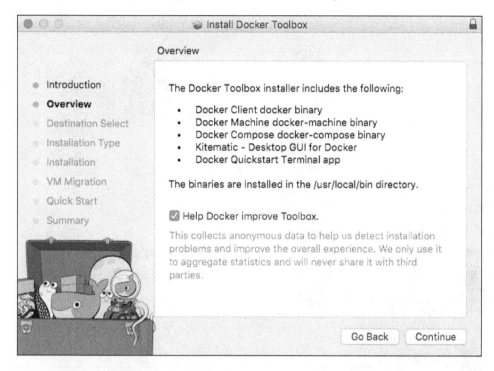

I always recommend keeping this box ticked, as it all goes toward Docker making a better product and improving the experience of future versions of the installer.

5. To progress to the next step of the installation, click on **Continue**.

6. The next screen will give you the option of which disk you would like to install the various tools on. In most cases, you should stick with the defaults, unless you are running applications across multiple drives:

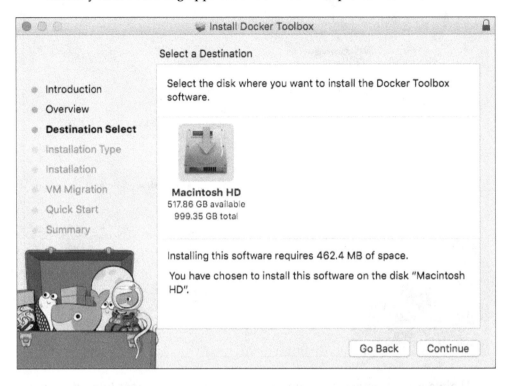

7. To move on to the next step of the installation, again click on the **Continue** button.

8. For majority of the people, a standard installation will be enough; however, if its not to install one of the tools, you can click the **Customize** button. The only two tools you have to install are the Docker Client and Docker Machine.

As I want to install all of the tools, I have chosen to go with the standard installation:

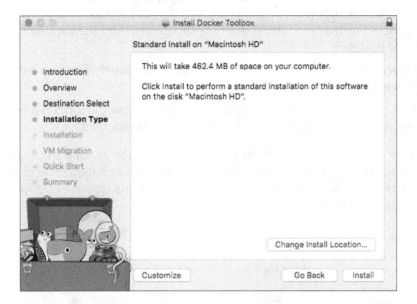

9. Once you have chosen either a standard or custom installation, you can perform the installation by clicking the **Install** button.

10. The installation itself takes a few minutes, during which you will get feedback on the task the installer is running:

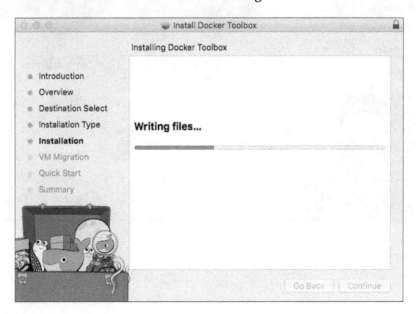

11. Once the installation is complete, click on the **Continue** button.

    As running the installer also acts as an upgrader for any components you have installed, it will run a check to see if any of the files managed by the services (such as the virtual machine images used by the various tools) need to be updated.

    Depending on the size of any updates and how much data you have, this process can take several minutes.

    This process only applies to updates, so if you have performed a fresh installation like I have done, this section will be skipped.

12. Now that the tools have been installed, you will be given the options of launching either the Docker Quickstart Terminal or Kitematic. For the purpose of this book, we will be skipping past this screen by clicking on the **Continue** button:

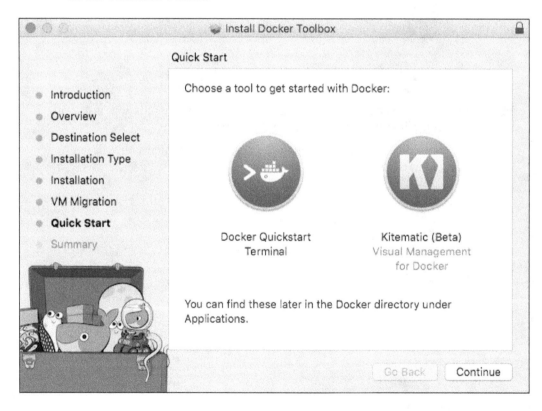

13. If everything has gone as planned, you will see a message confirming that the installation has been completed and you can click on the **Close** button to quit the installer:

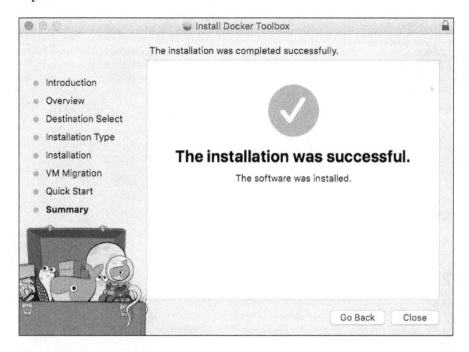

Now, you have all of the tools installed on your local machine to continue with the rest of the chapter and the book.

Before we start to look at the individual tools, we need to configure the Docker agent. To do this, run the **Docker Quickstart Terminal** application. If you have multiple terminal emulators installed, it will pop up a prompt asking you which one you would like to use; I prefer to use the one that ships with Mac OS X, so I chose Terminal.

Once you have made your selection, a new terminal window will open and the application will configure your local installation of Docker for you:

```
● ● ●                          russ — bash --login — 109×54
Creating CA: /Users/russ/.docker/machine/certs/ca.pem
Creating client certificate: /Users/russ/.docker/machine/certs/cert.pem
Running pre-create checks...
(default) Image cache directory does not exist, creating it at /Users/russ/.docker/machine/cache...
(default) No default Boot2Docker ISO found locally, downloading the latest release...
(default) Latest release for github.com/boot2docker/boot2docker is v1.9.1
(default)
(default) Boot2Docker v1.9.1 has a known issue with AUFS.
(default) See here for more details: https://github.com/docker/docker/issues/18180
(default) Consider specifying another storage driver (e.g. 'overlay') using '--engine-storage-driver' instead
.
(default)
(default) Downloading /Users/russ/.docker/machine/cache/boot2docker.iso from https://github.com/boot2docker/b
oot2docker/releases/download/v1.9.1/boot2docker.iso...
(default) 0%....10%....20%....30%....40%....50%....60%....70%....80%....90%....100%
Creating machine...
(default) Copying /Users/russ/.docker/machine/cache/boot2docker.iso to /Users/russ/.docker/machine/machines/d
efault/boot2docker.iso...
(default) Creating VirtualBox VM...
(default) Creating SSH key...
(default) Starting the VM...
(default) Waiting for an IP...
Waiting for machine to be running, this may take a few minutes...
Machine is running, waiting for SSH to be available...
Detecting operating system of created instance...
Detecting the provisioner...
Provisioning with boot2docker...
Copying certs to the local machine directory...
Copying certs to the remote machine...
Setting Docker configuration on the remote daemon...
Checking connection to Docker...
Docker is up and running!
To see how to connect Docker to this machine, run: /usr/local/bin/docker-machine env default


                         ##         .
                   ## ## ##        ==
                ## ## ## ## ##    ===
            /"""""""""""""""""""\___/ ===
       ~~~ {~~ ~~~~ ~~~ ~~~~ ~~~ ~ /  ===- ~~~
            _____ o          __/
              \    \        __/
               _____/


docker is configured to use the default machine with IP 192.168.99.100
For help getting started, check out the docs at https://docs.docker.com

russ in
⚡ docker --version
Docker version 1.9.1, build a34a1d5
russ in
⚡ ▯
```

In my case, I got the preceding terminal output when launching the **Docker Quickstart Terminal** application.

Docker Machine

So, when you ran the **Docker Quickstart Terminal** application, it created a bunch of certificates, SSH keys, and configured your user's environment to run Docker. It also launched a virtual machine running Docker.

Developing locally

The **Docker Quickstart Terminal** application did this using Docker machine, you can check the status of the machine launched by the application by running the following command:

```
docker-machine active
```

This will list the names of any active machines, the default machine launched when you first install Docker is called `default`, if you run:

```
docker-machine status default
```

It should tell you that the virtual machine is currently running. Finally, you should be able to SSH into the virtual machine by running the following command:

```
docker-machine ssh default
```

You will notice that when you SSH into the virtual machine, it is running the Boot2Docker distribution.

> Boot2Docker is an extremely lightweight Linux distribution based on Tiny Core Linux, and its one purpose is to run Docker. Due to this, the entire distribution comes in at less than 30 MB, and it boots in around five seconds, which makes it perfect for running local development machines. For more information on Boot2Docker, refer to http://boot2docker. io/, and for Tiny Core Linux, refer to http://tinycorelinux.net/.

You should something similar to the following terminal session when running these commands:

```
● ● ●                           russ — bash --login — 111×37
russ in
ϟ docker-machine active
default
russ in
ϟ docker-machine status default
Running
russ in
ϟ docker-machine ssh default
                        ##         .
                  ## ## ##        ==
               ## ## ## ## ##    ===
           /""""""""""""""""\___/ ===
      ~~~ {~~ ~~~~ ~~~ ~~~~ ~~ ~ /  ===- ~~~
           _____ o           __/
             \    \         __/
              _____/

  _                 _   ____     _            _
 | |__   ___   ___ | |_|___ \ __| | ___   ___| | _____ _ __
 | '_ \ / _ \ / _ \| __| __) / _` |/ _ \ / __| |/ / _ \ '__|
 | |_) | (_) | (_) | |_ / __/ (_| | (_) | (__|   <  __/ |
 |_.__/ \___/ \___/ \__|_____,_|\___/ \___|_|\_\___|_|
Boot2Docker version 1.9.1, build master : cef800b - Fri Nov 20 19:33:59 UTC 2015
Docker version 1.9.1, build a34a1d5
docker@default:~$ cat /etc/*release
NAME=Boot2Docker
VERSION=1.9.1
ID=boot2docker
ID_LIKE=tcl
VERSION_ID=1.9.1
PRETTY_NAME="Boot2Docker 1.9.1 (TCL 6.4.1); master : cef800b - Fri Nov 20 19:33:59 UTC 2015"
ANSI_COLOR="1;34"
HOME_URL="http://boot2docker.io"
SUPPORT_URL="https://github.com/boot2docker/boot2docker"
BUG_REPORT_URL="https://github.com/boot2docker/boot2docker/issues"
docker@default:~$ exit
russ in
ϟ ▯
```

There isn't much need to SSH into the virtual machine, though, as the Docker client that was installed by toolbox has been configured to connect to the Docker Engine on the virtual machine, this means that when you run the Docker commands locally, it passes all the calls through Docker on the virtual machine, try running the `hello-world` container:

```
docker run hello-world
```

You should see the following output:

```
● ○ ●                          russ — bash --login — 111×37
russ in ~
⚡  docker-machine active
default
russ in ~
⚡  docker-machine status default
Running
russ in ~
⚡  docker-machine ssh default
                        ##         .
                  ## ## ##        ==
               ## ## ## ## ##    ===
           /"""""""""""""""""""\___/ ===
      ~~~ {~~ ~~~~ ~~~ ~~~~ ~~ ~ /  ===- ~~~
           _____ o           __/
             \    \         __/
              _____/


 _                 _   ____     _            _
| |__   ___   ___ | |_|___ \ __| | ___   ___| | _____ _ __
| '_ \ / _ \ / _ \| __| __) / _` |/ _ \ / __| |/ / _ \ '__|
| |_) | (_) | (_) | |_ / __/ (_| | (_) | (__|   <  __/ |
|_.__/ \___/ \___/ \__|_____,_|\___/ \___|_|\_\___|_|
Boot2Docker version 1.9.1, build master : cef800b - Fri Nov 20 19:33:59 UTC 2015
Docker version 1.9.1, build a34a1d5
docker@default:~$ cat /etc/*release
NAME=Boot2Docker
VERSION=1.9.1
ID=boot2docker
ID_LIKE=tcl
VERSION_ID=1.9.1
PRETTY_NAME="Boot2Docker 1.9.1 (TCL 6.4.1); master : cef800b - Fri Nov 20 19:33:59 UTC 2015"
ANSI_COLOR="1;34"
HOME_URL="http://boot2docker.io"
SUPPORT_URL="https://github.com/boot2docker/boot2docker"
BUG_REPORT_URL="https://github.com/boot2docker/boot2docker/issues"
docker@default:~$ exit
russ in ~
⚡  ▯
```

At this stage, you may be thinking to yourself, this all is very good, but it's hardly a tool to get excited about. Well, you are wrong. Docker Machine has a few more tricks up its sleeve than being able to launch a Boot2Docker virtual machine locally.

Heading into the cloud

Docker Machine is able to connect to the following services, provision an instance, and configure your local Docker client to be able to communicate to the cloud-based instance.

The public cloud providers that currently are supported are as follows:

- **Amazon Web Services (AWS)**: https://aws.amazon.com/
- **DigitalOcean**: https://www.digitalocean.com/
- **Microsoft Azure**: https://azure.microsoft.com/
- **Google Compute Engine**: https://cloud.google.com/compute/
- **Rackspace**: http://www.rackspace.co.uk/cloud/

- **IBM SoftLayer**: `http://www.softlayer.com`
- **Exoscale**: `https://www.exoscale.ch/`
- **VMware vCloud Air**: `http://vcloud.vmware.com/`

The following self-hosted platforms can also be used:

- **OpenStack**: `https://www.openstack.org/`
- **Microsoft Hyper-V**: `http://www.microsoft.com/virtualization/`
- **VMware vSphere**: `http://www.vmware.com/uk/products/vsphere/`

The DigitalOcean driver

Let's start creating some instances in the cloud. First, let's launch a machine in DigitalOcean.

There are two prerequisites for launching an instance with Docker Machine in DigitalOcean, the first is a DigitalOcean account and the second is an API token.

To sign up for a DigitalOcean account, visit `https://www.digitalocean.com/` and click on the **Sign Up** button. Once you have logged in to your account, you can generate an API token by clicking on the **API** link in the top menu.

To grab your token, click on the **Generate New Token** button and follow the on-screen instructions:

 You only get one chance to make a record of your token, make sure that you store it somewhere safe, as it will allow anyone who has it to launch instances into your account.

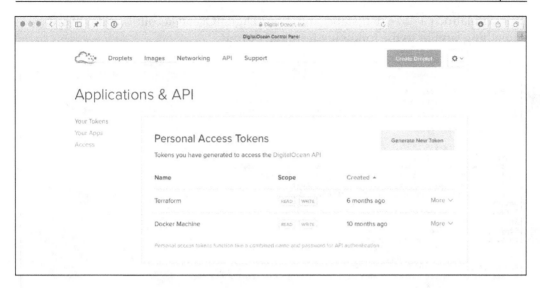

Once you have the token, you can launch your instance using Docker Machine. To do this, run the following command; make sure to replace the example API token with your own:

> Using a backslash: As we have a lot options to pass to the `docker-machine` command, we are using \ to split the command over multiple lines so that it's easier to follow what is going on.

```
docker-machine create \
    --driver digitalocean \
    --digitalocean-access-token
sdnjkjdfgkjb345kjdgljknqwetkjwhgoih314rjkwergoiyu34rjkherglkhrg0 \
    dotest
```

This will launch a `dotest` instance into your DigitalOcean account, you will see something similar to the following terminal output:

```
russ in
⚡ docker-machine create \
    --driver digitalocean \
    --digitalocean-access-token sdnjkjdfgkjb345kjdgljknqwetkjwhgoih314rjkwergoiyu34rjkherglkhrg0 \
    dotest
Running pre-create checks...
Creating machine...
(dotest) Creating SSH key...
(dotest) Creating Digital Ocean droplet...
(dotest) Waiting for IP address to be assigned to the Droplet...
Waiting for machine to be running, this may take a few minutes...
Machine is running, waiting for SSH to be available...
Detecting operating system of created instance...
Detecting the provisioner...
Provisioning with ubuntu(systemd)...
Installing Docker...
Copying certs to the local machine directory...
Copying certs to the remote machine...
Setting Docker configuration on the remote daemon...
Checking connection to Docker...
Docker is up and running!
To see how to connect Docker to this machine, run: docker-machine env dotest
russ in
⚡ ▯
```

If you check your DigitalOcean control panel, you will now see that the instance that was created by Docker Machine is listed here:

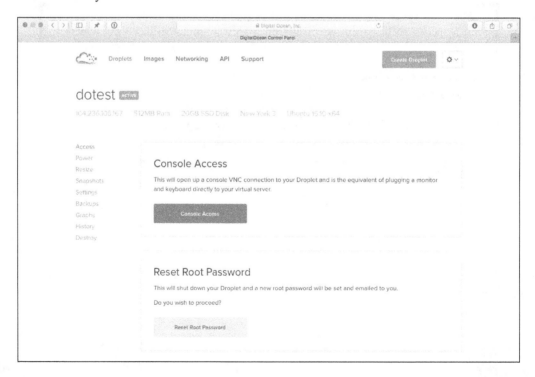

Now we have two instances launched by Docker Machine, one running locally running on our machine called `default` and one hosted in DigitalOcean called `dotest`. We can confirm this by running the following command:

docker-machine ls

This will return all of the machines we have running and confirm their state, IP address, Docker version, and name. There is also a column that allows you to know which of the two machines your local environment is configured to communicate with:

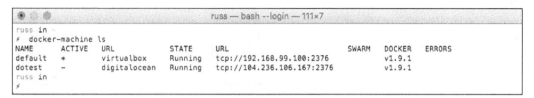

In the preceding example, our local Docker client is configured to communicate with the `default` instance, which is the run running locally. Let's change it so that it interacts with the DigitalOcean instance.

To do this, you have change some local environment variables, luckily, Docker Machine provides an easy way to find out what these are and also change them.

To find out what they all you have to do is simple, run the following command:

docker-machine env dotest

This will tell you exactly what you need to run to change from the `default` machine to `dotest`. The best thing is that the command itself formats the results in such a way that they can be executed, so we run the command again, but this time in a way where the output will be executed:

eval $(docker-machine env dotest)

Now if you get a listing from Docker Machine, you will notice that the `dotest` environment is now the active one:

```
                              russ — bash --login — 111×17
russ in
⚡ docker-machine env dotest
export DOCKER_TLS_VERIFY="1"
export DOCKER_HOST="tcp://104.236.106.167:2376"
export DOCKER_CERT_PATH="/Users/russ/.docker/machine/machines/dotest"
export DOCKER_MACHINE_NAME="dotest"
# Run this command to configure your shell:
# eval $(docker-machine env dotest)
russ in
⚡ eval $(docker-machine env dotest)
russ in
⚡ docker-machine ls
NAME       ACTIVE   URL           STATE     URL                          SWARM   DOCKER   ERRORS
default    -        virtualbox    Running   tcp://192.168.99.100:2376            v1.9.1
dotest     *        digitalocean  Running   tcp://104.236.106.167:2376           v1.9.1
russ in
⚡ 
```

Now that we have our DigitalOcean instance active, you can run the `docker` command on your local machine, and they will have been executed on the DigitalOcean instance. Let's test this by running the hello-world container.

If you run the following command, you should see the image download and then the output of running the hello-world container:

```
docker run hello-world
```

If you then run the following command, you will see that the hello-world image exited a few seconds ago:

```
docker ps -a
```

This is demonstrated by the following Terminal output:

```
● ● ●                              russ — bash --login — 145×50
russ in
↯  docker run hello-world
Unable to find image 'hello-world:latest' locally
latest: Pulling from library/hello-world

b901d36b6f2f: Pull complete
0a6ba66e537a: Pull complete
Digest: sha256:8be990ef2aeb16dbcb9271ddfe2610fa6658d13f6dfb8bc72074cc1ca36966a7
Status: Downloaded newer image for hello-world:latest

Hello from Docker.
This message shows that your installation appears to be working correctly.
russ in
↯  docker ps -a
CONTAINER ID      IMAGE           COMMAND          CREATED          STATUS                   PORTS        NAMES
b0fc0e11b3b0      hello-world     "/hello"         11 seconds ago   Exited (0) 10 seconds ago             dreamy_nobel
russ in
↯  docker-machine ssh dotest
Welcome to Ubuntu 15.10 (GNU/Linux 4.2.0-16-generic x86_64)

 * Documentation:  https://help.ubuntu.com/
Last login: Sun Jan 17 10:32:14 2016 from 86.141.181.55
root@dotest:~# docker ps -a
CONTAINER ID      IMAGE           COMMAND          CREATED          STATUS                   PORTS        NAMES
b0fc0e11b3b0      hello-world     "/hello"         39 seconds ago   Exited (0) 38 seconds ago             dreamy_nobel
root@dotest:~# docker images
REPOSITORY        TAG             IMAGE ID         CREATED          VIRTUAL SIZE
hello-world       latest          0a6ba66e537a     3 months ago     960 B
root@dotest:~# exit
logout
russ in
↯  []
```

As you can see, I used `ssh` to get into the DigitalOcean instance and ran the `docker ps -a` and `docker images` commands to demonstrate that the commands I ran locally were executed on the DigitalOcean instance; however, the beauty of this setup is that you shouldn't have to SSH instance often.

One thing you may have noticed is that all we told Docker Machine is that we want to use DigitalOcean and our API token; at no point did we tell it which region to launch the instance in, what specification we wanted, or which SSH key to use.

Docker Machine has some following sensible defaults:

- `digitalocean-image = ubuntu-15-10-x64`
- `digitalocean-region = nyc3`
- `digitalocean-size = 512mb`

As I am based in the UK, let's look at changing the region and the specifications of the machine. First of all, we should remove the dotest instance by running the following command:

```
docker-machine rm dotest
```

This will terminate the 512mb instance running in NYC3.

 It is important to terminate instances that you are not using, as they will be costing you for each hour they are active. Remember one of the key advantages of using Docker Machine is that you can spin up instances both quickly and with as little interaction as possible.

Now that we have removed the old instance, let's add some additional flags to our docker-machine command to launch the new instance in the desired region and specification, we will be calling our new instance douktest. The updated docker-machine create command now looks similar to the following (remember to replace the example API token with your own):

```
docker-machine create \
    --driver digitalocean \
    --digitalocean-access-token
sdnjkjdfgkjb345kjdgljknqwetkjwhgoih314rjkwergoiyu34rjkherglkhrg0 \
    --digitalocean-region lon1 \
    --digitalocean-size 1gb \
    douktest
```

You should see similar output from the command as before, once the instance has been deployed, you can make it active by running:

```
eval $(docker-machine env douktest)
```

```
russ in
↯ docker-machine ls
NAME      ACTIVE   URL          STATE     URL                          SWARM   DOCKER   ERRORS
default   -        virtualbox   Running   tcp://192.168.99.100:2376            v1.9.1
russ in
↯ docker-machine create \
     --driver digitalocean \
     --digitalocean-access-token sdnjkjdfgkjb345kjdgljknqwetkjwhgoih314rjkwergoiyu34rjkherglkhrg0 \
     --digitalocean-region lon1 \
     --digitalocean-size 1gb \
     douktest
Running pre-create checks...
Creating machine...
(douktest) Creating SSH key...
(douktest) Creating Digital Ocean droplet...
(douktest) Waiting for IP address to be assigned to the Droplet...
Waiting for machine to be running, this may take a few minutes...
Machine is running, waiting for SSH to be available...
Detecting operating system of created instance...
Detecting the provisioner...
Provisioning with ubuntu(systemd)...
Installing Docker...
Copying certs to the local machine directory...
Copying certs to the remote machine...
Setting Docker configuration on the remote daemon...
Checking connection to Docker...
Docker is up and running!
To see how to connect Docker to this machine, run: docker-machine env douktest
russ in
↯ docker-machine ls
NAME      ACTIVE   URL            STATE     URL                          SWARM   DOCKER   ERRORS
default   -        virtualbox     Running   tcp://192.168.99.100:2376            v1.9.1
douktest  -        digitalocean   Running   tcp://46.101.91.64:2376              v1.9.1
russ in
↯ eval $(docker-machine env douktest)
russ in
↯ []
```

When you enter the control panel, you will notice that the instance has launched in the specified region and at the desired specification:

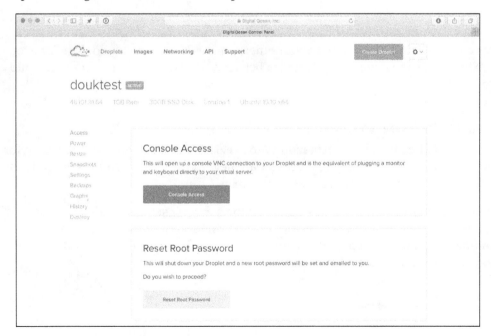

For full details on each of the regions and what machine types are available in each one, you can query the DigitalOcean API by running the following command (remember to replace the API token):

```
curl -X GET -H "Content-Type: application/json" -H "Authorization:
Bearer sdnjkjdfgkjb345kjdgljknqwetkjwhgoih314rjkwergoiyu34rjkherglkhrg0"
"https://api.digitalocean.com/v2/regions" | python -mjson.tool
```

This will output information about each region.

One last thing, we still haven't found out about the SSH key. Each time you run Docker Machine, a new SSH key for the instance you are launching is created and uploaded to the provider, each key is stored in the `.docker` folder in your user's home directory. For example, the key for `douktest` can be found by running the following command:

```
cd ~/.docker/machine/machines/douktest/
```

Here, you will also find the certificates used to authenticate the Docker agent with the Docker installation on the instance and also the configuration:

```
douktest — -bash — 111×8
russ in
⚡ cd ~/.docker/machine/machines/douktest/
russ in
⚡ ls
ca.pem          config.json    id_rsa.pub     server-key.pem
cert.pem        id_rsa         key.pem        server.pem
russ in
⚡
```

This covers DigitalOcean, what about other services? Let's quickly look at Amazon Web Services so that we can get an idea between the drivers for the different cloud providers.

The Amazon Web Services driver

If you don't already have an Amazon Web Services account, you should sign up for one at http://aws.amazon.com/. If you are new to AWS, then you will eligible for their free tier at http://aws.amazon.com/free/.

I would recommend reading through Amazon's getting started guide if you are unfamiliar with AWS before working through this section of the chapter, you can find the guide at http://docs.aws.amazon.com/gettingstarted/latest/awsgsg-intro/gsg-aws-intro.html.

The AWS driver is similar to the DigitalOcean driver and it has some sensible defaults, rather than going into too much detail about how to customize the EC2 instance launched by Docker Machine, I will stick to the defaults. For AWS driver, the defaults are as follows:

- `amazonec2-region = us-east-1` (North Virginia)
- `amazonec2-ami = ami-26d5af4c` (Ubuntu 15.10)
- `amazonec2-instance-type = t2.micro`
- `amazonec2-root-size = 16GB`
- `amazonec2-security-group = docker-machine`

Before we launch our instance, we will also need to know our AWS access and secret keys, and also the VPC ID will be launching our instance. To get these, log in to the AWS console that can be found at `https://console.aws.amazon.com/`.

You should already have a copy of your access and secret ID as these are created when your user was first created in AWS. If you have lost these, then you can generate a new pair by navigating to **Services** | **IAM** | **Users**, then selecting your user, and finally going to the **Security Credentials** tab. There you should see a button that says **Create Access Key**.

> Amazon describes Amazon **Virtual Private Cloud** (**VPC**) as letting you provision a logically-isolated section of the AWS cloud, where you can launch resources in a virtual network that you define. You have complete control over your virtual networking environment, including selection of your own IP address range, creation of subnets, and configuration of route tables and network gateways.

Before you find your VPC ID, you should make sure that you are in the correct region by ensuring that it says **N. Virginia** at the top right-hand corner of your AWS console, if it doesn't select it from the drop-down list.

Once you have ensured you are in the correct region, go to **Services | VPC** and click on **Your VPCs**. You don't need to worry about creating and configuring a VPC as Amazon provides you with a default VPC in each region. Select the VPC and you should see the something similar to the following screenshot:

Make a note of the VPC ID, you should now have enough information to launch your instance using Docker Machine. To do this, run the following command:

```
docker-machine create \
    --driver amazonec2 \
    --amazonec2-access-key JHFDIGJKBDS8639FJHDS \
    --amazonec2-secret-key sfvjbkdsvBKHDJBDFjbfsdvlkb+JLN873JKFLSJH \
    --amazonec2-vpc-id vpc-35c91750 \
    awstest
```

If all goes well, you should see something similar to the following output:

```
russ in
⚡  docker-machine create \
→  --driver amazonec2 \
→  --amazonec2-access-key JHFDIGJKBDS8639FJHDS \
→  --amazonec2-secret-key sfvjbkdsvBKHDJBDFjbfsdvlkb+JLN873JKFLSJH \
→  --amazonec2-vpc-id vpc-35c91750 \
→  awstest
Running pre-create checks...
Creating machine...
(awstest) Launching instance...
Waiting for machine to be running, this may take a few minutes...
Machine is running, waiting for SSH to be available...
Detecting operating system of created instance...
Detecting the provisioner...
Provisioning with ubuntu(systemd)...
Installing Docker...
Copying certs to the local machine directory...
Copying certs to the remote machine...
Setting Docker configuration on the remote daemon...
Checking connection to Docker...
Docker is up and running!
To see how to connect Docker to this machine, run: docker-machine env awstest
russ in
⚡  ☐
```

You should also be able to see an EC2 instance launched in the AWS Console by navigating to **Services | EC2 | Instances**:

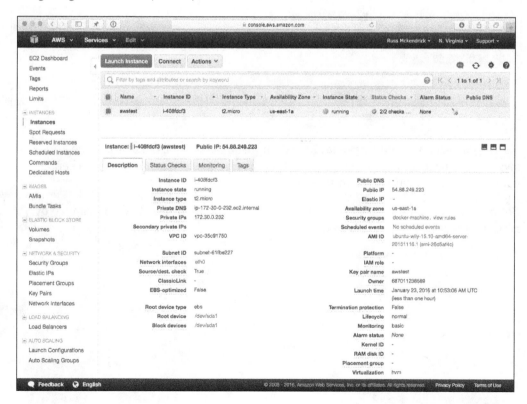

You may have noticed that Docker Machine created the security group and also assigned an SSH key to the instance without any need for us to get involved, keeping within the principle that you don't need to be an expert in configuring the environments that you are launching your Docker instance into.

Before we terminate the instance, let's switch our local Docker client over to use the AWS instance and launch the Hello World container:

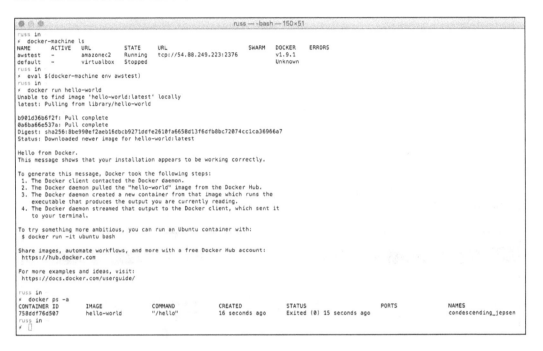

As you can see, once you have launched an instance using Docker Machine and switched your local Docker client to it, there is no difference in usage between running Docker locally and on a cloud provider.

Before we start to rack up the cost, we should terminate our test AWS instance by running the following command:

```
docker-machine rm awstest
```

Then confirm that the instance has been terminated correctly in the AWS console:

If you don't do this, the EC2 instance will quite happily sit there costing you **$0.013** per hour until it is terminated.

 Note that this is not Amazon's **Elastic Container Service (ECS)**. We will be covering Amazon ECS in *Chapter 7, Looking at Schedulers*.

Other considerations

As you can see from examples we have worked through, Docker Machine is a powerful part of Docker Toolbox as it allows users of all skill levels to be able to launch an instance either locally or in a cloud provider without having to roll their sleeves up and get stuck in configuring server instances or their local Docker client.

The examples we have used in this chapter have been launching either Boot2Docker or Ubuntu. Docker machine also supports the following:

- **Debian (8.0+)**: https://www.debian.org/
- **Red Hat Enterprise Linux (7.0+)**: https://www.redhat.com/
- **CentOS (7+)**: https://www.centos.org/
- **Fedora (21+)**: https://getfedora.org/
- **RancherOS (0.3)**: http://rancher.com/rancher-os/

The other thing to mention about Docker Machine is that, by default,
it operates and opts in for crash reporting, considering the amount of different
configuration/environment combinations Docker Machine can be used with, it
is important that Docker get notified of any problems to help them make a better
product. If, for any reason, you want to opt-out, then running the following
command will disable crash reporting:

```
mkdir -p ~/.docker/machine && touch ~/.docker/machine/no-error-report
```

For more information on Docker Machine, you can refer to the official
documentation:

- **Docker Machine**: `https://docs.docker.com/machine/`
- **Docker Machine Drivers**: `https://docs.docker.com/machine/drivers/`
- **Docker Machine Command Reference**: `https://docs.docker.com/machine/reference/`

Docker Swarm

Now that we have discussed how to launch individual Docker instances using
Docker Machine, let's get a little more adventurous and create a cluster of instances.
To do this, Docker ships a tool called Swarm. When deployed, it acts as a scheduler
between your Docker client and host Docker instances, deciding where to launch
containers based on scheduling rules.

Creating a local cluster

To start off, we are going to be using Docker Machine to create a cluster locally
using VirtualBox (`https://www.virtualbox.org`), which is bundled with Docker
Toolbox. To start, we are going to launch a VM to generate a discovery token. To do
this, run the following commands:

```
docker-machine create -d virtualbox discover
```

Then configure your Docker client to use the newly created local instance:

```
eval "$(docker-machine env discover)"
```

You can check that your Docker client is configured to use the `discover` instance
by running `docker-machine ls` and making sure that `discover` has a star in the
active column.

Finally, you can install the discovery service by running the following command:

```
docker run swarm create
```

This will download and run the discovery service and generate the token. At the end of the process, you will be given a token; it is important that you keep a note of this for the next steps. If everything went as planned, you should see something similar to the following output:

```
● ● ●                              russ — -bash — 137×45
russ in
⚡ docker-machine create -d virtualbox discover
Running pre-create checks...
Creating machine...
(discover) Copying /Users/russ/.docker/machine/cache/boot2docker.iso to /Users/russ/.docker/machine/machines/discover/boot2docker.iso...
(discover) Creating VirtualBox VM...
(discover) Creating SSH key...
(discover) Starting the VM...
(discover) Waiting for an IP...
Waiting for machine to be running, this may take a few minutes...
Machine is running, waiting for SSH to be available...
Detecting operating system of created instance...
Detecting the provisioner...
Provisioning with boot2docker...
Copying certs to the local machine directory...
Copying certs to the remote machine...
Setting Docker configuration on the remote daemon...
Checking connection to Docker...
Docker is up and running!
To see how to connect Docker to this machine, run: docker-machine env discover
russ in
⚡ eval "$(docker-machine env discover)"
russ in
⚡ docker-machine ls
NAME       ACTIVE   URL         STATE      URL                           SWARM   DOCKER    ERRORS
default    -        virtualbox  Stopped                                          Unknown
discover   *        virtualbox  Running    tcp://192.168.99.100:2376             v1.9.1
russ in
⚡ docker run swarm create
Unable to find image 'swarm:latest' locally
latest: Pulling from library/swarm

d681c900c6e3: Pull complete
188de6f24f3f: Pull complete
90b2ffb8d338: Pull complete
237af4efea94: Pull complete
3b3fc6f62107: Pull complete
7e6c9135b308: Pull complete
986340ab62f0: Pull complete
a9975e2cc0a3: Pull complete
Digest: sha256:c21fd414b0488637b1f05f13a59b032a3f9da5d818d31da1a4ca98a84c0c781b
Status: Downloaded newer image for swarm:latest
40c3bf4866eed5ad14ade6633fc4cefc
russ in
⚡ 
```

In the preceding example, the token is `40c3bf4866eed5ad14ade6633fc4cefc`. Now that we have our token, we need to launch an instance that will act as the scheduler, this is know as a Swarm manager.

To do this, enter the following command, making sure that you replace the token with the one you generated:

```
docker-machine create \
    -d virtualbox \
    --swarm \
    --swarm-master \
    --swarm-discovery token://40c3bf4866eed5ad14ade6633fc4cefc \
    swarm-master
```

Now that we have the Swarm manager VM up and running, we can start launching VMs that act as nodes within the cluster. Again, using the discovery token, run the following commands to launch two nodes:

```
docker-machine create \
    -d virtualbox \
    --swarm \
    --swarm-discovery token://40c3bf4866eed5ad14ade6633fc4cefc \
    swarm-node-01
```

Then launch the second node using the following command:

```
docker-machine create \
    -d virtualbox \
    --swarm \
    --swarm-discovery token://40c3bf4866eed5ad14ade6633fc4cefc \
    swarm-node-02
```

We can check our VMs by running the `docker-machine ls` command and then switch our Docker client to use the cluster by running the following command:

```
eval $(docker-machine env --swarm swarm-master)
```

Now that your Docker client is communicating with the cluster, you can run `docker info` to find information about all the nodes and the cluster itself, you will see something similar to the following screenshot:

```
● ● ●                                          russ — -bash — 151×44
russ in
⚡ docker-machine ls
NAME           ACTIVE   URL          STATE     URL                            SWARM                    DOCKER    ERRORS
default        -        virtualbox   Stopped                                                           Unknown
discover       *        virtualbox   Running   tcp://192.168.99.100:2376                               v1.9.1
swarm-master   -        virtualbox   Running   tcp://192.168.99.101:2376      swarm-master (master)    v1.9.1
swarm-node-01  -        virtualbox   Running   tcp://192.168.99.102:2376      swarm-master             v1.9.1
swarm-node-02  -        virtualbox   Running   tcp://192.168.99.103:2376      swarm-master             v1.9.1
russ in
⚡ eval $(docker-machine env --swarm swarm-master)
russ in
⚡ docker info
Containers: 4
Images: 3
Role: primary
Strategy: spread
Filters: health, port, dependency, affinity, constraint
Nodes: 3
 swarm-master: 192.168.99.101:2376
  └ Status: Healthy
  └ Containers: 2
  └ Reserved CPUs: 0 / 1
  └ Reserved Memory: 0 B / 1.021 GiB
  └ Labels: executiondriver=native-0.2, kernelversion=4.1.13-boot2docker, operatingsystem=Boot2Docker 1.9.1 (TCL 6.4.1); master : cef800b - Fri Nov 20
19:33:59 UTC 2015, provider=virtualbox, storagedriver=aufs
 swarm-node-01: 192.168.99.102:2376
  └ Status: Healthy
  └ Containers: 1
  └ Reserved CPUs: 0 / 1
  └ Reserved Memory: 0 B / 1.021 GiB
  └ Labels: executiondriver=native-0.2, kernelversion=4.1.13-boot2docker, operatingsystem=Boot2Docker 1.9.1 (TCL 6.4.1); master : cef800b - Fri Nov 20
19:33:59 UTC 2015, provider=virtualbox, storagedriver=aufs
 swarm-node-02: 192.168.99.103:2376
  └ Status: Healthy
  └ Containers: 1
  └ Reserved CPUs: 0 / 1
  └ Reserved Memory: 0 B / 1.021 GiB
  └ Labels: executiondriver=native-0.2, kernelversion=4.1.13-boot2docker, operatingsystem=Boot2Docker 1.9.1 (TCL 6.4.1); master : cef800b - Fri Nov 20
19:33:59 UTC 2015, provider=virtualbox, storagedriver=aufs
CPUs: 3
Total Memory: 3.064 GiB
Name: swarm-master
russ in
⚡ ▯
```

So, now we have a three CPU, 3-GB cluster running over three nodes. To test it, let's run the `Hello World` container and then run `docker ps -a` so that we can see which node the container launched on:

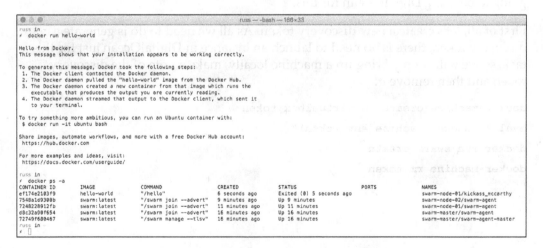

```
● ● ●                                          russ — -bash — 166×33
russ in
⚡ docker run hello-world

Hello from Docker.
This message shows that your installation appears to be working correctly.

To generate this message, Docker took the following steps:
 1. The Docker client contacted the Docker daemon.
 2. The Docker daemon pulled the "hello-world" image from the Docker Hub.
 3. The Docker daemon created a new container from that image which runs the
    executable that produces the output you are currently reading.
 4. The Docker daemon streamed that output to the Docker client, which sent it
    to your terminal.

To try something more ambitious, you can run an Ubuntu container with:
 $ docker run -it ubuntu bash

Share images, automate workflows, and more with a free Docker Hub account:
 https://hub.docker.com

For more examples and ideas, visit:
 https://docs.docker.com/userguide/

russ in
⚡ docker ps -a
CONTAINER ID   IMAGE          COMMAND                 CREATED          STATUS                    PORTS    NAMES
ef174e2103f9   hello-world    "/hello"                6 seconds ago    Exited (0) 5 seconds ago           swarm-node-01/kickass_mccarthy
7548a1d9308b   swarm:latest   "/swarm join --advert"  9 minutes ago    Up 9 minutes                       swarm-node-02/swarm-agent
7248228912fb   swarm:latest   "/swarm join --advert"  11 minutes ago   Up 11 minutes                      swarm-node-01/swarm-agent
d8c32a90f654   swarm:latest   "/swarm join --advert"  16 minutes ago   Up 16 minutes                      swarm-master/swarm-agent
72749f688467   swarm:latest   "/swarm manage --tlsv"  16 minutes ago   Up 16 minutes                      swarm-master/swarm-agent-master
russ in
⚡ ▯
```

As you can see from the terminal output, the container was launched on
`swarm-node-01`, running the container again should launch it on our second node:

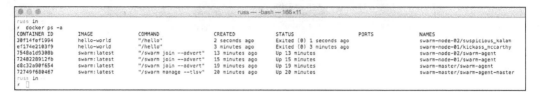

So there you have it, a really basic Docker Swarm cluster that you can launch
your containers into using your local Docker client, all launched a managed
using Docker Machine.

Before we move onto the next section, we should remove the local cluster. To do this,
just run the following command:

```
docker-machine rm discover swarm-master swarm-node-01 swarm-node-02
```

Click on `yes` when prompted. You can then check whether the VMs have been
terminated by running the `docker-machine ls` command.

Creating a Remote Cluster

Before we move onto looking at the next tool, let's launch a cluster in the cloud. I am
going to be using DigitalOcean for this.

First of all, let's create a new discovery token. As all we need to do is generate a
discovery token, there is no need to launch an instance in DigitalOcean just for this
task, so we will simply bring up a machine locally, make a note of the discovery
token and then remove it:

```
docker-machine create -d virtualbox token

eval "$(docker-machine env token)"

docker run swarm create

docker-machine rm token
```

Now that we have our discovery token, let's launch our Swarm cluster in DigitalOcean, first of all we will look into Swarm manager:

```
docker-machine create \
    --driver digitalocean \
    --digitalocean-access-token
sdnjkjdfgkjb345kjdgljknqwetkjwhgoih314rjkwergoiyu34rjkherglkhrg0 \
    --digitalocean-region lon1 \
    --swarm \
    --swarm-master \
    --swarm-discovery token://453sdfjbnfvlknmn3435mwedvmndvnwe \
    swarm-master
```

Then the we will use the two nodes:

```
docker-machine create \
    --driver digitalocean \
    --digitalocean-access-token
sdnjkjdfgkjb345kjdgljknqwetkjwhgoih314rjkwergoiyu34rjkherglkhrg0 \
    --digitalocean-region lon1 \
    --digitalocean-size 1gb \
    --swarm \
    --swarm-discovery token://453sdfjbnfvlknmn3435mwedvmndvnwe \
    swarm-node-01


docker-machine create \
    --driver digitalocean \
    --digitalocean-access-token
sdnjkjdfgkjb345kjdgljknqwetkjwhgoih314rjkwergoiyu34rjkherglkhrg0 \
    --digitalocean-region lon1 \
    --digitalocean-size 1gb \
    --swarm \
    --swarm-discovery token://453sdfjbnfvlknmn3435mwedvmndvnwe \
    swarm-node-02
```

As you can see in the following screenshot, I launched the cluster in DigitalOcean's London datacenter and gave the two nodes additional resources:

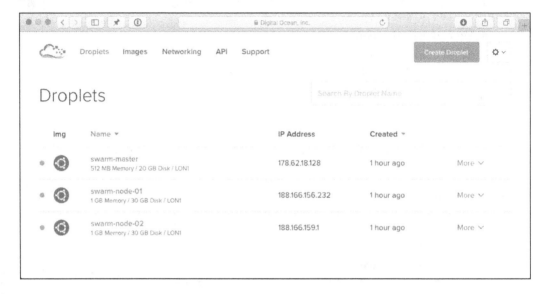

We will configure our local Docker client to use the remote cluster using the following command:

```
eval $(docker-machine env --swarm swarm-master)
```

This will give us the following information:

```
russ in
⚡ docker info
Containers: 4
Images: 3
Role: primary
Strategy: spread
Filters: health, port, dependency, affinity, constraint
Nodes: 3
 swarm-master: 178.62.18.128:2376
  └ Status: Healthy
  └ Containers: 2
  └ Reserved CPUs: 0 / 1
  └ Reserved Memory: 0 B / 513.4 MiB
  └ Labels: executiondriver=native-0.2, kernelversion=4.2.0-16-generic, operatingsystem=Ubuntu 15.10, provider=digitalocean, storagedriver=aufs
 swarm-node-01: 188.166.156.232:2376
  └ Status: Healthy
  └ Containers: 1
  └ Reserved CPUs: 0 / 1
  └ Reserved Memory: 0 B / 1.018 GiB
  └ Labels: executiondriver=native-0.2, kernelversion=4.2.0-16-generic, operatingsystem=Ubuntu 15.10, provider=digitalocean, storagedriver=aufs
 swarm-node-02: 188.166.159.1:2376
  └ Status: Healthy
  └ Containers: 1
  └ Reserved CPUs: 0 / 1
  └ Reserved Memory: 0 B / 1.018 GiB
  └ Labels: executiondriver=native-0.2, kernelversion=4.2.0-16-generic, operatingsystem=Ubuntu 15.10, provider=digitalocean, storagedriver=aufs
CPUs: 3
Total Memory: 2.538 GiB
Name: swarm-master
russ in
⚡ 
```

We are going to be using this cluster for the next part of this chapter, so try to keep it running for now. If you can't, then you can remove the cluster by running the following command:

```
docker-machine rm swarm-master swarm-node-01 swarm-node-02
```

You should also double the DigitalOcean control panel to ensure that your instances have terminated correctly.

> Remember that with public cloud services, you are paying for that you use, so if you have an instance sat powered on, even if it is an `errored` state, with Docker Machine, the meter is running and you will be incurring cost.

Discovery backends

At this point, it is worth pointing out that Docker allows you to swap out the Discovery backends, at the moment we are using the default one which the Hosted Discovery with Docker Hub, which isn't recommend for production.

Swarm supports the following discovery services:

- **etcd**: https://coreos.com/etcd/
- **Consul**: https://www.consul.io/
- **ZooKeeper**: https://zookeeper.apache.org/

For the time being, we are just going to be looking at the tools Docker provides rather than any third-party options, so we are going to stick to the default Discovery backend.

Unfortunately, the one thing that the default Discovery backend doesn't give you is high availability, this means that our Swarm manager is a single point of failure. For our needs, this isn't a problem; however, I would not recommend running this configuration in production.

For more information on the different discovery backends and high availability with Swarm, refer to the following URLs:

- **Discovery backends**: https://docs.docker.com/swarm/discovery/
- **Swarm High Availability**: https://docs.docker.com/swarm/multi-manager-setup/

We are going to be looking a lot more at schedulers in later chapters, so for now, let's move onto the final service installed by Docker Toolbox.

Docker Compose

So far in our exploration of the tools that ship with Docker Toolbox, we have been using services which manage our Docker host machines, the final service that we are going to look at in this chapter deals with containers. I am sure that you will agree that so far the tools provided by Docker are quite intuitive, Docker Compose is no different. It start off life as third-party service called Fig and was written by Orchard Labs (the project's original website is still available at http://fig.sh/).

The original project's goal was the following:

> *"Provide fast, isolated development environments using Docker"*

Since Fig became part of Docker, they haven't strayed too far from the original goal:

> *"Compose is a tool for defining and running multi-container Docker applications. With Compose, you use a Compose file to configure your application's services. Then, using a single command, you create and start all the services from your configuration."*

Before we start looking at Compose files and start containers up, let's think of why a tool such as Compose is useful.

Why Compose?

Launching individual containers is as simple as running the following command:

```
docker run -i -t ubuntu /bin/bash
```

This will launch and then attach to an Ubuntu container. As we have already touched upon, there is a little more to it than just launching simple containers though. Docker is not here to replace virtual machines, it is here to run a single application.

This means that you shouldn't really run an entire LAMP stack in single container, instead, you should look at running Apache and PHP in one container, which is then linked with a second container running MySQL. You could take this further, running a NGINX container, a PHP-FPM container, and also a MySQL container. This is where it gets complicated. All of sudden, your simple line for launching is now several lines, all of which have to executed in the correct order with the correct flags.

This is exactly the problem Docker Compose tries to fix. Rather than several long commands, you can define your containers using a YAML file. This means that you will be able to launch your application with a single command and leave the logic of the order in which the containers will be launched to Compose.

YAML Ain't Markup Language (YAML) is a human-friendly data serialization standard for all programming languages.

It also means that you can ship your application's Compose file with your code base or directly to another developer/administrator and they will be able to launch your application exactly how you intended it be executed.

Compose files

Almost everyone at some point would have installed, used, or read about WordPress, so for the next few examples, we will be using the official WordPress container from the Docker Hub, you can find details on the container at https://hub.docker. com/_/wordpress/.

 WordPress is web software that you can use to create a beautiful website, blog, or app. We like to say that WordPress is both free and priceless at the same time. For more information, check out https://wordpress.org/.

Let's start by getting a basic WordPress installation up and running, first of all create a folder called wordpress and then add the following content to a file called docker-compose.yml:

```
wordpress:
  container_name: my-wordpress-app
  image: wordpress
  ports:
    - "80:80"
  links:
    - "mysql:mysql"
mysql:
  container_name: my-wordpress-database
  image: mysql
  environment:
    MYSQL_ROOT_PASSWORD: "password"
```

You will be able to launch the application using your Swarm cluster by making sure that your local Docker client is configured to use it, run docker-machine ls and make sure that it is active and then run the following command:

```
eval $(docker-machine env --swarm swarm-master)
```

Once your client is configured to communicate with your Swarm cluster, run the following command within the folder containing the `docker-compose.yml` file:

```
docker-compose up -d
```

Using the `-d` flag at the end of the command launches the containers in detached mode, this means that they will run in the background. If we didn't use the -d flag, then our containers would have launched in the foreground and we would not have been able to carry on using the same terminal session without stopping the running containers.

You will see something similar to the following output:

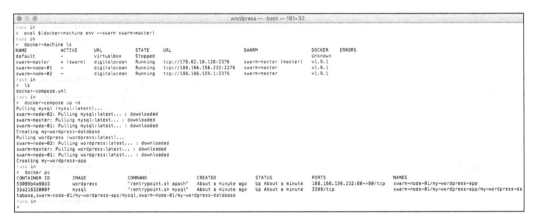

As you can see, you can find out the IP address of the node where the WordPress application has been launched by running `docker ps`. If you were to go to the IP address shown in the figure, where `port 80` is listed, you will see a WordPress installation screen:

One of the interesting things to note is that although the `my-wordpress-app` container was defined first in the `docker-compose.yml` file, Compose recognized that it was linked to the `my-wordpress-database` container and it launched that one first. Also, you may have noticed that the `wordpress:latest` and `mysql:latest` images were pulled down on all of the nodes in the Swarm cluster.

So, what of the `docker-compose.yml` file itself? Let's look at it again, but this time with some comments.

As far as Compose is concerned, our WordPress application is split into two applications, one called **wordpress** and another called **mysql**. Let's look at the `docker-compose.yml` file again:

```
wordpress:
  container_name: my-wordpress-app
  image: wordpress
  ports:
    - "80:80"
  links:
    - "mysql:mysql"
mysql:
  container_name: my-wordpress-database
  image: mysql
  environment:
    MYSQL_ROOT_PASSWORD: "password"
```

At the top level, we have the application name. From here, we then start to define the configuration for the application by giving a key and value, making sure that you pay close attention to the indentation. I tend to use two spaces to make it clear that the indent is there, but not so much that it becomes unreadable.

The first key that we are defining is `container_name`, we don't have to do this as Compose will name our containers automatically, based on the name of the folder we are in and the application name. If we hadn't defined this key, then our containers would have been called `wordpress_wordpress_01` and `wordpress_mysql_01`.

The next key tells the application which `image` to use, this will pull the image straight from the Docker Hub.

Then we define the `ports`, not that we only define the ports for the **wordpress** application and not the **mysql** one. As we want our **wordpress** application to listen on port of the host machine, we have given 80:80. In this case, the first 80 is the **host** port and the second one is the **container** port that we want to expose.

Again, the next key is only used on the **wordpress** application, this defines the `links`. Links are used to link containers together, exposing, in this case, the **mysql** container to the **wordpress** container. This means that when the **wordpress** container is launched, it will know the IP address of the **mysql** container and only its ports will be exposed to the **wordpress** container.

The final key we are defining is `environment`, here are we passing further keys and values that will be set as environment variables on the containers when they launch.

A full break down of all of the keys available in compose files can be found in the official documentation at `https://docs.docker.com/compose/compose-file/`.

Launching more

One of the advantages of using Compose is that each of the environments it launches is isolated, let's launch another WordPress installation using the following `docker-compose.yml` file:

```
wordpress:
  container_name: my-other-wordpress-app
  image: wordpress
  ports:
    - "80:80"
  links:
    - "mysql:mysql"
mysql:
  container_name: my-other-wordpress-database
```

```
image: mysql
environment:
    MYSQL_ROOT_PASSWORD: "password"
```

As you can see, other than the container names, it is exactly the same as the previous environment we launched:

```
                                        other-wordpress — -bash — 181×19
russ in                                                      on master
$ docker-compose up -d
Creating my-other-wordpress-database
Creating my-other-wordpress-app
russ in                                                      on master
$ docker ps -a
CONTAINER ID    IMAGE          COMMAND                 CREATED          STATUS           PORTS                         NAMES
12ee4a2dbe02    wordpress      "/entrypoint.sh apach"  6 seconds ago    Up 5 seconds     188.166.159.1:80->80/tcp      swarm-node-02/my-other-wordpress-app
665b9c93bce2    mysql          "/entrypoint.sh mysql"  8 seconds ago    Up 6 seconds     3306/tcp                      swarm-node-02/my-other-wordpress-app/my-other-w
ordpress-database,swarm-node-02/my-other-wordpress-app/mysql,swarm-node-02/my-other-wordpress-database
53089b4a98d3    wordpress      "/entrypoint.sh apach"  About an hour ago Up About an hour 188.166.156.232:80->80/tcp   swarm-node-01/my-wordpress-app
32a21632008f    mysql          "/entrypoint.sh mysql"  About an hour ago Up About an hour 3306/tcp                     swarm-node-01/my-wordpress-app/my-wordpress-dat
abase,swarm-node-01/my-wordpress-app/mysql,swarm-node-01/my-wordpress-database
f37a9c1ccb20    swarm:latest   "/swarm join --advert"  19 hours ago     Up 19 hours                                    swarm-node-02/swarm-agent
d53725cb1027    swarm:latest   "/swarm join --advert"  19 hours ago     Up 19 hours                                    swarm-node-01/swarm-agent
760860f530fe    swarm:latest   "/swarm join --advert"  19 hours ago     Up 19 hours                                    swarm-master/swarm-agent
16b8cb472d74    swarm:latest   "/swarm manage --tlsv"  19 hours ago     Up 19 hours                                    swarm-master/swarm-agent-master
russ in                                                      on master
$ []
```

The other thing you will notice is that the `my-other-wordpress` containers launched on the second node in the cluster. At the moment, each Compose environment will launch on a single node. As we launch more, we will start to have to change port assignments as they will start to clash on the hosts (that is, you can't have two `port` `80` assigned to a single host).

 Don't forget to remove any cloud-based instances that you have launched by using the `docker-machine rm` command and also check your cloud provider's control panel to ensure that the instances have correctly terminated.

Summary

In this chapter, we have covered the additional client tools provided by Docker to extend the functionality of your core Docker installation, all of the tools that we have looked at have been designed to slot into your workflow and be as simple as possible to use. In the later chapters, we will be looking at how to expand some of the core functionality of Docker using third-party services. When we do, we will revisit a few of the tools that we have been through in this chapter and look at how they add additional functionality to them.

3
Volume Plugins

In this chapter, you will get an overview of both first and third-party volume plugins. We will be discussing installing, configuring, and using the following storage plugins:

- **Docker Volumes**: `https://docs.docker.com/engine/userguide/containers/dockervolumes/`

- **Convoy**: `https://github.com/rancher/convoy/`

- **REX-Ray**: `https://github.com/emccode/rexray/`

- **Flocker**: `https://clusterhq.com/flocker/introduction/`

You will also get an understanding of how to interact with Docker plugins and how they both differ and work with the supporting tools that we covered in *Chapter 2, Introducing First-party Tools*.

 This chapter assumes that you are using Docker 1.10+. Note that some commands may not work in previous versions.

Zero volumes

Before we look at volumes, let's look at what happens when you do not use any volumes at all and store everything directly on the containers.

To start with, let's create a new Docker instance called `chapter03` locally using Docker Machine:

```
docker-machine create chapter03 --driver=virtualbox

eval $(docker-machine env chapter03)
```

```
● ● ●                      wordpress — -bash — 111×31
russ in ~/Documents/Code/extending-docker/chapter03/wordpress on master*
⚡ docker-machine create chapter03 --driver=virtualbox
Running pre-create checks...
Creating machine...
(chapter03) Copying /Users/russ/.docker/machine/cache/boot2docker.iso to /Users/russ/.docker/machine/machines/c
hapter03/boot2docker.iso...
(chapter03) Creating VirtualBox VM...
(chapter03) Creating SSH key...
(chapter03) Starting the VM...
(chapter03) Check network to re-create if needed...
(chapter03) Waiting for an IP...
Waiting for machine to be running, this may take a few minutes...
Detecting operating system of created instance...
Waiting for SSH to be available...
Detecting the provisioner...
Provisioning with boot2docker...
Copying certs to the local machine directory...
Copying certs to the remote machine...
Setting Docker configuration on the remote daemon...
Checking connection to Docker...
Docker is up and running!
To see how to connect your Docker Client to the Docker Engine running on this virtual machine, run: docker-mach
ine env chapter03
russ in ~/Documents/Code/extending-docker/chapter03/wordpress on master*
⚡ eval $(docker-machine env chapter03)
russ in ~/Documents/Code/extending-docker/chapter03/wordpress on master*
⚡ docker-machine ls
NAME        ACTIVE    DRIVER       STATE      URL                         SWARM    DOCKER    ERRORS
chapter03   *         virtualbox   Running    tcp://192.168.99.100:2376            v1.10.0
russ in ~/Documents/Code/extending-docker/chapter03/wordpress on master*
⚡ ▯
```

Now that we have our machine, we can use Docker Compose to run through a scenario with WordPress. First of all, we will need to launch our WordPress containers, we are using the official WordPress and MySQL images from the Docker Hub as we did earlier, our `docker-compose.yml` file looks similar to the following code:

```
version: '2'
services:
  wordpress:
    container_name: my-wordpress-app
    image: wordpress
```

```
ports:
  - "80:80"
links:
  - mysql
environment:
  WORDPRESS_DB_HOST: "mysql:3306"
  WORDPRESS_DB_PASSWORD: "password"
mysql:
container_name: my-wordpress-database
image: mysql
environment:
  MYSQL_ROOT_PASSWORD: "password"
```

As you can see, there is nothing special about the compose file. You can launch it by running the following command:

```
docker-compose up -d
```

Once you have launched the containers, check their status by running the following command:

```
docker-compose ps
```

If they both have state of Up, you can go to the WordPress installation screen by running the following command:

```
open http://$(docker-machine ip chapter03)/
```

This will open your browser and go to the IP address of your Docker instance. In my case, this is http://192.168.99.100/. You should see the following screen:

Let's click on **Continue** button and install WordPress:

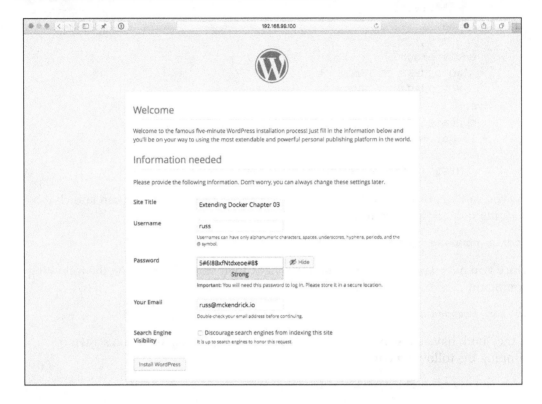

Once the information has been filled in, click on Install WordPress to complete the installation. When you do, the MySQL database will be updated with your settings and the test posts and comments will also be added. When this is completed, you will be shown a success screen:

You should now be able to rerun the following command:

```
open http://$(docker-machine ip chapter03)
```

This will take you to your very empty WordPress site:

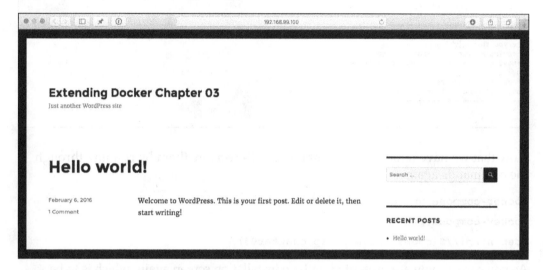

Your command line history should look something similar to the following terminal output:

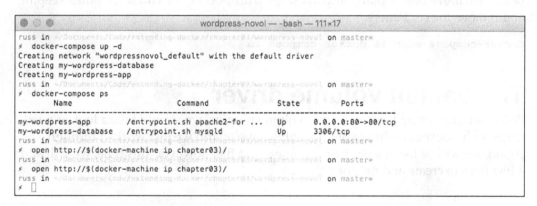

Now that we have our WordPress site installed, let's destroy the containers by running the following command:

```
docker-compose stop && docker-compose rm
```

Make sure you type y when prompted. You will then receive a confirmation message that your two containers have been removed:

```
                                    wordpress-novol — -bash — 111×14
russ in                                                         on master∗
⚡ docker-compose stop && docker-compose rm
Stopping my-wordpress-app ... done
Stopping my-wordpress-database ... done
Going to remove my-wordpress-app, my-wordpress-database
Are you sure? [yN] y
Removing my-wordpress-app ... done
Removing my-wordpress-database ... done
russ in                                                         on master∗
⚡ docker-compose ps
Name   Command   State   Ports
------------------------------
russ in                                                         on master∗
⚡ ▯
```

Now that we have removed our containers, let's recreate them by running through the commands again:

```
docker-compose up -d
```

```
docker-compose ps
```

```
open http://$(docker-machine ip chapter03)/
```

As you can see, you are presented with an installation screen again, which is to be expected as the MySQL database was stored on the `mysql` container that we removed.

Before we move onto looking at what ships with Docker, let's do some housekeeping and remove the containers:

```
docker-compose stop && docker-compose rm
```

The default volume driver

Before we start using the third-party volume plugins, we should take a look at what ships with Docker and how volumes solve the scenario we just worked through. Again, we will be using a `docker-compose.yml` file; however, this time, we will add a few lines to create and mount volumes:

```
version: '2'
services:
  wordpress:
    container_name: my-wordpress-app
    image: wordpress
    ports:
      - "80:80"
    links:
```

```
        - mysql
      environment:
        WORDPRESS_DB_HOST: "mysql:3306"
        WORDPRESS_DB_PASSWORD: "password"
      volumes:
        - "uploads:/var/www/html/wp-content/uploads/"
    mysql:
      container_name: my-wordpress-database
      image: mysql
      environment:
        MYSQL_ROOT_PASSWORD: "password"
      volumes:
        - "database:/var/lib/mysql"
volumes:
  uploads:
    driver: local
  database:
    driver: local
```

As you can see, here we are creating two volumes, one called uploads, which is being mounted to the WordPress uploads folder on the WordPress container. The second volume called database, which is being mounted in /var/lib/mysql on our MySQL container.

You can launch the containers and open WordPress, using the following commands:

```
docker-compose up -d
docker-compose ps
open http://$(docker-machine ip chapter03)/
```

Before we complete the WordPress installation in the browser, we should make sure that the uploads folder has the right permissions by running docker exec:

```
docker exec -d my-wordpress-app chmod 777 /var/www/html/wp-content/
uploads/
```

Now that the permissions are correctly set on the uploads folder, we can go through the WordPress installation as per the previous test.

As WordPress creates a `Hello World!` test post as part of the installation, we should go and edit the post. To do this, log in to WordPress using the credentials that you entered during the installation. Once logged in, go to **Posts | Hello World** and then upload a featured image by clicking on **Set featured image** button. Your edit should look similar to the following screenshot once you have uploaded the featured image:

Once your image has been uploaded, click on **Update** button and then go to your WordPress homepage by clicking on the title on the top left-hand side of the screen. Once the home page opens, you should see your featured image:

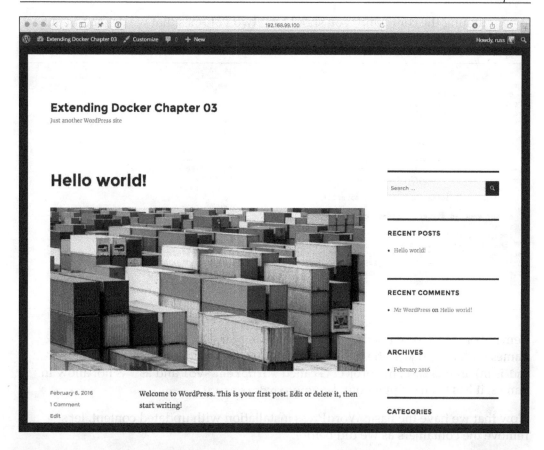

Before we remove our containers, you can run the following command to show all the volumes that have been created in Docker:

```
docker volume ls
```

When running the command, you should the two volumes that we defined in our
`docker-compose.yml` file:

```
● ● ●                            wordpress-vol — -bash — 111×24
russ in ~/Documents/Code/extending-docker/chapter03/wordpress-vol on master*
⚡ docker-compose up -d
Creating network "wordpressvol_default" with the default driver
Creating my-wordpress-database
Creating my-wordpress-app
russ in ~/Documents/Code/extending-docker/chapter03/wordpress-vol on master*
⚡ docker-compose ps
        Name              Command             State       Ports
--------------------------------------------------------------------------
my-wordpress-app       /entrypoint.sh apache2-for ...  Up    0.0.0.0:80->80/tcp
my-wordpress-database  /entrypoint.sh mysqld           Up    3306/tcp
russ in ~/Documents/Code/extending-docker/chapter03/wordpress-vol on master*
⚡ open http://$(docker-machine ip chapter03)/
russ in ~/Documents/Code/extending-docker/chapter03/wordpress-vol on master*
⚡ docker exec -d my-wordpress-app chmod 777 /var/www/html/wp-content/uploads/
russ in ~/Documents/Code/extending-docker/chapter03/wordpress-vol on master*
⚡ docker volume ls
DRIVER              VOLUME NAME
local               3700068a37798029ad5c90893c7fd8200405b62cfdc47f202850b567e0fd8537
local               5e3f76c08b303245e59fe73e453dc6637de1d0941e1b1b3701110c33df7b611a
local               wordpressvol_uploads
local               wordpressvol_database
russ in ~/Documents/Code/extending-docker/chapter03/wordpress-vol on master*
⚡ ▯
```

Remember, as we discussed in the previous chapter, Docker Compose will prefix
names with the project title (which is the name of the folder that `docker-compose.
yml` is in), in this case, the project is called `wordpress-vol` and as - is not allow in
names, it has been stripped out, leaving `wordpressvol`.

Now that we have the basic WordPress installation with updated content, let's
remove the containers as we did before:

docker-compose stop && docker-compose rm

docker-compose ps

```
● ● ●                            wordpress-vol — -bash — 111×14
russ in ~/Documents/Code/extending-docker/chapter03/wordpress-vol on master*
⚡ docker-compose stop && docker-compose rm
Stopping my-wordpress-app ... done
Stopping my-wordpress-database ... done
Going to remove my-wordpress-app, my-wordpress-database
Are you sure? [yN] y
Removing my-wordpress-app ... done
Removing my-wordpress-database ... done
russ in ~/Documents/Code/extending-docker/chapter03/wordpress-vol on master*
⚡ docker-compose ps
Name   Command   State   Ports
------------------------------
russ in ~/Documents/Code/extending-docker/chapter03/wordpress-vol on master*
⚡ ▯
```

At this stage, you can probably guess what is going to happen next, let's relaunch our containers and open the WordPress site in our browser:

```
docker-compose up -d
```

```
open http://$(docker-machine ip chapter03)/
```

It may take a few seconds for everything to start up, so if you don't see your WordPress when the browser opens, refresh the page. If everything goes as planned, you should be presented with your edited `Hello World!` post:

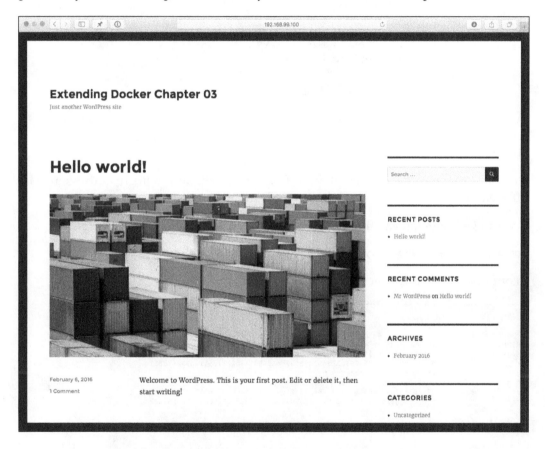

While it looks like the same screenshot as earlier, you will notice that you have been logged out of WordPress. This is because, by default, WordPress stores its sessions on the filesystem, and as they are not stored in the uploads directory, the session files were lost when we removed the containers.

Volumes can also be shared between containers, if we add the following to our `docker-compose.yml` file anywhere in the `Services` section:

```
wordpress8080:
  container_name: my-wordpress-app-8080
  image: wordpress
  ports:
    - "8080:80"
  links:
    - mysql
  environment:
    WORDPRESS_DB_HOST: "mysql:3306"
    WORDPRESS_DB_PASSWORD: "password"
  volumes:
    - "uploads:/var/www/html/wp-content/uploads/"
```

You can launch a second container with WordPress running on `port 8080` and access the file we uploaded at `http://192.168.99.100:8080/wp-content/uploads/2016/02/containers-1024x512.png`.

Note that the preceding URL will differ for your installation as the IP address may be different, along with the upload date and file name.

You can get more information on a volume by running the following command:

`docker volume inspect <your_volume_name>`

In our case, this returns the following information:

```
● ● ●                          wordpress-vol — -bash — 111×20
russ in ~/Documents/Code/extending-docker/chapter03/wordpress-vol on master↯
↯  docker volume ls
DRIVER              VOLUME NAME
local               3700068a37798029ad5c90893c7fd8200405b62cfdc47f202850b567e0fd8537
local               5e3f76c08b303245e59fe73e453dc6637de1d0941e1b1b3701110c33df7b611a
local               wordpressvol_uploads
local               wordpressvol_database
local               73ab63f0143f0d03197ed279c8f385301d9ffa619d696207987472b76a955e7a
local               e05cce4c4e2d133ee80346551e715b0b32b2e323f8c91360dac3db1ba1928e23
russ in ~/Documents/Code/extending-docker/chapter03/wordpress-vol on master↯
↯  docker volume inspect wordpressvol_uploads
[
    {
        "Name": "wordpressvol_uploads",
        "Driver": "local",
        "Mountpoint": "/mnt/sda1/var/lib/docker/volumes/wordpressvol_uploads/_data"
    }
]
russ in ~/Documents/Code/extending-docker/chapter03/wordpress-vol on master↯
↯  
```

You will have noticed that we have been using the `local` driver for our two volumes, this creates the volume on our Docker instance and mounts a folder from host machine, which is the Docker Machine host running under VirtualBox in this case.

You can view the contents on the folder by SSHing into the host machine and going to the folder listed under the mount point returned by the `docker volume inspect` command. To SSH into the host and change to the root user, run the following commands:

```
docker-machine ssh chapter03
```

```
sudo su -
```

You will then be able to change to the folder containing the volume, the reason for changing to the root user is to make sure that you have permissions to see the contents on the folder:

As you can see from the preceding terminal output, the files are owned by an unknown user with a user ID and group ID of 32, in the container, this is the Apache user. Be careful if you add files directly or make any changes, as you may find yourself causing all sorts of permission errors when it comes to your containers accessing the files you have added/changed.

So far so good, but what are the limits? The biggest one is that your data is tied to a single instance. In the last chapter, we looked at clustering Docker using Swarm, we discussed that the containers launched with Docker Compose are tied to a single instance, which is great for development, but not so hot for production, where we may have several host instances that we want to start spreading our containers across, this is where third-party volume drivers come into play.

Third-party volume drivers

There are several third-party volume drivers available, they all bring different functionality to the table. To start with, we are going to be looking at Convoy by Rancher.

Before we look at installing Convoy, we should look at launching a Docker instance somewhere in the cloud. As we already have launched Docker instance in both DigitalOcean and Amazon Web Services, we should terminate our local chapter03 instance and relaunch it in one of these providers, I am going to be using DigitalOcean:

```
docker-machine stop chapter03 && docker-machine rm chapter03

docker-machine create \
    --driver digitalocean \
    --digitalocean-access-token
sdnjkjdfgkjb345kjdgljknqwetkjwhgoih314rjkwergoiyu34rjkherglkhrg0\
    --digitalocean-region lon1 \
    --digitalocean-size 1gb \
    chapter03

eval "$(docker-machine env chapter03)"
```

```
●  ●  ●                        russ — -bash — 111×40
russ in
⚡  docker-machine stop chapter03 && docker-machine rm chapter03
Stopping "chapter03"...
Machine "chapter03" was stopped.
About to remove chapter03
Are you sure? (y/n): y
Successfully removed chapter03
russ in
⚡  docker-machine create \
    --driver digitalocean \
    --digitalocean-access-token sdnjkjdfgkjb345kjdgljknqwetkjwhgoih314rjkwergoiyu34rjkherglkhrg0 \
    --digitalocean-region lon1 \
    --digitalocean-size 1gb \
    chapter03
Running pre-create checks...
Creating machine...
(chapter03) Creating SSH key...
(chapter03) Creating Digital Ocean droplet...
(chapter03) Waiting for IP address to be assigned to the Droplet...
Waiting for machine to be running, this may take a few minutes...
Detecting operating system of created instance...
Waiting for SSH to be available...
Detecting the provisioner...
Provisioning with ubuntu(systemd)...
Installing Docker...
Copying certs to the local machine directory...
Copying certs to the remote machine...
Setting Docker configuration on the remote daemon...
Checking connection to Docker...
Docker is up and running!
To see how to connect your Docker Client to the Docker Engine running on this virtual machine, run: docker-mach
ine env chapter03
russ in
⚡  eval "$(docker-machine env chapter03)"
russ in
⚡  docker-machine ls
NAME          ACTIVE    DRIVER          STATE      URL                           SWARM    DOCKER      ERRORS
chapter03     *         digitalocean    Running    tcp://178.62.77.62:2376                v1.10.0
russ in
⚡  []
```

One of the reasons that we have launched the instance in a cloud provider is that
we need a full underlying operating system to be able install and use Convoy, while
the image provided by Boot2Docker is good, it is a little too lightweight for our
requirement.

 Before we do anything further, I would recommend you to attach a
floating IP address to your DigitalOcean droplet. The reason for this
is that, in this section of the chapter, we are going to be installing
WordPress and then moving the installation to a new machine. Without
a floating IP address, your WordPress installation may appear broken.
You can find more details on floating IPs on the DigitalOcean website
at https://www.digitalocean.com/community/tutorials/
how-to-use-floating-ips-on-digitalocean.

Installing Convoy

As already mentioned, we need to install Convoy on our underlying Docker hosts operating system. To do this, you should first SSH onto your Docker host:

```
docker-machine ssh chapter03
```

 As the machine has been launched in DigitalOcean, we have connected as the root user; this means that we don't have to use sudo in front of the commands, however, as you could have launched the instance in another provider, I will keep them there so that you don't end up getting permission errors if you are not the root user.

Now that you have used ssh command to get into our Docker host, we can install and start Convoy. Convoy is written in Go and ships as a static binary. This means that we don't have to compile it manually; instead, we just need to grab the binary and copy it into place:

```
wget https://github.com/rancher/convoy/releases/download/v0.4.3/convoy.
tar.gz

tar xvf convoy.tar.gz

sudo cp convoy/convoy convoy/convoy-pdata_tools /usr/local/bin/
```

There are later versions of Convoy available at https://github.com/rancher/convoy/releases; however, these are flagged for use with Rancher only. We will be looking at Rancher in detail in a later chapter.

Now that we have our binary in place, we need to set up our Docker installation so that it loads the plugin:

```
sudo mkdir -p /etc/docker/plugins/

sudo bash -c 'echo "unix:///var/run/convoy/convoy.sock" > /etc/docker/
plugins/convoy.spec'
```

The convoy.spec file tells Docker where it can access Convoy; for more details on how plugins work refer to *Chapter 5, Building Your Own Plugin*.

Convoy is installed and ready to go, now we just have to add some storage. For testing purposes, we are going to be creating and using a loopback device; however, do not do this in production!

 A Loopback Device is a mechanism used to interpret files as real devices. The main advantage of this method is that all tools used on real disks can be used with a loopback device. Refer to http://wiki.osdev.org/Loopback_Device.

To create the loopback device and mount it, run the following commands:

```
truncate -s 4G data.vol

truncate -s 1G metadata.vol

sudo losetup /dev/loop5 data.vol

sudo losetup /dev/loop6 metadata.vol
```

Now that we have our storage ready, we can start Convoy by running the following command:

```
sudo convoy daemon --drivers devicemapper --driver-opts dm.datadev=/dev/
loop5 --driver-opts dm.metadatadev=/dev/loop6 &
```

You should see something similar to the following output:

```
root@chapter03:~# sudo convoy daemon --drivers devicemapper --driver-opts dm.datadev=/dev/loop5 --driver-opts dm.metadatadev=/dev/loop6 &
[1] 3727
root@chapter03:~# DEBU[0000] Found existing config. Ignoring command line opts, loading config from /var/lib/convoy  pkg=daemon
DEBU[0000]                                          driver=devicemapper driver_opts=map[dm.datadev:/dev/loop5 dm.metadatadev:/dev/loo
DEBU[0000] Found created pool, skip pool reinit     pkg=devmapper
DEBU[0000]                                          driver=devicemapper event=init pkg=daemon reason=complete
DEBU[0000] Registering GET, /volumes/               pkg=daemon
DEBU[0000] Registering GET, /snapshots/             pkg=daemon
DEBU[0000] Registering GET, /backups/list           pkg=daemon
DEBU[0000] Registering GET, /backups/inspect        pkg=daemon
DEBU[0000] Registering GET, /info                   pkg=daemon
DEBU[0000] Registering GET, /uuid                   pkg=daemon
DEBU[0000] Registering GET, /volumes/list           pkg=daemon
DEBU[0000] Registering POST, /volumes/create        pkg=daemon
DEBU[0000] Registering POST, /volumes/mount         pkg=daemon
DEBU[0000] Registering POST, /volumes/umount        pkg=daemon
DEBU[0000] Registering POST, /snapshots/create      pkg=daemon
DEBU[0000] Registering POST, /backups/create        pkg=daemon
DEBU[0000] Registering DELETE, /volumes/            pkg=daemon
DEBU[0000] Registering DELETE, /snapshots/          pkg=daemon
DEBU[0000] Registering DELETE, /backups             pkg=daemon
DEBU[0000] Registering plugin handler POST, /Plugin.Activate  pkg=daemon
DEBU[0000] Registering plugin handler POST, /VolumeDriver.Create  pkg=daemon
DEBU[0000] Registering plugin handler POST, /VolumeDriver.Remove  pkg=daemon
DEBU[0000] Registering plugin handler POST, /VolumeDriver.Mount   pkg=daemon
DEBU[0000] Registering plugin handler POST, /VolumeDriver.Unmount  pkg=daemon
DEBU[0000] Registering plugin handler POST, /VolumeDriver.Path  pkg=daemon

root@chapter03:~# ps aux | grep convoy
root      3727  0.0  0.3  52812  3760 pts/0    S    07:42   0:00 sudo convoy daemon --drivers devicemapper --driver-opts dm.datadev=/dev/l
root      3728  0.0  1.4 106408 14664 pts/0    Sl   07:42   0:00 convoy daemon --drivers devicemapper --driver-opts dm.datadev=/dev/loop5
root      3734  0.0  0.2   9736  2220 pts/0    S+   07:43   0:00 grep --color=auto convoy
root@chapter03:~#
```

Now that we have Convoy running, type `exit` to leave the Docker host and return to your local machine.

Launching containers with a Convoy volume

Now that we have Convoy up and running, we can make some changes to our `docker-compose.yml` file:

```
version: '2'
services:
  wordpress:
    container_name: my-wordpress-app
```

```
        image: wordpress
        ports:
          - "80:80"
        links:
          - mysql
        environment:
          WORDPRESS_DB_HOST: "mysql:3306"
          WORDPRESS_DB_PASSWORD: "password"
        volumes:
          - "uploads:/var/www/html/wp-content/uploads/"
    mysql:
        container_name: my-wordpress-database
        image: mariadb
        environment:
          MYSQL_ROOT_PASSWORD: "password"
        command: mysqld --ignore-db-dir=lost+found
        volumes:
          - "database:/var/lib/mysql/"
  volumes:
    uploads:
      driver: convoy
    database:
      driver: convoy
```

Put the `docker-compose.yml` file in a `wordpressconvoy` folder if don't you will find you will need change the name of the volume in some of the later steps in this section.

As you can see, I have highlighted a few changes. The first being that we have moved over to using MariaDB, the reason for this is that as we now using an actual filesystem rather just a folder on the host machine, we have a `lost + found` folder created, presently the official MySQL container fails to work as it believes there are already databases on the volume. To get around this, we can use the `--ignore-db-dir` directive when starting MySQL, which MariaDB supports.

Let's launch our containers and take a look at the volume that is created by running:

```
docker-compose up -d
open http://$(docker-machine ip chapter03)/
docker-compose ps
docker volume ls
docker volume inspect wordpressconvoy_database
```

You should see something similar to the following terminal output:

```
● ● ●                           wordpress-convoy — -bash — 111×31
russ in ~/Documents/Code/extending-docker/chapter03/wordpress-convoy on master*
⚡ docker-compose up -d
Creating network "wordpressconvoy_default" with the default driver
Creating my-wordpress-database
Creating my-wordpress-app
russ in ~/Documents/Code/extending-docker/chapter03/wordpress-convoy on master*
⚡ open http://$(docker-machine ip chapter03)/
russ in ~/Documents/Code/extending-docker/chapter03/wordpress-convoy on master*
⚡ docker-compose ps
         Name                    Command              State        Ports
-------------------------------------------------------------------------------
my-wordpress-app        /entrypoint.sh apache2-for ...  Up     0.0.0.0:80->80/tcp
my-wordpress-database   /docker-entrypoint.sh mysq ...  Up     3306/tcp
russ in ~/Documents/Code/extending-docker/chapter03/wordpress-convoy on master*
⚡ docker volume ls
list convoy: VolumeDriver.List: Handler not found: POST /VolumeDriver.List
DRIVER              VOLUME NAME
local               56200fbc5086a32e9f1f89186bb1834049ae34e42577107ed6dbc6d2973e5a4b
convoy              wordpressconvoy_database
convoy              wordpressconvoy_uploads
russ in ~/Documents/Code/extending-docker/chapter03/wordpress-convoy on master*
⚡ docker volume inspect wordpressconvoy_database
[
    {
        "Name": "wordpressconvoy_database",
        "Driver": "convoy",
        "Mountpoint": "/var/lib/convoy/devicemapper/mounts/8212de61-ea8c-4777-881e-d4bd07b800e3"
    }
]
russ in ~/Documents/Code/extending-docker/chapter03/wordpress-convoy on master*
⚡ ▯
```

Before we do anything further, complete the WordPress installation and upload some content:

```
open http://$(docker-machine ip chapter03)/
```

Remember to set the correct permissions on the volume before uploading content:

```
docker exec -d my-wordpress-app chmod 777 /var/www/html/wp-content/
uploads/
```

Creating a snapshot using Convoy

So far, it's no different from the default volume driver. Let's look at creating a snapshot and then backing up of the volume, you will see why later in the chapter.

First of call, let's jump back to the Docker host:

```
docker-machine ssh chapter03
```

Let's create our first snapshot by running the following the commands:

```
sudo convoy snapshot create wordpressconvoy_uploads --name snap_
wordpressconvoy_uploads_01
```

```
sudo convoy snapshot create wordpressconvoy_database --name snap_
wordpressconvoy_database_01
```

Once a snapshot has been created, you will receive a unique ID. In my case, these were `c00caa88-087d-45ad-9498-7610844c075e` and `4e2a2a6f-887c-4692-b2a8-e1f08aa42400`.

Backing up our Convoy snapshot

Now that we have our snapshots, we can use these as a basis to create our backups. To do this, we must first make sure that the destination directory where we are going to store it exists:

```
sudo mkdir /opt/backup/
```

Now that we have somewhere to store the backup, let's create it:

```
sudo convoy backup create snap_wordpressconvoy_uploads_01 --dest vfs:///
opt/backup/
```

```
sudo convoy backup create snap_wordpressconvoy_database_01 --dest vfs:///
opt/backup/
```

Once the backup has been completed, you will receive confirmation in the form of a URL. For the uploads, the URL returned is as follows:

```
vfs:///opt/backup/?backup=34ca255e-7164-4734-8b96-579b4e79f728\
u0026volume=26a5913e-4794-4df3-bbb9-7a6361c23a75
```

For the database, the URL was as follows:

```
vfs:///opt/backup/?backup=41731035-2760-4a1b-bba9-5e906e2471bc\
u0026volume=8212de61-ea8c-4777-881e-d4bd07b800e3
```

It is important that you make a note of the URLs, as you will need these to restore the backups. There is one flaw, the backups we have created are being stored on our Docker host machine. What if it was to go down? All our hard work would be then lost!

Convoy supports creating backups for Amazon S3, so let's do that. First, you will need to log in to your Amazon Web Services account and create an S3 bucket to store your backups.

Once you have created a bucket, you need to add your credentials to the server:

```
mkdir ~/.aws/
cat >>  ~/.aws/credentials << CONTENT
[default]
aws_access_key_id = JHFDIGJKBDS8639FJHDS
aws_secret_access_key = sfvjbkdsvBKHDJBDFjbfsdvlkb+JLN873JKFLSJH
CONTENT
```

> For more information on how to create an Amazon S3 bucket, refer to the getting started guide at https://aws.amazon.com/s3/getting-started/, and for details on credentials files, refer to http://blogs.aws.amazon.com/security/post/Tx3D6U6WSFGOK2H/A-New-and-Standardized-Way-to-Manage-Credentials-in-the-AWS-SDKs.

Now your Amazon S3 bucket is created. I have named mine chapter03-backup-bucket and created it in the us-west-2 region. Your Docker host has access to Amazon's API. You can make your backups again, but this time, push them to Amazon S3:

```
sudo convoy backup create snap_wordpressconvoy_uploads_01 --dest s3://
chapter03-backup-bucket@us-west-2/
sudo convoy backup create snap_wordpressconvoy_database_01 --dest s3://
chapter03-backup-bucket@us-west-2/
```

As you can see, the destination URL takes the following format:

```
s3://<bucket-name>@<aws-region>
```

Again, you will receive URLs once the backups has been completed. In my case, there are as follows:

```
s3://chapter03-backup-bucket@us-west-2/?backup=6cb4ed46-2084-42bc-8261-6b4da690bd5e\u0026volume=26a5913e-4794-4df3-bbb9-7a6361c23a75
```

For the database backup, we will see the following:

```
s3://chapter03-backup-bucket@us-west-2/?backup=75608b0b-93e7-4319-b212-7a1b0ccaf289\u0026volume=8212de61-ea8c-4777-881e-d4bd07b800e3
```

When running the preceding commands, your terminal output should have looked something similar to the following:

```
root@chapter03:~# sudo convoy snapshot create wordpressconvoy_uploads --name snap_wordpressconvoy_uploads_01
c00caa88-087d-45ad-9498-7610844c075e
root@chapter03:~# sudo convoy snapshot create wordpressconvoy_database --name snap_wordpressconvoy_database_01
4e2a2a6f-887c-4692-b2a8-e1f08aa42400
root@chapter03:~# mkdir /opt/backup/
root@chapter03:~# sudo convoy backup create snap_wordpressconvoy_uploads_01 --dest vfs:///opt/backup/
vfs:///opt/backup/?backup=34ca255e-7164-4734-8b96-579b4e79f728\u0026volume=26a5913e-4794-4df3-bbb9-7a6361c23a75
root@chapter03:~# sudo convoy backup create snap_wordpressconvoy_database_01 --dest vfs:///opt/backup/
root@chapter03:~# sudo convoy backup create snap_wordpressconvoy_uploads_01 --dest s3://chapter03-backup-bucket@us-west-2/
s3://chapter03-backup-bucket@us-west-2/?backup=6c4ed46-2084-42bc-8261-6b4da690bd5e\u0026volume=26a5913e-4794-4df3-bbb9-7a6361c23a75
root@chapter03:~# sudo convoy backup create snap_wordpressconvoy_database_01 --dest s3://chapter03-backup-bucket@us-west-2/
s3://chapter03-backup-bucket@us-west-2/?backup=75608b0b-93e7-4319-b212-7a1b0ccaf289\u0026volume=8212de61-ea8c-4777-881e-d4bd07b800e3
root@chapter03:~#
```

Now that we have off instance backups of our data volumes, let's terminate the Docker host and bring up a new one. If you haven't already, `exit` from the Docker host and terminate it by running the following command:

```
docker-machine stop chapter03 && docker-machine rm chapter03
```

Restoring our Convoy backups

As you can see from the following screen, we have backups of our snapshots in an Amazon S3 bucket:

Before we restore the backups, we need to recreate our Docker instance. Use the instructions for launching a Docker host in DigitalOcean, installing and starting Convoy, and also setting up your AWS credentials file from the previous sections of this chapter.

Remember to reassign your floating IP address to the Droplet before you continue.

Once you have everything backed up and running, you should be able to run the following commands to restore the volumes:

```
sudo convoy create wordpressconvoy_uploads --backup s3://chapter03-
backup-bucket@us-west-2/?backup=6cb4ed46-2084-42bc-8261-6b4da690bd5e\
u0026volume=26a5913e-4794-4df3-bbb9-7a6361c23a75
```

You should also be able to run the following command:

```
sudo convoy create wordpressconvoy_database --backup s3://chapter03-
backup-bucket@us-west-2/?backup=75608b0b-93e7-4319-b212-7a1b0ccaf289\
u0026volume=8212de61-ea8c-4777-881e-d4bd07b800e3
```

The process of restoring the volumes will take several minutes, during which you will see a lot of output streamed to your terminal. The output should look similar to the following screenshot:

```
● ● ●                           ↑ root@chapter03: ~ — ssh ◂ docker-machine ssh chapter03 — 134×44
root@chapter03:~# sudo convoy create wordpressconvoy_uploads --backup s3://chapter03-backup-bucket@us-west-2/?backup=6cb4ed46-2084-42b
c-8261-6b4da690bd5e\u0026volume=26a5913e-4794-4df3-bbb9-7a6361c23a75
DEBU[0172] Calling: POST, /volumes/create, request: POST, /v1/volumes/create  pkg=daemon
DEBU[0172]                                              event=create object=volume opts=map[PrepareForVM:false Size:0 BackupURL:s3://
chapter03-backup-bucket@us-west-2/?backup=6cb4ed46-2084-42bc-8261-6b4da690bd5e&volume=26a5913e-4794-4df3-bbb9-7a6361c23a75 VolumeName:
wordpressconvoy_uploads VolumeDriverID: VolumeType: VolumeIOPS:0]  pkg=daemon reason=prepare volume=033285b5-ce8c-4a5f-be8e-d11c1e87ed6
b volume_name=wordpressconvoy_uploads
DEBU[0173] Loaded driver for %vs3://chapter03-backup-bucket@us-west-2/  pkg=s3
DEBU[0173]                                              filepath=convoy-objectstore/volumes/26/a5/26a5913e-4794-4df3-bbb9-7a6361c23a7
5/volume.cfg kind=s3 object=config pkg=objectstore reason=start
DEBU[0173]                                              filepath=convoy-objectstore/volumes/26/a5/26a5913e-4794-4df3-bbb9-7a6361c23a7
5/volume.cfg kind=s3 object=config pkg=objectstore reason=complete
DEBU[0173] Current devID 1                              pkg=devmapper
DEBU[0173] Creating volume                              dm_volume_device=1 event=create object=volume pkg=devmapper reason=start volum
e=033285b5-ce8c-4a5f-be8e-d11c1e87ed6b
DEBU[0173] [devmapper] CreateDevice(poolName=/dev/mapper/convoy-pool, deviceId=1)
DEBU[0173] libdevmapper(7): ioctl/libdm-iface.c:1750 (4) dm message convoy-pool  OF  create_thin 1 [16384] (*1)
DEBU[0174] Activating device for volume                 dm_volume_device=1 event=activate object=volume pkg=devmapper reason=start vol
ume=033285b5-ce8c-4a5f-be8e-d11c1e87ed6b
DEBU[0174] libdevmapper(7): ioctl/libdm-iface.c:1750 (4) dm create 033285b5-ce8c-4a5f-be8e-d11c1e87ed6b  OF   [16384] (*1)
DEBU[0174] libdevmapper(7): libdm-common.c:1348 (4) 033285b5-ce8c-4a5f-be8e-d11c1e87ed6b: Stacking NODE_ADD (252,1) 0:0 0600 [verify_u
dev]
DEBU[0174] libdevmapper(7): ioctl/libdm-iface.c:1750 (4) dm reload 033285b5-ce8c-4a5f-be8e-d11c1e87ed6b  OF   [16384] (*1)
DEBU[0174] libdevmapper(7): ioctl/libdm-iface.c:1750 (4) dm resume 033285b5-ce8c-4a5f-be8e-d11c1e87ed6b  OF   [16384] (*1)
DEBU[0174] libdevmapper(7): libdm-common.c:1348 (4) 033285b5-ce8c-4a5f-be8e-d11c1e87ed6b: Processing NODE_ADD (252,1) 0:0 0600 [verify
_udev]
DEBU[0174] libdevmapper(7): libdm-common.c:983 (4) Created /dev/mapper/033285b5-ce8c-4a5f-be8e-d11c1e87ed6b
DEBU[0174] Loaded driver for %vs3://chapter03-backup-bucket@us-west-2/  pkg=s3
DEBU[0174]                                              filepath=convoy-objectstore/volumes/26/a5/26a5913e-4794-4df3-bbb9-7a6361c23a7
5/volume.cfg kind=s3 object=config pkg=objectstore reason=start
DEBU[0174]                                              filepath=convoy-objectstore/volumes/26/a5/26a5913e-4794-4df3-bbb9-7a6361c23a7
5/volume.cfg kind=s3 object=config pkg=objectstore reason=complete
DEBU[0174]                                              filepath=convoy-objectstore/volumes/26/a5/26a5913e-4794-4df3-bbb9-7a6361c23a7
5/backups/backup_6cb4ed46-2084-42bc-8261-6b4da690bd5e.cfg kind=s3 object=config pkg=objectstore reason=start
DEBU[0175]                                              filepath=convoy-objectstore/volumes/26/a5/26a5913e-4794-4df3-bbb9-7a6361c23a7
5/backups/backup_6cb4ed46-2084-42bc-8261-6b4da690bd5e.cfg kind=s3 object=config pkg=objectstore reason=complete
DEBU[0175]                                              backup_url=s3://chapter03-backup-bucket@us-west-2/?backup=6cb4ed46-2084-42bc-
8261-6b4da690bd5e&volume=26a5913e-4794-4df3-bbb9-7a6361c23a75 event=restore object=snapshot original_volume=26a5913e-4794-4df3-bbb9-7a
6361c23a75 pkg=objectstore reason=start snapshot=6cb4ed46-2084-42bc-8261-6b4da690bd5e volume_dev=/dev/mapper/033285b5-ce8c-4a5f-be8e-d
11c1e87ed6b
DEBU[0175] Restore for /dev/mapper/033285b5-ce8c-4a5f-be8e-d11c1e87ed6b: block dd9896f7abf18825808d2721ab382c693e2a5a4edd01ac358accbf2
071d369e0, 1/933  pkg=objectstore
DEBU[0175] Restore for /dev/mapper/033285b5-ce8c-4a5f-be8e-d11c1e87ed6b: block f1af6a6aa6410a1eea5a1ba2a8856cc7bb01b302483e819f3ff4ca4
6bb17bb16, 2/933  pkg=objectstore
DEBU[0379] Restore for /dev/mapper/033285b5-ce8c-4a5f-be8e-d11c1e87ed6b: block 731859029215873fdac1c9f2f8bd25a334abf0f3a9e1b057cf2cacc
2826d86b0, 932/933  pkg=objectstore
DEBU[0379] Restore for /dev/mapper/033285b5-ce8c-4a5f-be8e-d11c1e87ed6b: block ba32c76671d5b4dc48ba5571e9b71472a7453b3af2bca0fcfb30dc7
e01aa3a8e, 933/933  pkg=objectstore
DEBU[0380] Created volume                               event=create object=volume pkg=daemon reason=complete volume=033285b5-ce8c-4a
5f-be8e-d11c1e87ed6b
DEBU[0380] Response:  033285b5-ce8c-4a5f-be8e-d11c1e87ed6b  pkg=daemon
033285b5-ce8c-4a5f-be8e-d11c1e87ed6b
root@chapter03:~# 
```

As you can see towards the end of the preceding terminal session, the restore process restores each block from the S3 bucket so that you will most see these messages scroll past.

Once you have both volumes restored, go back to your Docker Compose file and run the following command:

```
docker-compose up -d
```

If everything goes as planned, you should be able to open a browser and see your content intact and how you left it using the following command:

```
open http://$(docker-machine ip chapter03)/
```

 Don't forget, if you have finished with the Docker host, you will need to stop and remove using `docker-machine stop chapter03 && docker-machine rm chapter03`, otherwise you may incur unwanted costs.

Summing up Convoy

Convoy is a great tool to start looking at Docker volumes, it is great to quickly move the content around different environments, which means that you can not only share your containers, but also share your volumes with fellow developers or sysadmins. It is also straightforward to install and configure, as it ships as a precompiled binary.

Block volumes using REX-Ray

So far, we have looked at drivers that use local storage with backups to remote storage. We are now going to take this one step further by looking at remote storage that is directly attached to our container.

In this example, we are you going to be launching a Docker instance in Amazon Web Services and launch our WordPress example and attach Amazon Elastic Block Store volumes to our containers using REX-Ray, a volume driver by EMC.

REX-Ray supports several storage types on both public clouds and EMC's own range, as follows:

- AWS EC2
- OpenStack
- Google Compute Engine
- EMC Isilon, ScaleIO, VMAX, and XtremIO

The driver is in active development and more types of supported storage are promised soon.

Installing REX-Ray

As we are going to be using Amazon EBS volumes, we will need to launch the Docker host in AWS, as EBS volumes can not be mounted as block devices to instances in other cloud providers. As per the previous chapter, this can be accomplished using Docker Machine and the following command:

```
docker-machine create \
    --driver amazonec2 \
    --amazonec2-access-key JHFDIGJKBDS8639FJHDS \
    --amazonec2-secret-key sfvjbkdsvBKHDJBDFjbfsdvlkb+JLN873JKFLSJH \
    --amazonec2-vpc-id vpc-35c91750 \
    chapter03
```

Switch Docker Machine to use the newly created host:

```
eval "$(docker-machine env chapter03)"
```

Then, SSH into the host, as follows:

```
docker-machine ssh chapter03
```

Once you are on the Docker host, run the following command to install REX-Ray:

```
curl -sSL https://dl.bintray.com/emccode/rexray/install | sh -
```

This will download and perform the basic configuration of the latest stable release of REX-Ray:

```
● ● ●                    ⬆ ubuntu@chapter03: ~ — ssh ‹ docker-machine ssh chapter03 — 111×17
ubuntu@chapter03:~$ curl -sSL https://dl.bintray.com/emccode/rexray/install | sh -
Selecting previously unselected package rexray.
(Reading database ... 67416 files and directories currently installed.)
Preparing to unpack rexray-latest-x86_64.deb ...
Unpacking rexray (0.3.1-1) ...
Setting up rexray (0.3.1-1) ...

REX-Ray has been installed to /usr/bin/rexray

Binary: /usr/bin/rexray
SemVer: 0.3.1
OsArch: Linux-x86_64
Branch: v0.3.1
Commit: bf4d6eec8c931b10d1ec187de052a23c09681ac6
Formed: Wed, 30 Dec 2015 21:12:44 UTC

ubuntu@chapter03:~$ ▯
```

Once REX-Ray is installed, we will need to configure it to use Amazon EBS volumes. This will need to be done as the root user, to the following to add a file called `config.yml` to `/etc/rexray/`:

```
sudo vim /etc/rexray/config.yml
```

The file should contain the following, remember to replace the values for AWS credentials:

```
rexray:
  storageDrivers:
  - ec2
aws:
  accessKey: JHFDIGJKBDS8639FJHDS
  secretKey: sfvjbkdsvBKHDJBDFjbfsdvlkb+JLN873JKFLSJH
```

Once you have added the configuration file, you should be able to use REX-Ray straight away, running the following command should return a list of EBS volumes:

```
sudo rexray volume ls
```

If you see the list of volumes, then you will need to start the process. If you don't see the volumes, check whether the user that you have provided accesskey and secretkey for has access to read and create EBS volumes. To start the process and check whether everything is OK, run the following commands:

```
sudo systemctl restart rexray
```
```
sudo systemctl status rexray
```

You should see something similar to the following terminal output if everything works as expected:

```
● ● ●                    ⇧ root@chapter03: ~ — ssh ‹ docker-machine ssh chapter03 — 111×37
root@chapter03:~# rexray volume ls
- name: ""
  volumeid: vol-7fa81edc
  availabilityzone: us-east-1a
  status: in-use
  volumetype: gp2
  iops: 48
  size: "16"
  networkname: ""
  attachments:
  - volumeid: vol-7fa81edc
    instanceid: i-eacbbf72
    devicename: /dev/sda1
    status: attached

root@chapter03:~# systemctl restart rexray
root@chapter03:~# systemctl status rexray
● rexray.service - rexray
   Loaded: loaded (/etc/systemd/system/rexray.service; enabled; vendor preset: enabled)
   Active: active (running) since Mon 2016-02-15 17:22:33 UTC; 6s ago
 Main PID: 22244 (rexray)
   Memory: 3.0M
      CPU: 12ms
   CGroup: /system.slice/rexray.service
           └─22244 /usr/bin/rexray start -f

Feb 15 17:22:33 chapter03 rexray[22244]: [[[,/[[['  [[cccc        '[[,,[['   [[[,/[[['  ,[[ '[[,  '[[,[[['
Feb 15 17:22:33 chapter03 rexray[22244]: $$$$$$c      $$"""""       Y$$$Pcccc $$$$$$c   c$$$cc$$$c   c$$"
Feb 15 17:22:33 chapter03 rexray[22244]: 888b "88bo,888oo,__     oP"''"Yo,   888b "88bo,888    888,,8P"'
Feb 15 17:22:33 chapter03 rexray[22244]: MMMM    "W" """"YUMMM,m"       "Mm, MMMM    "W" YMM    ""'mM"
Feb 15 17:22:33 chapter03 rexray[22244]: Binary: /usr/bin/rexray
Feb 15 17:22:33 chapter03 rexray[22244]: SemVer: 0.3.1
Feb 15 17:22:33 chapter03 rexray[22244]: OsArch: Linux-x86_64
Feb 15 17:22:33 chapter03 rexray[22244]: Branch: v0.3.1
Feb 15 17:22:33 chapter03 rexray[22244]: Commit: bf4d6eec8c931b10d1ec187de052a23c09681ac6
Feb 15 17:22:33 chapter03 rexray[22244]: Formed: Wed, 30 Dec 2015 21:12:44 UTC
root@chapter03:~# []
```

The final step of the installation is to restart Docker on the instance so that it picks up the new volume driver. To do this, run the following command:

```
sudo systemctl restart docker
```

Now its time to launch some containers. The only change we need make to the Docker Compose file from the Convoy one is to change the name of the volume driver, everything else stays the same:

```
version: '2'
services:
  wordpress:
    container_name: my-wordpress-app
    image: wordpress
    ports:
      - "80:80"
    links:
      - mysql
    environment:
      WORDPRESS_DB_HOST: "mysql:3306"
```

```
        WORDPRESS_DB_PASSWORD: "password"
      volumes:
        - "uploads:/var/www/html/wp-content/uploads/"
    mysql:
      container_name: my-wordpress-database
      image: mariadb
      environment:
        MYSQL_ROOT_PASSWORD: "password"
      command: mysqld --ignore-db-dir=lost+found
      volumes:
        - "database:/var/lib/mysql/"
  volumes:
    uploads:
      driver: rexray
    database:
      driver: rexray
```

Once the application has launched, set the permissions on the upload folder by
running the following command:

```
docker exec -d my-wordpress-app chmod 777 /var/www/html/wp-content/
uploads/
```

In the AWS Console, you will notice that now there are some additional volumes:

Open your new WordPress installation in a browser by running the following
command:

```
open http://$(docker-machine ip chapter03)/
```

If you have a problem opening the WordPress site in your browser, find the running instance in the AWS Console and add a rule for `port 80/HTTP` to the **DOCKER-MACHINE** security group. Your rules should look similar to the following image:

You will only have to add the rule once, as Docker Machine will reassign the `docker-machine` security group whenever you launch more Docker hosts.

Once you have the page open, complete the WordPress installation and edit or upload some content. You know the drill by now, once you have added your content, it's time to stop the containers, remove them, and then terminate the Docker host:

```
docker-compose stop
```

```
docker-compose rm
```

Before removing the host, you can check the status of the volumes by running the following command:

```
docker volume ls
```

You will see something similar to the following image:

Finally, it's time to remove the Docker host:

```
docker-machine stop chapter03 && docker-machine rm chapter03
```

Moving the REX-Ray volume

Before we bring up a new Docker host with Docker Machine, it is worth pointing out that our WordPress installation will probably look a little broken.

This is because moving our containers to a new host changes the IP address that we will be accessing the WordPress site on, meaning that until you change the settings to use the second node's IP address, you will see a broken site.

This is because it is trying to load content, such as CSS and JavaScript, from the first Docker host's IP address.

For more information on how to update these settings, refer to the WordPress Codex at https://codex.wordpress.org/Changing_The_Site_URL.

Also, if you have logged into the AWS Console, you may have noticed that your EBS volumes are not currently attached to any instance:

Now that we have this out of the way, let's launch our new Docker host using Docker Machine. If you followed the instructions in the previous section to launch the host, connect, install REX-Ray, and launch the WordPress and Database containers. As we have already discussed, you could update the site's IP address by connecting to the database:

1. Should you want to update the IP address, then you can run the following. First of all, connect to your database container:

```
docker exec -ti my-wordpress-database env TERM=xterm bash -l
```

2. Then make a connection to MariaDB using the MySQL client:

```
mysql -uroot -ppassword --protocol=TCP -h127.0.0.1
```

3. Switch to the `wordpress` database:

```
use wordpress;
```

4. Then finally run the following SQL. In my case, `http://54.175.31.251` is the old URL and `http://52.90.249.56` is the new one:

```
UPDATE wp_options SET option_value = replace(option_value,
'http://54.175.31.251', 'http://52.90.249.56') WHERE option_name =
'home' OR option_name = 'siteurl';
UPDATE wp_posts SET guid = replace(guid, 'http://54.175.31.251','h
ttp://52.90.249.56');
UPDATE wp_posts SET post_content = replace(post_content,
'http://54.175.31.251', 'http://52.90.249.56');
UPDATE wp_postmeta SET meta_value = replace(meta_value,'http://54.
175.31.251','http://52.90.249.56');
```

Your terminal session should look similar to the following screenshot:

```
russ in ~/Documents/Code/extending-docker/chapter03/wordpress-roxtay on master*
↯ docker exec -ti my-wordpress-database env TERM=xterm bash -l
root@6d8b398154bb:/# mysql -uroot -ppassword --protocol=TCP -h127.0.0.1
Welcome to the MariaDB monitor.  Commands end with ; or \g.
Your MariaDB connection id is 12
Server version: 10.1.11-MariaDB-1~jessie mariadb.org binary distribution

Copyright (c) 2000, 2015, Oracle, MariaDB Corporation Ab and others.

Type 'help;' or '\h' for help. Type '\c' to clear the current input statement.

MariaDB [(none)]> use wordpress;
Reading table information for completion of table and column names
You can turn off this feature to get a quicker startup with -A

Database changed
MariaDB [wordpress]> UPDATE wp_options SET option_value = replace(option_value, 'http://54.175.31.251', 'http://52.90.249.56')
Query OK, 2 rows affected (0.01 sec)
Rows matched: 2  Changed: 2  Warnings: 0

MariaDB [wordpress]> UPDATE wp_posts SET guid = replace(guid, 'http://54.175.31.251','http://52.90.249.56');
Query OK, 4 rows affected (0.00 sec)
Rows matched: 4  Changed: 4  Warnings: 0

MariaDB [wordpress]> UPDATE wp_posts SET post_content = replace(post_content, 'http://54.175.31.251', 'http://52.90.249.56');
Query OK, 1 row affected (0.00 sec)
Rows matched: 4  Changed: 1  Warnings: 0

MariaDB [wordpress]> UPDATE wp_postmeta SET meta_value = replace(meta_value,'http://54.175.31.251','http://52.90.249.56');
Query OK, 0 rows affected (0.00 sec)
Rows matched: 5  Changed: 0  Warnings: 0

MariaDB [wordpress]> exit
Bye
root@6d8b398154bb:/# exit
logout
russ in ~/Documents/Code/extending-docker/chapter03/wordpress-roxtay on master*
↯ ▯
```

However, we can see that the content is present, even though the site looks broken.

Summing up REX-Ray

REX-Ray is very much in early development, with more features being added all the time. Over the next few releases, I can foresee it getting more and more useful as it is slowly moving towards being a cluster-aware tool rather than the standalone tool it is at the moment.

However, even in this early stage of its development, it serves as a great introduction to using external storage with Docker Volumes.

Flocker and Volume Hub

The next tool that we are going to look at is Flocker by ClusterHQ. It's certainly the most feature-rich of the third-party volume drivers that we are going to be looking at in this chapter. As you can see from the following list of supported storage options, it has the widest coverage of storage backends out of all of the volume drivers:

- AWS Elastic Block Storage
- OpenStack Cinder with any supported backend
- EMC ScaleIO, XtremeIO, and VMAX
- VMware vSphere and vSan
- NetApp OnTap
- Dell Storage SC Series
- HPE 3PAR StoreServ and StoreVirtual (with OpenStack only)
- Huawei OceanStor
- Hedvig
- NexentaEdge
- ConvergeIO
- Saratoga Speed

There is also support for the following storage options coming soon:

- Ceph
- Google Persistent Disk

As most people will have access to AWS, we are going to look at launching a Flocker cluster in AWS.

Forming your Flock

Rather than rolling our sleeves up and installing Flocker manually, we are going to take a look at how to get Flocker up and running quickly.

For this part of the chapter, we will be launching a cluster using an AWS CloudFormation template provided by ClusterHQ to get a Flocker cluster up and running quickly.

AWS CloudFormation is the orchestration tool provided by Amazon that allows you to define how you would like your AWS infrastructure to look and be configured. CloudFormation is free to use; however, you do pay for the resources that are launched by it. At the time of writing, the estimated cost for running the template for one month is $341.13. For more information on CloudFormation, refer to https://aws.amazon.com/cloudformation/, or for a breakdown of the costs, refer to http://calculator.s3.amazonaws.com/index.html#r=IAD&s=EC2&key=calc-D96E035B-5A84-48DE-BF62-807FFE4740A8.

There are a few steps that we will need to perform before we launch the CloudFormation template. First of all, you will need to create a key pair to be used by the template. To do this, log in to the AWS console at `https://console.aws.amazon.com/`, select your region, then click on EC2, and then on the left-hand side **Key Pairs** menu, the key pair you create should be called something like flocker-test:

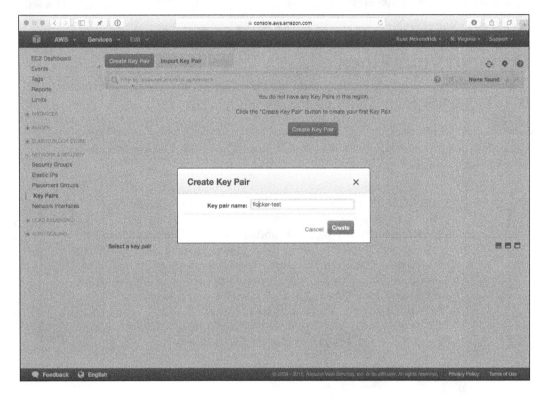

After you click on the **Create** button, your key pair will be downloaded, **keep this safe** as you will not be able to download it again. Now that you have your key pair created and safely downloaded, it's time to create an account on the ClusterHQ Volume Hub, you can do this by going to `https://volumehub.clusterhq.com/`.

The Volume Hub (at the time of writing this book, it is in Alpha testing) is a web-based interface to manage your Flocker volumes. You can either signup for an account using your e-mail address or signin using your Google ID.

Once you have signed up/in, you will be presented with a notice pointing out that *You don't appear to have a cluster yet.* and the option of either creating a new cluster or connect to an existing cluster:

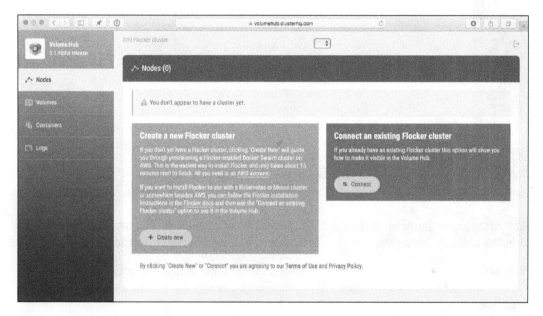

Clicking on **Create new** button will open an overlay with instructions about what you need to do to create a cluster using AWS CloudFormation. As we have already actioned step one, scroll down to step two. Here, you should see a button that says **Start CloudFormation Configuration Process**, click on this to open a new tab that will take you directly to the AWS CloudFormation page on the AWS console:

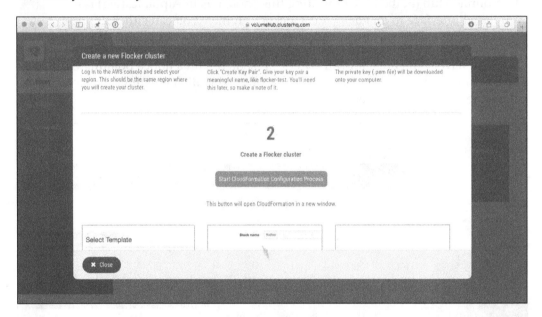

The first step of launching the AWS CloudFormation stack is selecting the template, this has already been done for us, so you can click on the **Next** button.

You will now be asked to give some details about your stack, this includes a name for the stack, EC2 key pair name, AWS access and secret keys, and also your Volume Hub token.

To get your Volume Hub token, visit `https://volumehub.clusterhq.com/v1/token` and you will be presented with a token. This token is unique to your Volume Hub account, it is important you don't share it:

Once you have filled in the details you can click on the **Next** button. On the next page, you will be asked to tag your resources, this is optional. You should follow your normal processes for tagging resources here. Once you have added your tags, click on the **Next** button.

 Note that clicking on create will launch resources in your AWS account that will incur hourly charges. Only click on create if you are planning on working through the next steps.

The next page gives you an overview of the details that you have provided. If you are happy with these, click on the **Create** button.

After you click on the **Create** button, you will be taken back to the AWS
CloudFormation page, where should see your stack with a **CREATE_IN_
PROGRESS** status:

If you don't see your stack, click on the refresh icon on the right-hand top corner.
Typically, it will take around 10 minutes to create your cluster. While the stack is
being created, you can click on one of the **Split pane** icons on the bottom-right
of the screen and view the events that are taking place to launch your cluster.

Also, as the cluster is launching, you should start seeing Nodes registering
themselves in your Volume Hub account. It is important, however tempting, to not
start using the Volume Hub until your stack has a **CREATE_COMPLETE** status.

Once your stack has been deployed, click on the **Outputs** tab. This will give you the details you will need to connect to the cluster. You should see something similar to the following:

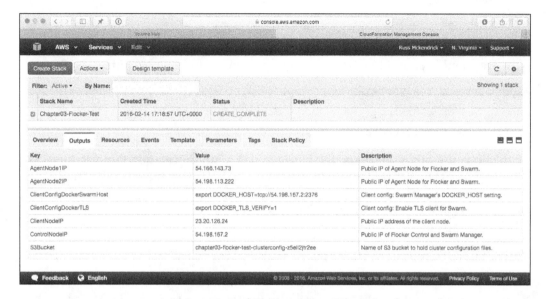

The first thing we need to do is set the correct permissions on the key pair that we created earlier. In my case, it is in my `Downloads` folder:

```
chmod 0400 ~/Downloads/flocker-test.pem.txt
```

Once you have set the permission, you will need to log in to the client node using `ubuntu` as the username and your key pair. In my case, the client node IP address is 23.20.126.24:

```
ssh ubuntu@23.20.126.24 -i ~/Downloads/flocker-test.pem.txt
```

Once you are logged in, you need to run a few more commands to get the cluster ready. For this, you will need to make a note of the IP addresses of the **Control Node**, which in the preceding screen is `54.198.167.2`:

```
export FLOCKER_CERTS_PATH=/etc/flocker
export FLOCKER_USER=user1
export FLOCKER_CONTROL_SERVICE=54.198.167.2
```

Now that you have connected to the control service, you should be able to get an overview of the cluster using the `flockerctl` command:

```
flockerctl status
flockerctl ls
```

When running the `flockerctl ls` command, you shouldn't see any datasets listed. Now we should connect to Docker. To do this, run the following commands:

```
export DOCKER_TLS_VERIFY=1
export DOCKER_HOST=tcp://$FLOCKER_CONTROL_SERVICE:2376
docker info | grep Nodes
```

At the time of writing this book, the Flocker AWS CloudFormation template installs and configures Docker 1.9.1 and Docker Compose 1.5.2. This means that you will not be able to use the new Docker Compose file format. There should be, however, Docker Compose files in both the old and new formats in the GitHub repository, which accompanies this book.

You can find the repository at `https://github.com/russmckendrick/extending-docker/`.

Your terminal output should look similar to the following session:

```
● ◎ ● ↥ ubuntu@ip-10-123-196-215: ~ — ssh ubuntu@23.20.126.24 -i ~/Downloads/flocker-test.pem.txt — 110×20
ubuntu@ip-10-123-196-215:~$ export FLOCKER_CERTS_PATH=/etc/flocker
ubuntu@ip-10-123-196-215:~$ export FLOCKER_USER=user1
ubuntu@ip-10-123-196-215:~$ export FLOCKER_CONTROL_SERVICE=54.198.167.2
ubuntu@ip-10-123-196-215:~$ flockerctl status
SERVER     ADDRESS
809beb96   10.182.54.66
9ccc6bf2   10.179.213.198

ubuntu@ip-10-123-196-215:~$ flockerctl ls
DATASET    SIZE    METADATA    STATUS    SERVER

ubuntu@ip-10-123-196-215:~$ export DOCKER_TLS_VERIFY=1
ubuntu@ip-10-123-196-215:~$ export DOCKER_HOST=tcp://54.198.167.2:2376
ubuntu@ip-10-123-196-215:~$ docker info |grep Nodes
Nodes: 2
ubuntu@ip-10-123-196-215:~$ docker --version
Docker version 1.9.1, build a34a1d5
ubuntu@ip-10-123-196-215:~$ docker-compose --version
docker-compose version 1.5.2, build 7240ff3
ubuntu@ip-10-123-196-215:~$ []
```

Now that we have everything up and running, let's launch our WordPress installation using Flocker volumes.

Deploying into the Flock

First thing we should do is create the volumes. We could let Flocker use its defaults, which is a 75 GB EBS volume, but this is a little overkill for our needs:

```
docker volume create -d flocker -o size=1G -o profile=bronze
--name=database
docker volume create -d flocker -o size=1G -o profile=bronze
--name=uploads
```

As you can see, this is a more sensible size and we are choosing the same volume names as we have done in the previous examples. Now that we have our volumes created, we can launch WordPress. To do this, we have two Docker Compose files, one will launch the containers on AgentNode1 and the other on AgentNode2. First of all, create a folder to store the files:

```
mkdir wordpress
cd wordpress
vim docker-compose-node1.yml
```

As already mentioned, at the time of writing this book, only the original Docker Compose file format is support, due to this, our file should have the following content:

```
wordpress:
   container_name: my-wordpress-app
   image: wordpress
   ports:
     - "80:80"
   links:
     - mysql
   environment:
     - "constraint:flocker-node==1"
     - "WORDPRESS_DB_HOST=mysql:3306"
     - "WORDPRESS_DB_PASSWORD=password"
   volume_driver: flocker
   volumes:
     - "uploads:/var/www/html/wp-content/uploads/"
mysql:
   container_name: my-wordpress-database
   image: mariadb
   environment:
     - "constraint:flocker-node==1"
     - "MYSQL_ROOT_PASSWORD=password"
```

```
command: mysqld --ignore-db-dir=lost+found
volume_driver: flocker
volumes:
  - "database:/var/lib/mysql/"
```

As you can see, it isn't too different from the new format. The important thing to note is the lines that bind the containers to a node, this has been highlighted in the preceding code.

To launch the containers, we have to pass the filename to docker-compose. To do this, run the following commands:

```
docker-compose -f docker-compose-node1.yml up -d

docker-compose -f docker-compose-node1.yml ps
```

Once the container's have launched, run the following to set the correct permissions on the uploads folder:

```
docker exec -d my-wordpress-app chmod 777 /var/www/html/wp-content/
uploads/
```

Now that we have our volumes created and containers launched, let's take a quick look at the Volume Hub:

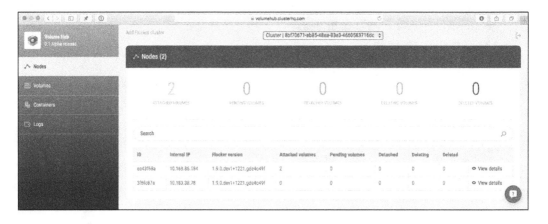

As you can see, there are two volumes being shown as attached to the node with the internal IP of 10.168.86.184. Looking at the Volumes page gives us a lot more detail:

As you can see, we have information on the size, name, its unique ID, and which node it is attached to. We can also see the information on the containers that are running within our cluster:

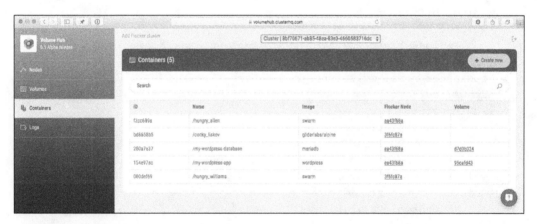

Before we stop and remove the containers, you should configure WordPress and then log in and upload a file. You will be able to get the IP address you can access WordPress on by running the following command and opening the IP address where port 80 is mapped to in your browser:

```
docker-compose -f docker-compose-node1.yml ps
```

Once you have made these changes, you can stop and remove the containers by running the following commands:

```
docker-compose -f docker-compose-node1.yml stop
docker-compose -f docker-compose-node1.yml rm -f
```

Now that you have removed the containers, it's time to launch them on the second node. You will need to create a second Docker Compose file, as follows:

```
vim docker-compose-node2.yml
```

```yaml
    wordpress:
        container_name: my-wordpress-app
        image: wordpress
        ports:
          - "80:80"
        links:
          - mysql
        environment:
          - "constraint:flocker-node==2"
          - "WORDPRESS_DB_HOST=mysql:3306"
          - "WORDPRESS_DB_PASSWORD=password"
        volume_driver: flocker
        volumes:
          - "uploads:/var/www/html/wp-content/uploads/"
    mysql:
        container_name: my-wordpress-database
        image: mariadb
        environment:
          - "constraint:flocker-node==2"
          - "MYSQL_ROOT_PASSWORD=password"
        command: mysqld --ignore-db-dir=lost+found
        volume_driver: flocker
        volumes:
          - "database:/var/lib/mysql/"
```

As you can see, all that has changed is the node number. To launch the containers, run the following command:

```
docker-compose -f docker-compose-node2.yml up -d
```

It will take a little longer to launch, as Flocker has to unattach and reattach the volumes to the second node. Once the containers are running, you will see that they are now showing as being attached to the second node in the Volume Hub, as shown in the following screenshot:

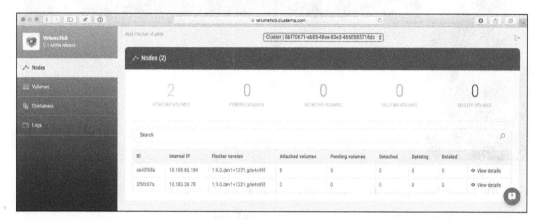

This is also reflected in the other sections of the Volume Hub:

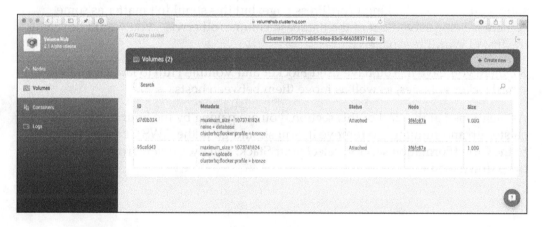

Finally, you can see your new containers on the **Containers** page:

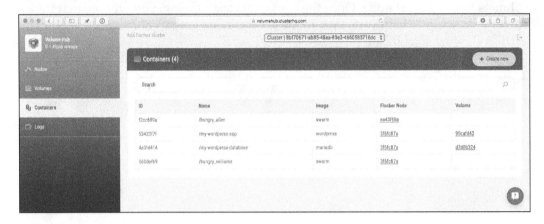

Run the following command and open the IP address in a browser:

```
docker-compose -f docker-compose-node2.yml ps
```

As mentioned in the REX-Rey section of this chapter, opening WordPress should show you a broken-looking WordPress page, but this shouldn't matter as some content is being served out of the database volume; otherwise, you would be seeing the Install WordPress page.

So, there you have it. You have used Flocker and Volume Hub to launch and view your Docker volumes, as well as move them between hosts.

As mentioned at the start of this section, you are paying by the hour to have the cluster up and running. To remove it, you should go to the AWS Console, switch to the CloudFormation service, select your Stack, and then delete from the actions drop-down menu:

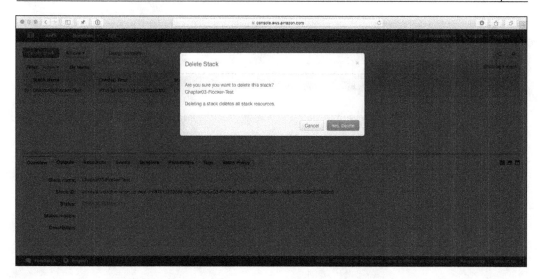

If you get an error about not being able to remove the S3 bucket, don't worry, all of the expensive stuff will have been terminated. To resolve the error, just go to the S3 bucket it is complaining about in the AWS Console and remove the content. Once you have removed the content, go back to the CloudFormation page and attempt to delete the stack again.

Summing up Flocker

Flocker is the grandfather of Docker volumes, it was one of the original solutions for managing volumes even before the volume plugin architecture was released. This means that it is both mature and easily the most complicated of the volume plugins that we have looked at.

To get an idea of its complexity, you can view the CloudFormation template at `https://s3.amazonaws.com/installer.downloads.clusterhq.com/flocker-cluster.cloudformation.json`.

As you can see, there are a lot of steps. Viewing the template in the CloudFormation visualizer gives you more of an idea of how everything is linked:

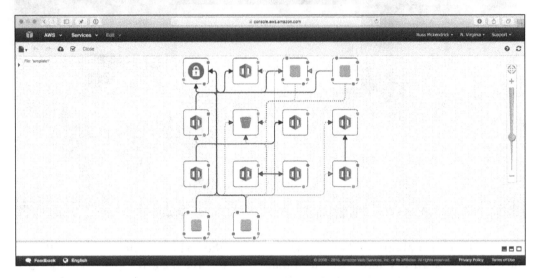

Add to the mix that Docker itself is regularly being updated and you have a very complex installation process. This is the reason why I have not gone into detail about how to manually install it in this chapter, as the process will no doubt have changed by the time you come to read it.

Luckily, Cluster Labs have an extremely good documentation that is regularly updated. It can be found at `https://docs.clusterhq.com/en/latest/`.

It's also worth pointing out that, at the time of writing this book, Volume Hub is in early alpha and more functionality is being added regularly. Eventually, I can see this being quite a powerful combination of tools.

Summary

In this chapter, we have looked at three different volume drivers that all work with Docker's plugin architecture.

While the three drivers offer three very different approaches to providing persistent storage for your containers, you may have noticed that Docker Compose files and how we interact with the volumes using the Docker client was pretty much the same experience across all three tools, probably to the point where I am sure it was starting to get a little repetitive.

This repetitiveness showcases, in my opinion, one of the best features of using Docker plugins, the consistent experience from the client's point of view. At no point, after we configured the tools, did we have to really think about or take into consideration how we were using the storage, we just got on with it.

This allows us to reuse our resources, such as Docker Compose files and containers, across multiple environments such as local VMs, cloud-based Docker hosts, or even Docker clusters.

However, at the moment, we are still bound to a single Docker host machine. In the next chapter, we will look at how to start spanning multiple Docker hosts by looking at Docker Networking plugins.

4
Network Plugins

In this chapter, we are going to be looking at the next type of plugin: networking. We will discuss how to make use of the new networking tools introduced with Docker 1.9, along with third-party tools that add even more functionality to the already powerful built-in tools. The two main tools that we are going to look at are as follows:

- **Docker Overlay Network**: `https://docs.docker.com/engine/userguide/networking/dockernetworks/`
- **Weave**: `https://weave.works/`

 This chapter assumes that you are using Docker 1.10+, some commands may not work in the previous versions.

Docker networking

Before we start to go into detail about Networking in Docker, I should mention that we have managed to make it to the fourth chapter in the book without having to really think about networking, this is because, by default, Docker creates a network bridge between the containers and your host machine's network interface. This is Docker networking at its most basic form.

Like basic storage, this limits you to bring up your containers on a single host even when using a clustering tool such as Docker Swarm, as you may have already noticed in *Chapter 2, Introducing First-party Tools*, when we were bringing up our WordPress installation, the web and database containers where launched on a single host within the cluster. If we were to try and bind each of the two containers to different host, they would not be able to talk to each other.

Luckily, Docker has you covered and provides its own multi-host networking layer to use with Docker Swarm.

Multi-host networking with overlays

Docker released its production-ready multi-host overlay networking functionality in Docker 1.9. Before this release, the functionality was classed as experimental.

 An overlay network is a computer network that is built on top of another network. Nodes in the overlay network can be thought of as being connected by virtual or logical links, each of which corresponds to a path, perhaps through many physical links, in the underlying network:
https://en.wikipedia.org/wiki/Overlay_network

In Docker terms, it allows containers on one Docker host to talk directly to containers on another Docker host as if they were on the same host, as shown in the following screenshot:

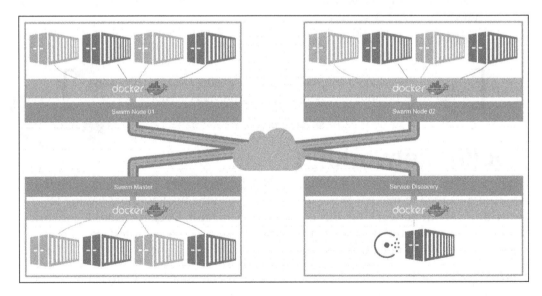

As you can see from the preceding diagram, there are some prerequisites. Firstly, you must be running a Docker Swarm cluster. Here we have a Docker Swarm cluster made up of two nodes and a master, all of which have the overlay network configured. You will also need a Service Discovery service, where it can be accessed by the Docker Swarm cluster. For this, you can use the following applications:

- **Consul**: `https://www.consul.io/`
- **Etcd**: `https://coreos.com/etcd/`
- **ZooKeeper**: `http://zookeeper.apache.org/`

For the purpose of this chapter, we will be using Consul by HashiCorp (`https://hashicorp.com/`) and we will also be launching our cluster using Docker Machine in DigitalOcean.

Launching Discovery

Back in *Chapter 2, Introducing First-party Tools*, we launched our Docker Swarm cluster using a one-off token from the Docker hub. One of the requirements of multi-host networking is a persistent key/value store so that we have permanent and accessible place to store values about our cluster, we will be using Consul to provide this in our example cluster.

Consul is an open source tool written by HashiCorp for discovering and configuring services in an infrastructure. It provides several key features, including Service Discovery, health checking, and a key/value store, all while being multi-datacenter aware.

To launch the Docker host, which will run Consul, run the following command:

```
docker-machine create \
    --driver digitalocean \
    --digitalocean-access-token
sdnjkjdfgkjb345kjdgljknqwetkjwhgoih314rjkwergoiyu34rjkherglkhrg0 \
    --digitalocean-region lon1 \
    --digitalocean-size 512mb \
    --digitalocean-private-networking \
    service-discovery
```

You may notice that we have added an additional line to the `docker-machine` command, this launches the DigitalOcean Droplet with private networking enabled. Once the Docker host has launched, we can launch the Consul service by running the following command:

```
docker $(docker-machine config service-discovery) run -d \
    -p "8400:8400" \
    -p "8500:8500" \
    -h "consul" \
    russmckendrick/consul agent -data-dir /data -server -bootstrap-expect
1 -ui-dir /ui -client=0.0.0.0
```

This will download a copy of my Consul container image, also now there is an official image that can be found at `https://hub.docker.com/_/consul/`; however, this image as it is new may not work with the preceding example.

As this is the only command we need to run on this host, we are not configuring our local Docker client to use the host; instead, we are passing the configuration over at runtime using `$(docker-machine config service-discovery)`. To check whether everything is running as expected, you can run the following command:

```
docker $(docker-machine config service-discovery) ps
```

Here, you should see a single container running something similar to the following terminal output:

Before we progress further, it should be noted that launching Consul with the `-bootstrap-expect 1` flag should never be attempted in production. You should consider bringing multiple Consul hosts. For more information on a highly available Consul cluster, refer to the following URL for details on how to configure a full Consul cluster:

`https://www.consul.io/docs/guides/bootstrapping.html`

You can also get an idea of what information Docker will be storing in Consul by opening the web interface, to do this type the following command:

```
open http://$(docker-machine ip service-discovery):8500/ui
```

You should see an almost empty Consul view, as shown in the following image:

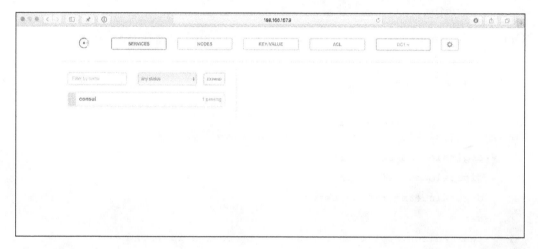

We will come back to the web interface once we have launched the Docker Swarm cluster. Now we have the service discover container running and accessible, it's time to start launching the rest of the cluster.

Readying the Swarm

Let's start to launch the Docker Swarm cluster, first of all the Swarm master. We will call this `chapter04-00`:

```
docker-machine create \
    --driver digitalocean \
    --digitalocean-access-token
sdnjkjdfgkjb345kjdgljknqwetkjwhgoih314rjkwergoiyu34rjkherglkhrg0 \
    --digitalocean-region lon1 \
```

```
    --digitalocean-size 1gb \
    --digitalocean-private-networking \
    --swarm --swarm-master \
    --swarm-discovery="consul://$(docker-machine ip service-
discovery):8500" \
    --engine-opt="cluster-store=consul://$(docker-machine ip service-
discovery):8500" \
    --engine-opt="cluster-advertise=eth1:2376" \
    chapter04-00
```

As you can see, the command is very similar to the one used in *Chapter 2, Introducing First-party Tools*; however, we are supplying details of our Consul installation. We are doing this by passing in the IP address of the service-discovery host using the docker-machine ip command.

Once the Swarm master is booted, we are going to launch two Swarm nodes using the following commands:

```
docker-machine create \
    --driver digitalocean \
    --digitalocean-access-token
sdnjkjdfgkjb345kjdgljknqwetkjwhgoih314rjkwergoiyu34rjkherglkhrg0 \
    --digitalocean-region lon1 \
    --digitalocean-size 1gb \
    --digitalocean-private-networking \
    --swarm \
    --swarm-discovery="consul://$(docker-machine ip service-
discovery):8500" \
    --engine-opt="cluster-store=consul://$(docker-machine ip service-
discovery):8500" \
    --engine-opt="cluster-advertise=eth1:2376" \
    chapter04-01
```

For the second node, we are going to use the following commands:

```
docker-machine create \
    --driver digitalocean \
    --digitalocean-access-token
sdnjkjdfgkjb345kjdgljknqwetkjwhgoih314rjkwergoiyu34rjkherglkhrg0 \
    --digitalocean-region lon1 \
    --digitalocean-size 1gb \
```

```
    --digitalocean-private-networking \

    --swarm \

    --swarm-discovery="consul://$(docker-machine ip service-
discovery):8500" \

    --engine-opt="cluster-store=consul://$(docker-machine ip service-
discovery):8500" \

    --engine-opt="cluster-advertise=eth1:2376" \

    chapter04-02
```

Now that we have our master and two nodes up and running, let's switch to the environment and make sure that the cluster is showing the correct number of hosts:

```
eval $(docker-machine env --swarm chapter04-00)

docker info
```

You should see something similar to the following screenshot when running `docker info`:

```
russ in
⚡ docker info
Containers: 4
 Running: 4
 Paused: 0
 Stopped: 0
Images: 3
Server Version: swarm/1.1.2
Role: primary
Strategy: spread
Filters: health, port, dependency, affinity, constraint
Nodes: 3
 chapter04-00: 188.166.153.89:2376
  └ Status: Healthy
  └ Containers: 2
  └ Reserved CPUs: 0 / 1
  └ Reserved Memory: 0 B / 1.018 GiB
  └ Labels: executiondriver=native-0.2, kernelversion=4.2.0-27-generic, operatingsystem=Ubuntu 15.10, provider=digitalocean, storagedriver=aufs
  └ Error: (none)
  └ UpdatedAt: 2016-02-21T16:07:28Z
 chapter04-01: 188.166.149.41:2376
  └ Status: Healthy
  └ Containers: 1
  └ Reserved CPUs: 0 / 1
  └ Reserved Memory: 0 B / 1.018 GiB
  └ Labels: executiondriver=native-0.2, kernelversion=4.2.0-27-generic, operatingsystem=Ubuntu 15.10, provider=digitalocean, storagedriver=aufs
  └ Error: (none)
  └ UpdatedAt: 2016-02-21T16:07:04Z
 chapter04-02: 188.166.149.159:2376
  └ Status: Healthy
  └ Containers: 1
  └ Reserved CPUs: 0 / 1
  └ Reserved Memory: 0 B / 1.018 GiB
  └ Labels: executiondriver=native-0.2, kernelversion=4.2.0-27-generic, operatingsystem=Ubuntu 15.10, provider=digitalocean, storagedriver=aufs
  └ Error: (none)
  └ UpdatedAt: 2016-02-21T16:07:31Z
Plugins:
 Volume:
 Network:
Kernel Version: 4.2.0-27-generic
Operating System: linux
Architecture: amd64
CPUs: 3
Total Memory: 3.054 GiB
Name: chapter04-00
russ in
⚡ []
```

So, we now have our cluster launched, and everything is talking to each other. We will now be able to create our overlay network.

Adding the overlay network

For testing purpose, we are going to be creating a very basic network and launching a very basic container. The following command will create the overlay network, and thanks to the service-discovery provided by Consul, the network settings will be distributed to each node within our Docker Swarm cluster:

```
docker network create --driver overlay --subnet=10.0.9.0/24 chapter04-
overlay-network
```

So, there you have it, we have created an overlay network called `chapter04-overlay-network` with a subnet of `10.0.9.0/24` on our cluster. To make sure that everything is OK, you can run the following commands to list the networks configured within the cluster:

```
docker network ls
```

You can also check on the individual nodes by running the following command:

```
docker $(docker-machine config chapter04-01) network ls
```

```
docker $(docker-machine config chapter04-02) network ls
```

```
russ — -bash — 143×29
russ in
⚡ docker network ls
NETWORK ID          NAME                          DRIVER
6ae07cf49992        chapter04-01/host             host
cb85774c3cf0        chapter04-02/host             host
e2e00f4858fb        chapter04-00/bridge           bridge
d25bc46c09c7        chapter04-00/host             host
48e3821e0771        chapter04-01/bridge           bridge
9f33bf31dfcb        chapter04-01/none             null
1be67d5713b7        chapter04-02/bridge           bridge
0ba01d48bee0        chapter04-02/none             null
bcc7dc7ecd5f        chapter04-overlay-network     overlay
aaac7717f288        chapter04-00/none             null
russ in
⚡ docker $(docker-machine config chapter04-01) network ls
NETWORK ID          NAME                          DRIVER
bcc7dc7ecd5f        chapter04-overlay-network     overlay
48e3821e0771        bridge                        bridge
9f33bf31dfcb        none                          null
6ae07cf49992        host                          host
russ in
⚡ docker $(docker-machine config chapter04-02) network ls
NETWORK ID          NAME                          DRIVER
bcc7dc7ecd5f        chapter04-overlay-network     overlay
1be67d5713b7        bridge                        bridge
0ba01d48bee0        none                          null
cb85774c3cf0        host                          host
russ in
⚡
```

As you can see, each node has its host and bridge networks available, meaning that you don't have to use the overlay network if you don't want to; however, we do so that its time to launch a container and configure it to use our newly added network.

Using the overlay network

To start with, we will be launching a container that runs NGINX:

```
docker run -itd \
    --name=chapter04-web \
    --net=chapter04-overlay-network \
    -p 80:80 \
    --env="constraint:node==chapter04-01" \
    russmckendrick/nginx
```

As you can see, we are configuring our container to use chapter04-overlay-network by passing the --net flag. We are also making sure that the container is launched on the chapter04-01 node. Next up, let's see if we can view the content being served by our NGINX container.

To do this, let's launch a container on our second node, chapter04-02, and run wget to fetch the page being served by NGINX:

```
docker run -it \
    --rm \
    --net=chapter04-overlay-network \
    --env="constraint:node==chapter04-02" \
    russmckendrick/base wget -q -O- http://chapter04-web
```

If everything went as planned, you will see Hello from NGINX returned by the command. We can also ping the NGINX container from the second node by running the following command:

```
docker run -it \
    --rm \
    --net=chapter04-overlay-network \
    --env="constraint:node==chapter04-02" \
    russmckendrick/base ping -c 3 chapter04-web
```

You should see an IP address within the 10.0.9.0/24 subnet returned, as shown in the following screenshot:

```
● ◌ ◉                                                    russ — -bash — 147×18
russ in
⚡ docker run -itd --name=chapter04-web --net=chapter04-overlay-network -p 80:80 --env="constraint:node==chapter04-01" russmckendrick/nginx
a6644d7a04394b09ed6e75f75a25ad4c6937265a9bb8833c6d746dceb4a09966
russ in
⚡ docker run -it --rm --net=chapter04-overlay-network --env="constraint:node==chapter04-02" russmckendrick/base wget -q -O- http://chapter04-web
Hello from NGINX
russ in
⚡ docker run -it --rm --net=chapter04-overlay-network --env="constraint:node==chapter04-02" russmckendrick/base ping -c 3 chapter04-web
PING chapter04-web (10.0.9.2): 56 data bytes
64 bytes from 10.0.9.2: seq=0 ttl=64 time=0.767 ms
64 bytes from 10.0.9.2: seq=1 ttl=64 time=0.509 ms
64 bytes from 10.0.9.2: seq=2 ttl=64 time=0.378 ms

--- chapter04-web ping statistics ---
3 packets transmitted, 3 packets received, 0% packet loss
round-trip min/avg/max = 0.378/0.551/0.767 ms
russ in
⚡ ▯
```

If you want to take a look at the network that has been configured on the chapter04-web container, you can run the following commands:

```
docker exec chapter04-web ip addr
docker exec chapter04-web route -n
docker exec chapter04-web ping -c 3 google.com
```

You should see something similar to the following terminal output returned:

```
● ◌ ◉                                                    russ — -bash — 111×39
russ in
⚡ docker exec chapter04-web ip addr
1: lo: <LOOPBACK,UP,LOWER_UP> mtu 65536 qdisc noqueue state UNKNOWN
    link/loopback 00:00:00:00:00:00 brd 00:00:00:00:00:00
    inet 127.0.0.1/8 scope host lo
       valid_lft forever preferred_lft forever
    inet6 ::1/128 scope host
       valid_lft forever preferred_lft forever
31: eth0@if32: <BROADCAST,MULTICAST,UP,LOWER_UP,M-DOWN> mtu 1450 qdisc noqueue state UP
    link/ether 02:42:0a:00:09:02 brd ff:ff:ff:ff:ff:ff
    inet 10.0.9.2/24 scope global eth0
       valid_lft forever preferred_lft forever
    inet6 fe80::42:aff:fe00:902/64 scope link
       valid_lft forever preferred_lft forever
33: eth1@if34: <BROADCAST,MULTICAST,UP,LOWER_UP,M-DOWN> mtu 1500 qdisc noqueue state UP
    link/ether 02:42:ac:12:00:02 brd ff:ff:ff:ff:ff:ff
    inet 172.18.0.2/16 scope global eth1
       valid_lft forever preferred_lft forever
    inet6 fe80::42:acff:fe12:2/64 scope link
       valid_lft forever preferred_lft forever
russ in
⚡ docker exec chapter04-web route -n
Kernel IP routing table
Destination     Gateway         Genmask         Flags Metric Ref    Use Iface
0.0.0.0         172.18.0.1      0.0.0.0         UG    0      0        0 eth1
10.0.9.0        0.0.0.0         255.255.255.0   U     0      0        0 eth0
172.18.0.0      0.0.0.0         255.255.0.0     U     0      0        0 eth1
russ in
⚡ docker exec chapter04-web ping -c 3 google.com
PING google.com (216.58.213.174): 56 data bytes
64 bytes from 216.58.213.174: seq=0 ttl=57 time=0.483 ms
64 bytes from 216.58.213.174: seq=1 ttl=57 time=0.703 ms
64 bytes from 216.58.213.174: seq=2 ttl=57 time=0.392 ms

--- google.com ping statistics ---
3 packets transmitted, 3 packets received, 0% packet loss
round-trip min/avg/max = 0.392/0.526/0.703 ms
russ in
⚡ ▯
```

Finally, you can access the container in your browser by running the following command:

```
open http://$(docker-machine ip chapter04-01)/
```

The page will look something similar to the following screenshot:

While the page itself isn't much to look at, there are actually some quite clever things going on in the background that you may not have noticed, the biggest of which is that we haven't had to link our containers together. In the previous chapters, we had used the link flag when launching multiple containers to link them together. Now we are launching our containers in the same Overlay Network, Docker assumes that all of the containers within this network will be able to talk each other, and it handles the linking of the containers automatically.

Docker has also configured a gateway for the containers in order to be able to route traffic outside of our Overlay Network by default. If you wanted to create an internal only networking, then you could add the ``--internal`` flag.

Back to Consul

Don't forget that while we have been creating the networks and launching our containers, the service discovery container has been running in the background. Going back to the Consul web interface, you should notice that under the **Key/Value** option, you will see a list of the nodes within our Docker Swarm cluster:

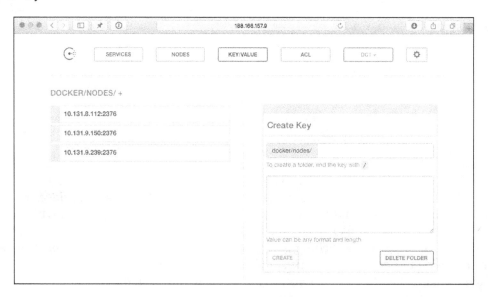

Clicking around, you should also see other values, such as the networking ones, that are being shared within the Docker Swarm cluster:

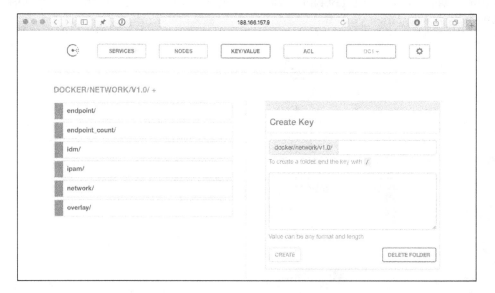

Before we tear down our Docker Swarm cluster, let's look at launching our WordPress stack using Docker Compose.

Composing multi-host networks

As in the previous chapters, we are going to launch our trusty WordPress installation. We are going to make it a little interesting by:

- Creating an external network called wpoutside. This network will be able to get external access, our webserver will be launched over here.

- Creating an internal network called wpinside. This network will not be able to get any external access, on containers on the same network will be able to access, we will be adding both web server and database containers to this network.

- Launching our web server container one node and the database container on our second node.

Before we launch our containers, we should terminate the chapter04-web container:

```
docker rm -f chapter04-web
```

Now, let's create two overlay networks:

```
docker network create --driver overlay --subnet=10.0.10.0/24 wpoutside
docker network create --driver overlay --internal --subnet=10.0.11.0/24 wpinside
```

As you can see, we are giving the networks different subnets, and for wpinside, we are passing the --internal flag, meaning that the network will not have an external gateway.

Now, let's take a look at our docker-compose.yml file:

```
version: '2'
services:
  wordpress:
    container_name: my-wordpress-app
    image: wordpress
    ports:
      - "80:80"
    networks:
      - wpoutside
      - wpinside
    environment:
      - "WORDPRESS_DB_HOST=mysql:3306"
```

```
          - "WORDPRESS_DB_PASSWORD=password"
        - "constraint:node==chapter04-01"
      volumes:
        - "uploads:/var/www/html/wp-content/uploads/"
    mysql:
      container_name: my-wordpress-database
      image: mysql
      networks:
        - wpinside
      environment:
        - "MYSQL_ROOT_PASSWORD=password"
        - "constraint:node==chapter04-02"
      volumes:
        - "database:/var/lib/mysql"
  volumes:
    uploads:
      driver: local
    database:
      driver: local
  networks:
    wpoutside:
      external: true
    wpinside:
      external: true
```

As you can see, I have highlighted the changes made in the file since the previous chapter. The interesting thing to note is that while it is possible to define your network within the `docker-compose.yml` file, you will get a lot more control by setting up the network using the `docker network create` command. To do this, we need to tell Docker Compose to use the externally defined networks for the project. We are also using labels to bind the containers to a host in our Docker Swarm cluster.

Now that we have the two overlay networks created, you can launch the WordPress stack by running the following command:

```
docker-compose up -d
```

You can check everything launched as expected by running the following command:

```
docker-compose ps
```

To make sure that the containers have launched on different hosts, run the following command and check the last column:

```
docker ps
```

To see what IP addresses are assigned to the containers, run the following commands:

```
docker inspect my-wordpress-app | grep IPAddress
docker inspect my-wordpress-database | grep IPAddress
```

You should see two IP addresses for `my-wordpress-app` and a single for `my-wordpress-database`:

Before we log in to WordPress, we can try some ping tests. First, we will run the tests on your `my-wordpress-app` container by running the following commands:

```
docker exec my-wordpress-app ping -c 3 google.com
docker exec my-wordpress-app ping -c 3 my-wordpress-database
```

For the first command, you will see Google's external IP address returned. For the second, you will get the IP of your `my-wordpress-database` container, which will be on the `10.0.11.0/24` subnet we defined for the `wpinside` overlay network:

Trying similar commands on `my-wordpress-database` should give you different results, try running the following commands:

```
docker exec my-wordpress-database ping -c 3 my-wordpress-app
docker exec my-wordpress-database ping -c 3 google.com
```

As you can see, pinging `my-wordpress-app` works fine; however, when you try and ping Google, you get an error saying something like `Network is unreachable` or some another error. This is exactly what we would expect to see as `my-wordpress-database` has no external network access and therefore it cannot route to `www.google.com`:

```
● ● ●                          wordpress-overlay — -bash — 111×20
russ in ~/Documents/Code/extending-docker/chapter04/wordpress-overlay on master*
⚡ docker exec my-wordpress-app ping -c 3 google.com
PING google.com (216.58.198.238): 56 data bytes
64 bytes from 216.58.198.238: icmp_seq=0 ttl=57 time=0.550 ms
64 bytes from 216.58.198.238: icmp_seq=1 ttl=57 time=0.376 ms
64 bytes from 216.58.198.238: icmp_seq=2 ttl=57 time=0.347 ms
--- google.com ping statistics ---
3 packets transmitted, 3 packets received, 0% packet loss
round-trip min/avg/max/stddev = 0.347/0.424/0.550/0.090 ms
russ in ~/Documents/Code/extending-docker/chapter04/wordpress-overlay on master*
⚡ docker exec my-wordpress-app ping -c 3 my-wordpress-database
PING my-wordpress-database (10.0.11.3): 56 data bytes
64 bytes from 10.0.11.3: icmp_seq=0 ttl=64 time=0.477 ms
64 bytes from 10.0.11.3: icmp_seq=1 ttl=64 time=0.463 ms
64 bytes from 10.0.11.3: icmp_seq=2 ttl=64 time=0.435 ms
--- my-wordpress-database ping statistics ---
3 packets transmitted, 3 packets received, 0% packet loss
round-trip min/avg/max/stddev = 0.435/0.458/0.477/0.000 ms
russ in ~/Documents/Code/extending-docker/chapter04/wordpress-overlay on master*
⚡ ▯
```

Finally, if you would like to access WordPress, you can type in either of the following commands. First of all, we need to confirm which host the `my-wordpress-app` container is launched on. To confirm the host, run:

```
docker ps
```

Then, depending on which host, run one of the following three commands:

```
open http://$(docker-machine ip chapter04-00)/
open http://$(docker-machine ip chapter04-01)/
open http://$(docker-machine ip chapter04-02)/
```

Your browser will open the now familiar WordPress installation page.

Before moving on further, you should tear down your Docker Swarm cluster. To do this, run the following command:

```
docker-machine stop chapter04-00 chapter04-01 chapter04-02 service-discovery
docker-machine rm chapter04-00 chapter04-01 chapter04-02 service-discovery
```

Summing up multi-host networking

Although overlay networks were classed as production-ready in Docker version 1.9, with the advancements in Docker version 1.10 and the new Docker Compose v2 file format, Docker networking has really come into its own.

While the overlay network functionality is built into Docker and Swarm, as you have seen in the examples we have worked through, it is extremely powerful. When used in conjunction with third-party volume plugins that we covered in *Chapter 3, Volume Plugins*, and Docker Swarm, we can start to build highly available deployments.

Weaving a network

Next up, we are going to take a look at Weave Net and Scope by Weaveworks. This is one of the original Docker networking tools, and at its core, it is a mature software-defined networking service.

Weave Net is described as follows:

> *"Weave Net creates a container SDN that can run across any mixture of public and private cloud, virtual machines and bare metal. The container SDN can carry any layer 2 and layer 3 traffic, including multicast. If you can run it over Ethernet, you can run it on Weave Net."*

In fact, there are two drivers provided by Weave, as follows:

- Weave Mesh is a local scope driver that operates without the need for a cluster store. It can be used to create networks that span non-clustered machines. With this, you get a single network called Weave, which spans all of the machines you have Weave launched on.

- Weave, like Docker's own overlay driver, is a global scope driver. This means that it can be used with Docker Swarm and Docker Compose, because of this, you will need to launch a cluster store.

First of all, let's look at the Weave driver and how to use it with Docker Swarm and then we will take a look at using the Weavemesh driver.

Configuring a Cluster again

Like Docker multi-host networking, we will need to launch a service discovery instance and our Swarm cluster. Let's launch the service discovery host with Docker Machine:

```
docker-machine create \
    --driver digitalocean \
    --digitalocean-access-token
sdnjkjdfgkjb345kjdgljknqwetkjwhgoih314rjkwergoiyu34rjkherglkhrg0 \
    --digitalocean-region lon1 \
    --digitalocean-size 512mb \
    --digitalocean-private-networking \
    service-discovery
```

This time, we don't need to enable the Consul web interface, so run the following command:

```
docker $(docker-machine config service-discovery) run -d \
    -p "8400:8400" \
    -p "8500:8500" \
    -h "consul" \
    russmckendrick/consul agent -data-dir /data -server -bootstrap-expect
1 -client=0.0.0.0
```

Now launch the Docker Swarm cluster, first the master:

```
docker-machine create \
    --driver digitalocean \
    --digitalocean-access-token
sdnjkjdfgkjb345kjdgljknqwetkjwhgoih314rjkwergoiyu34rjkherglkhrg0 \
    --digitalocean-region lon1 \
    --digitalocean-size 1gb \
    --digitalocean-private-networking \
    --swarm --swarm-master \
    --swarm-discovery="consul://$(docker-machine ip service-
discovery):8500" \
    --engine-opt="cluster-store=consul://$(docker-machine ip service-
discovery):8500" \
    --engine-opt="cluster-advertise=eth1:2376" \
    chapter04-00
```

Then we will launch our first node:

```
docker-machine create \
    --driver digitalocean \
    --digitalocean-access-token
sdnjkjdfgkjb345kjdgljknqwetkjwhgoih314rjkwergoiyu34rjkherglkhrg0 \
    --digitalocean-region lon1 \
    --digitalocean-size 1gb \
    --digitalocean-private-networking \
    --swarm \
    --swarm-discovery="consul://$(docker-machine ip service-
discovery):8500" \
```

```
    --engine-opt="cluster-store=consul://$(docker-machine ip service-
discovery):8500" \

    --engine-opt="cluster-advertise=eth1:2376" \

    chapter04-01
```

Finally, we will launch the second node:

```
docker-machine create \
    --driver digitalocean \
    --digitalocean-access-token
sdnjkjdfgkjb345kjdgljknqwetkjwhgoih314rjkwergoiyu34rjkherglkhrg0 \
    --digitalocean-region lon1 \
    --digitalocean-size 1gb \
    --digitalocean-private-networking \
    --swarm \
    --swarm-discovery="consul://$(docker-machine ip service-
discovery):8500" \
    --engine-opt="cluster-store=consul://$(docker-machine ip service-
discovery):8500" \
    --engine-opt="cluster-advertise=eth1:2376" \
    chapter04-02
```

To check whether everything is working as expected, run the following commands to switch our local Docker client to connect to the Swarm cluster and also check whether the three nodes are visible:

```
eval $(docker-machine env --swarm chapter04-00)
docker info
```

Installing and configuring Weave

Now that we have our cluster up and running, we can install and configure Weave. Installing Weave is simple, all you have to do is download the binary and give it the correct permissions. Let's do this on the Swarm master using `docker-machine ssh` to connect to the host and run the `install` command:

```
docker-machine ssh chapter04-00 'curl -L git.io/weave -o /usr/local/bin/
weave; chmod a+x /usr/local/bin/weave'
```

Next, we start Weave, again using `docker-machine ssh`, we can run the following command:

```
docker-machine ssh chapter04-00 weave launch --init-peer-count 3
```

You will have notice that Weave deployed three containers from the Docker Hub, they are as follows:

- weaveworks/weaveexec
- weaveworks/weave
- weaveworks/plugin

Also, we are telling Weave to expect three peers to join the cluster by passing the `--init-peer-count 3` flag, that's pretty much all we have to do to configure Weave on our first cluster node.

Next, we need to install Weave onto our other two cluster nodes, again using the `docker-machine ssh` command run the following:

```
docker-machine ssh chapter04-01 'curl -L git.io/weave -o /usr/local/bin/
weave; chmod a+x /usr/local/bin/weave'
docker-machine ssh chapter04-01 weave launch --init-peer-count 3
```

Now that we have Weave up and running on the node, we need to tell it to connect to the Weave installation running on the Swarm master. To do this, run the following command:

```
docker-machine ssh chapter04-01 weave connect "$(docker-machine ip
chapter04-00)"
```

Then on our last cluster node, we will run the following command:

```
docker-machine ssh chapter04-02 'curl -L git.io/weave -o /usr/local/bin/
weave; chmod a+x /usr/local/bin/weave'
docker-machine ssh chapter04-02 weave launch --init-peer-count 3
docker-machine ssh chapter04-02 weave connect "$(docker-machine ip
chapter04-00)"
```

Once all three nodes in the Swarm cluster have Weave installed and configured, we will run the following command to ensure that all three nodes are talking to each other:

```
docker-machine ssh chapter04-00 weave status
```

The command should return confirmation that there are three peers with six established connections along with other information about the installation, as shown in the following screenshot:

```
●  ○  ●                            russ — -bash — 111×31
russ in
⚡ docker-machine ssh chapter04-00 weave status

         Version: 1.4.4

         Service: router
        Protocol: weave 1..2
            Name: 12:a0:fa:0e:ef:31(chapter04-00)
      Encryption: disabled
   PeerDiscovery: enabled
         Targets: 0
     Connections: 2 (2 established)
           Peers: 3 (with 6 established connections)
  TrustedSubnets: none

         Service: ipam
          Status: idle
           Range: 10.32.0.0-10.47.255.255
   DefaultSubnet: 10.32.0.0/12

         Service: dns
          Domain: weave.local.
        Upstream: 8.8.8.8, 8.8.4.4
             TTL: 1
         Entries: 0

         Service: proxy
         Address: unix:///var/run/weave/weave.sock

         Service: plugin
      DriverName: weave
```

Now that we have confirmation that everything is working as expected, we will list the networks in Docker using the following command:

```
docker network ls
```

As per the following terminal session, you should see that there is a weavemesh network called weave on each of the nodes within the cluster; we will discuss more about that later:

```
●  ○  ●                            russ — -bash — 111×16
russ in
⚡ docker network ls
NETWORK ID      NAME                  DRIVER
7bd175171134    chapter04-00/bridge   bridge
38408938be81    chapter04-01/bridge   bridge
04ffa837678f    chapter04-01/none     null
c7acb4cb2ef6    chapter04-01/host     host
153bc86653d6    chapter04-02/none     null
7a2b9b03e934    chapter04-02/weave    weavemesh
784b0d913c5b    chapter04-00/weave    weavemesh
d2912acaf231    chapter04-00/none     null
9224a0c4a98d    chapter04-00/host     host
52fd1021c514    chapter04-01/weave    weavemesh
7bbe31b1dd8e    chapter04-02/bridge   bridge
f96ddc0ccf3a    chapter04-02/host     host
russ in
```

Docker Compose and Weave

So, let's launch our WordPress installation. The Docker Compose file looks a little different from the overlay network one:

```
version: '2'
services:
  wordpress:
    container_name: "my-wordpress-app"
    image: wordpress
    ports:
      - "80:80"
    environment:
      - "WORDPRESS_DB_HOST=mysql.weave.local:3306"
      - "WORDPRESS_DB_PASSWORD=password"
      - "constraint:node==chapter04-01"
    hostname: "wordpress.weave.local"
    dns: "172.17.0.1"
    dns_search: "weave.local"
    volumes:
      - "uploads:/var/www/html/wp-content/uploads/"
  mysql:
    container_name: "my-wordpress-database"
    image: mysql
    environment:
      - "MYSQL_ROOT_PASSWORD=password"
      - "constraint:node==chapter04-02"
    hostname: "mysql.weave.local"
    dns: "172.17.0.1"
    dns_search: "weave.local"
    volumes:
      - "database:/var/lib/mysql"
volumes:
  uploads:
    driver: local
  database:
    driver: local
networks:
  default:
    driver: weave
```

I have highlighted a few changes from the Overlay Docker Compose file: first off, we will define a hostname and provide a DNS server and search domain. To get the right values for the `dns` and `dns_search` keys, you can run the following command to have Weave let you know what it has configured:

```
docker-machine ssh chapter04-00 weave dns-args
```

As you can see, in my case, it returned `172.17.0.1` and `weave.local`:

```
russ in
⚡  docker-machine ssh chapter04-00 weave dns-args
--dns 172.17.0.1 --dns-search=weave.local.russ in
⚡
```

Also, for the MySQL connection from the WordPress container to the Database one, we are using the internal DNS name as well.

We are also letting Docker Compose create a network for us using the Weave driver, this will add a single network named after the project. Docker Compose gets the project name from the folder our Docker Compose file is, in my case, it's a folder called `wordpress`.

To launch your containers and check whether they are running as expected, run the following commands:

```
docker-compose up -d
```

```
docker-compose ps
```

```
docker ps
```

You should see something similar to the following terminal output:

```
russ in                                                                    on master+
⚡  docker-compose up -d
Creating network "wordpressweave_default" with driver "weave"
Creating my-wordpress-app
Creating my-wordpress-database
russ in                                                                    on master+
⚡  docker-compose ps
        Name                    Command            State          Ports
--------------------------------------------------------------------------------------
my-wordpress-app        /entrypoint.sh apache2-for ...   Up    188.166.146.185:80->80/tcp
my-wordpress-database   /entrypoint.sh mysqld            Up    3306/tcp
russ in                                                                    on master+
⚡  docker ps
CONTAINER ID   IMAGE                          COMMAND                  CREATED          STATUS          PORTS                         NAMES
b53b05142dac   mysql                          "/entrypoint.sh mysql"   11 seconds ago   Up 12 seconds   3306/tcp                      chapter04-02/my-wordpress-database
4d0f54db3f62   wordpress                      "/entrypoint.sh apach"   12 seconds ago   Up 13 seconds   188.166.146.185:80->80/tcp    chapter04-01/my-wordpress-app
f1e8400e1fb5   weaveworks/plugin:1.4.4        "/home/weave/plugin"     2 hours ago      Up 2 hours                                    chapter04-02/weaveplugin
8d7d389384a0   weaveworks/weaveexec:1.4.4     "/home/weave/weavepro"   2 hours ago      Up 2 hours                                    chapter04-02/weaveproxy
06e1a566c4ba   weaveworks/weave:1.4.4         "/home/weave/weaver -"   2 hours ago      Up 2 hours                                    chapter04-02/weave
8dfa72e22509   weaveworks/plugin:1.4.4        "/home/weave/plugin"     2 hours ago      Up 2 hours                                    chapter04-01/weaveplugin
a2614027b139   weaveworks/weaveexec:1.4.4     "/home/weave/weavepro"   2 hours ago      Up 2 hours                                    chapter04-01/weaveproxy
9b36cd91005c   weaveworks/weave:1.4.4         "/home/weave/weaver -"   2 hours ago      Up 2 hours                                    chapter04-01/weave
04901a5c0b17   weaveworks/plugin:1.4.4        "/home/weave/plugin"     2 hours ago      Up 2 hours                                    chapter04-00/weaveplugin
b9a0d49233b5   weaveworks/weaveexec:1.4.4     "/home/weave/weavepro"   2 hours ago      Up 2 hours                                    chapter04-00/weaveproxy
ebb8aee65b64   weaveworks/weave:1.4.4         "/home/weave/weaver -"   2 hours ago      Up 2 hours                                    chapter04-00/weave
russ in                                                                    on master+
⚡  []
```

If you really want to, you can access your WordPress installation by running the following command:

```
open http://$(docker-machine ip chapter04-01)/
```

There are some things happening in the background that Docker's multi-host networking doesn't give you, such as internal DNS. Weave has its own internal DNS system that you can register your containers with, as you saw in the Docker Compose file that we provided details for records for both containers. Run the following command:

```
docker-machine ssh chapter04-00 weave status dns
```

It will show you all the DNS records that Weave has configured. In my case, it looks like the following screenshot:

Weave Scope

While we have our three-node Swarm cluster up and running, let's quickly install Scope. Scope is a tool for visualizing your Containers and host. We will just be installing it to run locally, but Weave Works will be offering a cloud-based service, which can be found at http://scope.weave.works/ (at the time of writing this book, it was in private beta).

Similar to the way we installed Weave Net, we will be using the docker-machine ssh command to download the binary and launch and configure the service.

We will write the code on the Swarm master first:

```
docker-machine ssh chapter04-00 'curl -L git.io/scope -o /usr/local/bin/
scope; chmod a+x /usr/local/bin/scope'
docker-machine ssh chapter04-00 scope launch
```

Then, we will write the code for remaining two nodes:

```
docker-machine ssh chapter04-01 'curl -L git.io/scope -o /usr/local/bin/
scope; chmod a+x /usr/local/bin/scope'
docker-machine ssh chapter04-01 scope launch $(docker-machine ip
chapter04-00)
```

```
docker-machine ssh chapter04-02 'curl -L git.io/scope -o /usr/local/bin/
scope; chmod a+x /usr/local/bin/scope'
docker-machine ssh chapter04-02 scope launch $(docker-machine ip
chapter04-00)
```

As you can see on the two remaining nodes, we are telling Scope to connect to the Scope instance running on the Swarm master.

Now that Scope is installed, open it in your browser by running the following command:

```
open http://$(docker-machine ip chapter04-00):4040/
```

When your browser opens, you will be presented with a visual representation of your Swarm cluster, and the containers that are running.

I am not going to go into any more detail on Scope here, as at the moment, it doesn't have much to do with networking, have a look around to start seeing more information on your cluster and how it all hangs together. Mine looked similar to the following screenshot:

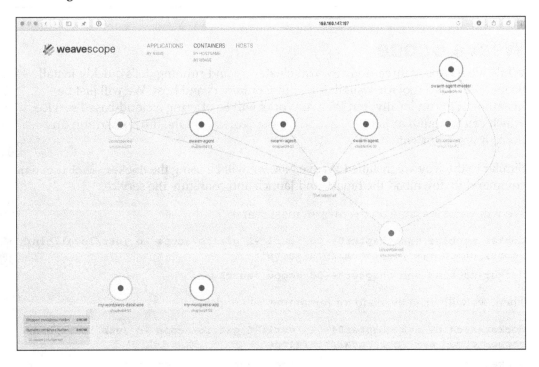

Calling off the Swarm

As you can see, while Weave is quite a powerful SDN, it is straightforward to configure. However, replicating the multi-host networking Docker provides is only one of its tricks.

Let's shut down our Swarm cluster and terminate the hosts before we start to look at the Weavemesh network driver:

```
docker-machine stop chapter04-00 chapter04-01 chapter04-02 service-discovery
docker-machine rm chapter04-00 chapter04-01 chapter04-02 service-discovery
```

Before you move on, log in to your DigitalOcean control panel and make sure that you don't have any machines labelled with chapter04 running, remember that you will be charged per hour whether you are using them or not.

Weavemesh Driver

We have looked at how Weave Net can by used alongside a Docker Swarm cluster to create multi-host networking, now let's take a look at the second Weave network driver, Weavemesh. As you may recall, when we first installed Weave Net, a network called "weave" was automatically create using the "weavemesh" driver on each node within our cluster.

This time, let's bring up two independent Docker hosts DigitalOcean using Docker Machine. To make it interesting, we will launch one host in London and the other in New York City. As these are going to be acting as individual hosts, we do not need to launch a key/value store, or configure Docker Swarm.

First, type the following command to launch a host in London host:

```
docker-machine create \
    --driver digitalocean \
    --digitalocean-access-token
sdnjkjdfgkjb345kjdgljknqwetkjwhgoih314rjkwergoiyu34rjkherglkhrg0 \
    --digitalocean-region lon1 \
    --digitalocean-size 1gb \
    mesh-london
```

Then, the following command is to launch another host is New York City.

```
docker-machine create \
    --driver digitalocean \
    --digitalocean-access-token
sdnjkjdfgkjb345kjdgljknqwetkjwhgoih314rjkwergoiyu34rjkherglkhrg0 \
    --digitalocean-region nyc2 \
    --digitalocean-size 1gb \
    mesh-nyc
```

Now that we have our two Docker hosts up and running, let's install and configure Weave:

```
docker-machine ssh mesh-london 'curl -L git.io/weave -o /usr/local/bin/
weave; chmod a+x /usr/local/bin/weave'
docker-machine ssh mesh-london weave launch --password 3UnFh4jhahFC
```

As you can see, this time we are telling Weave to launch with a password. This flag will enable encryption between the networking layer on our two hosts. Now that we have the London host configured, let's do the one in New York City and then get it talking to the host in London:

```
docker-machine ssh mesh-nyc 'curl -L git.io/weave -o /usr/local/bin/
weave; chmod a+x /usr/local/bin/weave'
docker-machine ssh mesh-nyc weave launch --password 3UnFh4jhahFC
docker-machine ssh mesh-nyc weave connect "$(docker-machine ip mesh-
london)"
```

Now that we have Weave configured on our two hosts, we can check the status of Weave by running the following command:

```
docker-machine ssh mesh-nyc weave status
```

As you can see from the following terminal output, encryption is enabled and we have two peers within our Weave network:

```
                                        russ — -bash — 111×34
russ in ~
⚡ docker-machine ssh mesh-nyc weave status

        Version: 1.4.4

        Service: router
       Protocol: weave 1..2
           Name: 2a:7d:07:5f:af:b1(mesh-nyc)
     Encryption: enabled
  PeerDiscovery: enabled
        Targets: 1
    Connections: 1 (1 established)
          Peers: 2 (with 2 established connections)
  TrustedSubnets: none

        Service: ipam
         Status: idle
          Range: 10.32.0.0-10.47.255.255
  DefaultSubnet: 10.32.0.0/12

        Service: dns
         Domain: weave.local.
       Upstream: 8.8.8.8, 8.8.4.4
            TTL: 1
        Entries: 0

        Service: proxy
        Address: unix:///var/run/weave/weave.sock

        Service: plugin
     DriverName: weave

russ in ~
⚡ ▯
```

So, let's take a look at Weave's party trick. We will keep it basic to start with by launching our NGINX container:

```
docker $(docker-machine config mesh-nyc) run -itd \
    --name=nginx \
    --net=weave \
    --hostname="nginx.weave.local" \
    --dns="172.17.0.1" \
    --dns-search="weave.local" \
    russmckendrick/nginx
```

Now we can check whether the container is up and running:

```
docker $(docker-machine config mesh-nyc) ps
```

Let's also check whether it's responding on port 80:

```
docker $(docker-machine config mesh-london) run -it \
    --rm \
    --net=weave \
    --dns="172.17.0.1" \
    --dns-search="weave.local" \
    russmckendrick/base wget -q -O- http://nginx.weave.local
```

Finally, let's do a ping test:

```
docker $(docker-machine config mesh-london) run -it \
    --rm \
    --net=weave \
    --dns="172.17.0.1" \
    --dns-search="weave.local" \
    russmckendrick/base ping -c 3 nginx.weave.local
```

Your terminal session should look something like the following screenshot:

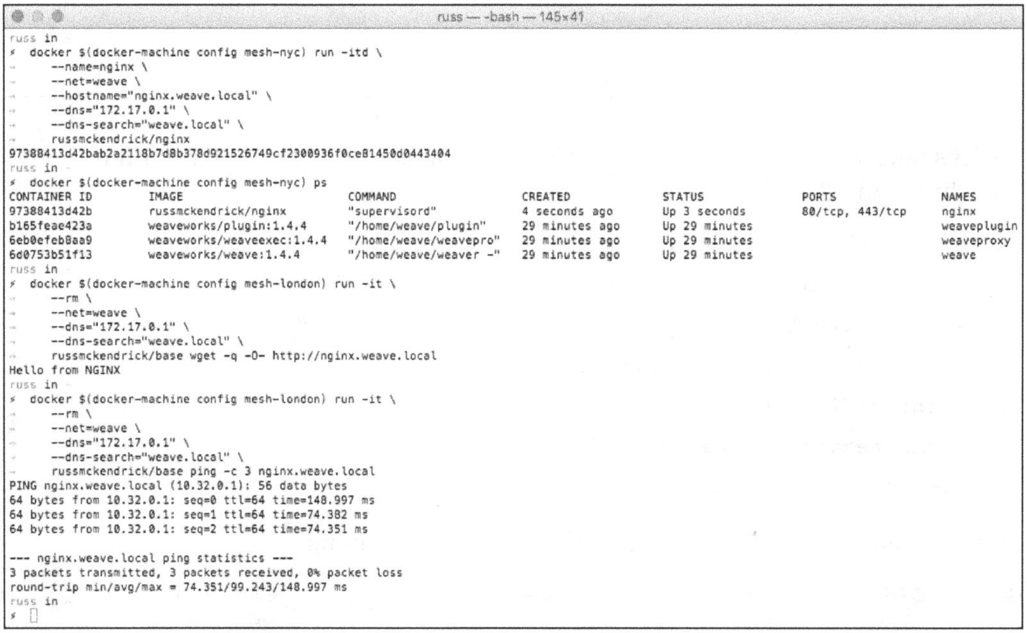

On the surface, this test doesn't look like much; however, if you look closely at the commands we used, you will see just how powerful the weavemesh driver is.

First of all, when we launched our NGINX container on the New York City Docker host, we did not publish any ports, meaning that port 80 was only available on the weave network that we attached it to.

Secondly, when we ran the check on port 80 and did the ping test, we did that from our Docker host in London. We temporally launched a basic container, attached it to the `weave` network and configured it use Weave DNS service so that it could resolve the `nginx.weave.local` domain.

Let's do our tests again, but this time, using a local virtual machine:

```
docker-machine create -d virtualbox mesh-local
```

Now, install Weave as we did on our other two Docker hosts:

```
docker-machine ssh mesh-local 'sudo curl -L git.io/weave -o /usr/local/
bin/weave; sudo chmod a+x /usr/local/bin/weave'
docker-machine ssh mesh-local sudo weave launch --password 3UnFh4jhahFC
docker-machine ssh mesh-local sudo weave connect "$(docker-machine ip
mesh-london)"
```

Then run the tests again:

```
docker $(docker-machine config mesh-local) run -it \
    --rm \
    --net=weave \
    --dns="172.17.0.1" \
    --dns-search="weave.local" \
    russmckendrick/base wget -q -O- http://nginx.weave.local
```

Run the ping test, as follows:

```
docker $(docker-machine config mesh-local) run -it \
    --rm \
    --net=weave \
    --dns="172.17.0.1" \
    --dns-search="weave.local" \
    russmckendrick/base ping -c 3 nginx.weave.local
```

As you can see, it worked!

```
● ○ ●                              russ — -bash — 111×25
russ in
⚡ docker $(docker-machine config mesh-local) run -it \
        --rm \
        --net=weave \
        --dns="172.17.0.1" \
        --dns-search="weave.local" \
        russmckendrick/base wget -q -O- http://nginx.weave.local
Hello from NGINX
russ in
⚡ docker $(docker-machine config mesh-local) run -it \
        --rm \
        --net=weave \
        --dns="172.17.0.1" \
        --dns-search="weave.local" \
        russmckendrick/base ping -c 3 nginx.weave.local
PING nginx.weave.local (10.32.0.1): 56 data bytes
64 bytes from 10.32.0.1: seq=0 ttl=64 time=163.910 ms
64 bytes from 10.32.0.1: seq=1 ttl=64 time=81.007 ms
64 bytes from 10.32.0.1: seq=2 ttl=64 time=81.922 ms

--- nginx.weave.local ping statistics ---
3 packets transmitted, 3 packets received, 0% packet loss
round-trip min/avg/max = 81.007/108.946/163.910 ms
russ in
⚡ ▯
```

We now have three Docker hosts in our Weavemesh network, all of which can talk to each other. To prove this, we are going to do one final test. Let's launch a container on our local Docker host and try the tests from the New York City host.

Create a NGINX container called vm.weave.local on our local Docker host:

```
docker $(docker-machine config mesh-local) run -itd \
    --name=vm \
    --net=weave \
    --hostname="vm.weave.local" \
    --dns="172.17.0.1" \
    --dns-search="weave.local" \
    russmckendrick/nginx
```

Then try connecting to port 80 and pinging the new container from the Docker host in New York City:

```
docker $(docker-machine config mesh-nyc) run -it \
    --rm \
    --net=weave \
    --dns="172.17.0.1" \
    --dns-search="weave.local" \
    russmckendrick/base wget -q -O- http://vm.weave.local
```

```
docker $(docker-machine config mesh-nyc) run -it \

    --rm \

    --net=weave \

    --dns="172.17.0.1" \

    --dns-search="weave.local" \

    russmckendrick/base ping -c 3 vm.weave.local
```

My terminal session looked similar to the following screenshot:

```
russ in
⚡ docker $(docker-machine config mesh-local) run -itd \
    --name=vm \
    --net=weave \
    --hostname="vm.weave.local" \
    --dns="172.17.0.1" \
    --dns-search="weave.local" \
    russmckendrick/nginx
cda9ec3f2b43283ce7acffac5670fc7621d504cb6599db05a512b662df73c76f
russ in
⚡ docker $(docker-machine config mesh-nyc) run -it \
    --rm \
    --net=weave \
    --dns="172.17.0.1" \
    --dns-search="weave.local" \
    russmckendrick/base wget -q -O- http://vm.weave.local
Hello from NGINX
russ in
⚡ docker $(docker-machine config mesh-nyc) run -it \
    --rm \
    --net=weave \
    --dns="172.17.0.1" \
    --dns-search="weave.local" \
    russmckendrick/base ping -c 3 vm.weave.local
PING vm.weave.local (10.43.255.255): 56 data bytes
64 bytes from 10.43.255.255: seq=0 ttl=64 time=162.760 ms
64 bytes from 10.43.255.255: seq=1 ttl=64 time=101.865 ms
64 bytes from 10.43.255.255: seq=2 ttl=64 time=82.171 ms

--- vm.weave.local ping statistics ---
3 packets transmitted, 3 packets received, 0% packet loss
round-trip min/avg/max = 82.171/115.598/162.760 ms
russ in
⚡ 
```

Now that we don't have the constants of the Docker Swarm cluster, we can also start to do some tasks that are only available outside of Swarm.

First of all, you attach container to the Weave network after they have been launched, let's launch an NGINX container called `lonely` on our London Docker host:

```
docker $(docker-machine config mesh-london) run -itd \
    --name=lonely \
    russmckendrick/nginx
```

Now, let's connect to the London Docker host and attached the container to the weave network:

```
docker-machine ssh mesh-london weave attach lonely
```

When you run the command, it will return an IP address. This will be the new IP address of our container; in my case, it is 10.40.0.0. Let's run our test from both the New York City and Local Docker hosts:

```
docker $(docker-machine config mesh-nyc) run -it \
    --rm \
    --net=weave \
    --dns="172.17.0.1" \
    --dns-search="weave.local" \
    russmckendrick/base wget -q -O- 10.40.0.0
docker $(docker-machine config mesh-local) run -it \
    --rm \
    --net=weave \
    --dns="172.17.0.1" \
    --dns-search="weave.local" \
    russmckendrick/base ping -c 3 10.40.0.0
```

Your terminal session should look similar to the following screenshot:

```
● ○ ●                              russ — -bash — 111×33
russ in ~
⚡ docker $(docker-machine config mesh-london) run -itd \
     --name=lonely \
     russmckendrick/nginx
95f226ecd5ea496a56f39fda67e56c76e686fcde75e9ba6938510c6bbe2d6c18
russ in ~
⚡ docker-machine ssh mesh-london weave attach lonely
10.40.0.0
russ in ~
⚡ docker $(docker-machine config mesh-nyc) run -it \
     --rm \
     --net=weave \
     --dns="172.17.0.1" \
     --dns-search="weave.local" \
     russmckendrick/base wget -q -O- 10.40.0.0
Hello from NGINX
russ in ~
⚡ docker $(docker-machine config mesh-local) run -it \
     --rm \
     --net=weave \
     --dns="172.17.0.1" \
     --dns-search="weave.local" \
     russmckendrick/base ping -c 3 10.40.0.0
PING 10.40.0.0 (10.40.0.0): 56 data bytes
64 bytes from 10.40.0.0: seq=0 ttl=64 time=32.636 ms
64 bytes from 10.40.0.0: seq=1 ttl=64 time=17.996 ms
64 bytes from 10.40.0.0: seq=2 ttl=64 time=17.718 ms

--- 10.40.0.0 ping statistics ---
3 packets transmitted, 3 packets received, 0% packet loss
round-trip min/avg/max = 17.718/22.783/32.636 ms
russ in ~
⚡ ▯
```

Now that we have our container on the network, we can manually add a DNS for the host by running the following command:

```
docker-machine ssh mesh-london weave dns-add lonely -h lonely.weave.local
```

As you can see, we can now access port 80 using http://lonely.weave.local from our New York City Docker host:

```
docker $(docker-machine config mesh-nyc) run -it \
    --rm \
    --net=weave \
    --dns="172.17.0.1" \
    --dns-search="weave.local" \
    russmckendrick/base wget -q -O- lonely.weave.local
```

The only downside is that there is no easy way of adding the DNS resolution to the host we have attached to the "weave" network.

Now that we are finished with our Docker hosts, let's terminate them so that we don't incur unnecessary cost:

```
docker-machine stop mesh-local mesh-london mesh-nyc
docker-machine rm mesh-local mesh-london mesh-nyc
```

Again, remember to check your DigitalOcean control panel to ensure that your hosts have been correctly terminated.

Summarizing Weave

As you have seen and I have already mentioned, Weave is an incredibly powerful software-defined network, which is really easy to configure. Speaking from experience, this is a difficult combination to pull off, as most SDN solutions are incredibly complex to install, configure, and maintain.

We have only touched on what is possible with "weave" and "weavemesh" drivers. For a full feature list, along with instructions on some most of the advanced use cases, refer to `http://docs.weave.works/weave/latest_release/features.html`.

Summary

In this chapter, we have looked at three different network drivers, all three of which add quite powerful functionality to your basic Docker installation. These, along with the volume drivers, really extend Docker to the point where you can run large fault-tolerant clusters of containers.

Personally, when I first installed Weave and started to communicate with containers across different Docker hosts in different hosting providers so easily, I was absolutely blown away.

In the next chapter, we will look at how you should approach to creating your own extension.

5
Building Your Own Plugin

Along with providing the core tools, Docker also documents an API that allows the core Docker engine to talk to the plugin services written by third-party developers. At the moment, this API allows you to hook your own storage and networking engines into Docker.

This may seem like it is limiting you to a very niche set of plugins, and it is. However, there is a good reason that Docker has taken this decision.

Let's have a look at some of the plugins that we have already installed in the previous chapters; however, rather than covering the functionality, we will take a look at what goes on behind the scenes.

Third-party plugins

The first page about plugins on the Docker documentation site lists a lot of third-party plugins. As already mentioned, let's get an idea of what's going on in the background of the plugins that we have already installed and used in *Chapter 3*, *Volume Plugins*, and *Chapter 4*, *Network Plugins*.

Convoy

Convoy was the first third-party plugin we looked at in *Chapter 3*, *Volume Plugins*. To install it, we launched a Docker host in DigitalOcean as we needed a more complete underlying operating system than is provided by the Boot2Docker operating system, which is favored by Docker Machine.

To install Convoy, we downloaded a release file from GitHub. This tar archive contained the static binaries required to run Convoy on a Linux system, once the static binaries were in place, we created a Docker plugin folder and then added a symbolic link to the socket file that Convoy creates when it is first executed.

We then went on to configure a loopback device that we created on a volume. We then instructed Convoy to use the newly created volume by launching Convoy as a daemon using the Convoy static binary that we downloaded.

> In multitasking computer operating systems, a daemon is a computer program that runs as a background process, rather than being under the direct control of an interactive user:
>
> `https://en.wikipedia.org/wiki/Daemon(computing)`.

As far as Docker is concerned, for each request it gets when the `--volume-driver=convoy` flag is used to launch a container, it will simply offload anything to do with volume the daemonized Convoy process.

If you review the *Convoy* section of *Chapter 3, Volume Plugins*, you will notice that all of our interaction with Convoy is using the `convoy` command and not the `docker` one, in fact, the Convoy client is using the same socket file as we symbolically linked to the `Docker plugins` folder.

REX-Ray

Next up, we installed REX-Ray. To do this, we ran a command, which downloaded and executed a bash script from `https://dl.bintray.com/emccode/rexray/install`.

This script works out the operating system you are running and then downloads and installs either the DEB or RPM file. These packages, as you may have already guessed, install the correct static binaries for your operating system.

REX-Ray goes one step further by also installing init, upstart, or systemd service scripts for the daemon, meaning that you can start and stop it as you would with any other services on your Docker host.

Again, once we have installed REX-Ray, the only interaction we had with the tool is by using the `rexray` command.

Flocker

Flocker went one step further, rather than installing an installation script, we used the AWS CloudFormation templates supplied by Cluster HQ to bootstrap the environment for us.

This did the obvious task of launching the Docker host, setting up the security groups, and installing and configuring both Docker and Flocker.

Flocker goes one step further than Convoy and REX-Ray by installing an agent that interacts with the remotely-hosted web API, the volume hub.

Also, as mentioned in this chapter, Flocker existed before the concept of volume plugins existed. So again, a lot of interaction with Flocker is done outside of Docker; in fact, Cluster HQ wrote their own wrapper for Docker so that you could easily create Flocker volumes before the option existed within Docker.

Weave

This was the only third-party network plugin we looked at. Like Flocker, Weave existed before Docker launched its plugin functionality.

Weave is slightly different from the other third-party tools that we have looked at. In this, what is downloaded is actually a bash script rather than a static binary.

 This script is used to configure the host and download containers from the Weaveworks Docker Hub account, which can be found at `https://hub.docker.com/u/weaveworks/`.

The script launches and configures the containers with enough permissions to interact with the host machine. The script is also responsible for sending commands via the `docker exec` command to the running containers and also configure `iptables` on the host machine.

The commonalities among the plugins

As you can see, and as you have experienced, all of these plugins have scripts and binaries that are external to Docker itself.

They are also pretty much all written in the same language as Docker:

Plugin	Language
Convoy	Go
REX-Ray	Go
Flocker	Python
Weave	Go

Majority of the services are written in Go, the only exception is Flocker, which is mostly written in Python:

> *Go is expressive, concise, clean, and efficient. Its concurrency mechanisms make it easy to write programs that get the most out of multicore and networked machines, while its novel type system enables flexible and modular program construction. Go compiles quickly to machine code yet has the convenience of garbage collection and the power of run-time reflection. It's a fast, statically typed, compiled language that feels like a dynamically typed, interpreted language.* `https://golang.org/`.

Understanding a plugin

So far, we have established that all the plugins that we have installed have actually nothing to do with Docker directly, so what does a plugin do?

Docker describes a plugin as:

> *"Docker plugins are out-of-process extensions which add capabilities to the Docker Engine."*

This is exactly what we have seen when installing third-party tools, they all run alongside Docker as separate daemons.

Let's assume that we are going to be creating a volume plugin called `mobyfs` for the remainder of this chapter. The mobyfs plugin is a fictional service which is written in Go and it runs as a daemon.

Discovery

Typically, a plugin will be installed on the same host as the Docker binary. We can register our mobyfs plugin with Docker by creating the following files in either `/run/docker/plugins` if it's a Unix socket file, or `/etc/docker/plugins` or `/usr/lib/docker/plugins` if it is one of the other two files:

- `mobyfs.sock`
- `mobyfs.spec`
- `mobyfs.json`

Plugins that use a Unix socket file must run on the same hosts as your Docker installation. Ones which use either a `.spec` or `.json` file can run on external hosts if your daemon supports TCP connections.

If you were using a .spec file, your file would just contain a single URL to either a TCP host and port or local socket file. Any of the following three examples are valid:

```
tcp://192.168.1.1:8080
tcp://localhost:8080
unix:///other.sock
```

If you wanted to use a .json file, it must look something similar to the following code:

```json
{
  "Name": "mobyfs",
  "Addr": "https:// 192.168.1.1:8080",
  "TLSConfig": {
    "InsecureSkipVerify": false,
    "CAFile": "/usr/shared/docker/certs/example-ca.pem",
    "CertFile": "/usr/shared/docker/certs/example-cert.pem",
    "KeyFile": "/usr/shared/docker/certs/example-key.pem",
  }
}
```

The TLSConfig section of the JSON file is optional; however, if you are running your service on host other than your Docker host, I would recommend using HTTPS for communication between Docker and your plugin.

Startup order

Ideally, your plugin service should be started before Docker. If you are running a host, which has systemd installed, this can be achieved by using a systemd service file similar to the following one, which should be called mobyfs.service:

```
[Unit]
Description= mobyfs
Before=docker.service

[Service]
EnvironmentFile=/etc/mobyfs/mobyfs.env
ExecStart=/usr/bin/mobyfs start -p 8080
ExecReload=/bin/kill -HUP $MAINPID
KillMode=process

[Install]
WantedBy=docker.service
```

This will ensure that your plugin service is always started before the main Docker service.

If you are hosting your Plugin service on an external host, you may have to restart Docker for Docker to start communicating with your plugin service.

It is possible to package your plugin inside a container. To get around Docker having to be started before the plugin service, each activation request will retry several times over 30 seconds.

This will give the container enough time to start and to run the plugin service run though any bootstrapping processes before binding itself to a port on the container.

Activation

Now that the plugin service has started, and we need to let Docker know where it should send requests to if the plugin service is called. According to our example, service is a volume plugin and we should run something similar to the following command:

```
docker run -ti -v volumename:/data --volume-driver=mobyfs russmckendrick/
base bash
```

This will mount the `volumename` volume, which we have already configured in our plugin service to `/data` in a container, which runs my base container image and attaches us to a shell.

When the mobyfs volume driver is called, Docker will search through the three plugin directories that we covered in the *Discovery* section. By default, Docker will always look for a socket file, then either a `.spec` or `.json` file. The plugin name must match the filename in front of the file extension. If it is doesn't, the plugin will not be recognized by Docker.

API calls

Once the plugin has been called, the Docker daemon will make a post request using RPC-style JSON over HTTP to the plugin service using either the socket file or the URL defined in the `.spec` or `.json` file.

This means that your plugin service must implement an HTTP server and bind itself to the socket or port that you defined in the Discovery section.

The first request that is made by Docker will be to `/Plugin.Activate`. Your plugin service must respond to one of three responses. As mobyfs is a volume plugin, the response would be as follows:

```
{
    "Implements": ["VolumeDriver"]
}
```

If it was a network driver, then the response our plugin service should give would be as follows:

```
{
    "Implements": ["NetworkDriver"]
}
```

The final response of plugin service is as shown in the following code:

```
{
    "Implements": ["authz"]
}
```

Any other responses will be rejected and the activation will fail. Now that Docker has activated the plugin, it will continue to make post requests to the plugin service depending on the response it got when calling `/Plugin.Activate`.

Writing your plugin service

As mentioned in the previous section, Docker will interact with your plugin service by making HTTP calls. These calls are documented on the following pages:

- **Volume Driver Plugins**: `https://docs.docker.com/engine/extend/plugins_volume/`
- **Network Driver Plugins**: `https://docs.docker.com/engine/extend/plugins_network/`
- **Authorization Plugins**: `https://docs.docker.com/engine/extend/plugins_authorization/`

Docker also provides an SDK as a collection for Go helpers, these can be found at the following URL:

`https://github.com/docker/go-plugins-helpers`

Each helper comes with examples, as well as links to open source projects, which serve as further examples on how to implement the helper.

These API requests should not be confused with the Docker Remote API, which is documented at the following URL:

`https://docs.docker.com/engine/reference/api/docker_remote_api/`

This is the API, which allows your applications to interact with Docker, and not Docker to interact with your application.

Summary

As you can see, we only discussed how Docker will interact with the plugin service that you have written and didn't cover how you can actually write a plugin service.

The reason for this is that due to the plugin service that we would have had to cover, we would also need the following features:

- To be written in Go
- To be able run as a daemon
- To contain an HTTP server bound to a Unix socket or TCP port
- To be able to accept and answer requests made to it by the Docker daemon
- To translate the API requests that Docker is making to a filesystem or network service

As you can imagine, this has the potential of being an entire book by itself.

Also, building your own plugin is quite an undertaking as you already have to have the foundations of a service written. While it seems like there are a lot of Docker plugins out there, searching GitHub for Docker plugins only returns a few dozen plugins that have been written to use the Docker plugin API.

The other projects returned are all tools or plugins for third-party services (such as Jenkins, Maven, and so on) that communicate with the Docker Remote API.

In the next chapter, we are going to look at third-party tools to extend your infrastructure past using Docker Machine.

Extending Your Infrastructure

6

In *Chapter 2, Introducing First-party Tools*, we looked at the tools Docker provides for extending the functionality of the core Docker engine. In this chapter, we will look at third-party tools that extend the way you manage your Docker configuration and build and launch containers. The tools that we are going to be discussing are as follows:

- **Puppet**: `http://puppetlabs.com/`
- **Ansible**: `http://www.ansible.com/docker/`
- **Vagrant**: `https://docs.vagrantup.com/v2/docker/`
- **Packer**: `https://www.packer.io/docs/builders/docker.html`
- **Jenkins**: `https://jenkins-ci.org/content/jenkins-and-docker/`

For each of the tools, we will look at how to install, configure, and use them with Docker. Before we look at how to use the tools, let's discuss why we would want to use them.

Why use these tools?

So far, we have been looking at tools that either use the main Docker client or use the tools that are provided by Docker and other third parties to support the main Docker client.

For quite a while, the functionality that some of these tools have now did not exist within a Docker support product. For example, if you wanted to launch a Docker host, you couldn't just use Docker Machine, instead you had to use something such as Vagrant to launch a virtual machine (locally or in the cloud) and then install Docker using a bash script, Puppet, or Ansible.

Once you had your Docker host up and running, you could use these tools to place your containers on hosts as there was no Docker Swarm or Docker Compose (remember Docker Compose started off as a third-party tool called Fig).

So while Docker has slowly been releasing their own tooling, some of these third-party options are actually more mature and have quite an active community behind them.

Let's start by looking at Puppet.

Puppetize all the things

Long before the following *Containerize all the things* meme regularly started to pop up in people's presentations:

People were saying the same thing about Puppet. So, what is Puppet and why would you want to use it on all things?

Puppet Labs, the makers of Puppet, describe Puppet as:

> *"With Puppet, you define the state of your IT infrastructure, and Puppet automatically enforces the desired state. Puppet automates every step of the software delivery process, from provisioning of physical and virtual machines to orchestration and reporting; from early-stage code development through testing, production release and updates."*

Before tools such as Puppet, working as a sysadmin could sometimes be quite a tedious process: if you weren't looking into problems, you were writing your own scripts to bootstrap servers once they had been built, or even worse, you were copying and pasting commands from an internal wiki to install your software stack and configure it.

Servers would very quickly evolve away from your initial installation and when they broke, which all servers eventually do, things could get really interesting, complicated, scary, very bad, or all of them quickly.

This is where Puppet comes in; you define what you need your server to look like and Puppet does the heavy lifting for you, making sure that your configuration is not only applied, but also maintained.

For example, if I had several servers behind a load balancer for my PHP-powered website, it's important that the servers are all configured in the same way, meaning that they all have the following:

- The same NGINX or Apache configuration
- The same version of PHP along with the same configuration
- The same PHP modules installed, at the same version

To do this before Puppet, I would have to ensure that not only I kept a script that is used to do the initial installation, but I would also have to carefully manually apply the same configuration changes across the servers or write a script to synchronize my changes across the cluster.

I would also have to ensure that anyone who has access to the servers adheres to the processes and procedures I have put in place in order to maintain consistency across my load balanced web servers.

If they didn't, I would start to get configuration drift, or worse, still one in every x requests could be being served from a server that is running a different codebase/ configuration from the other machines.

With Puppet, if I need to run an up-to-date version of PHP 5.6 because my application doesn't work correctly under PHP 7, then I can use the following definition to ensure that my requirements are met:

```
package { 'php' :
  ensure => '5.6',
}
```

This will make sure that the php package is installed and that the version is and stays at 5.6, I can then take this single configuration and apply it across all of my web servers.

So, what's this got to do with Docker?

Docker and Puppet

Before Docker Machine, Docker Compose, and Docker Swarm, I used Puppet to bootstrap and manage my Docker hosts and containers. Let's take a look at the excellent Docker Puppet module written by Gareth Rushgrove.

To start off, we need a virtual machine to work on. In the previous chapters, we have been using Docker Machine to launch virtual machines that we can run our containers on.

However, as we want Puppet to manage the installation of Docker and the container on which we are going to be launching a local virtual machine using Vagrant, confusingly, we are also going to be looking at Vagrant later in this chapter, so we will not go into much detail here.

First of all, you need to ensure that you have Vagrant installed, you can get the latest release from `https://www.vagrantup.com/` and you can find a guide to perform the installation at `https://www.vagrantup.com/docs/getting-started/`.

Once you have Vagrant installed, you can a launch an Ubuntu 14.04 virtual server using VirtualBox by running the following command:

```
mkdir  ubuntu && cd ubuntu/
vagrant init ubuntu/trusty64; vagrant up --provider VirtualBox
```

This will download and launch the virtual server, storing everything in the `ubuntu` folder. It will also mount the `ubuntu` folder as a filesystem share using the `/vagrant` path:

```
ubuntu — -bash — 118×57
russ in ~/Desktop
⚡  mkdir ubuntu && cd ubuntu
russ in ~/Desktop/ubuntu
⚡  vagrant init ubuntu/trusty64; vagrant up --provider virtualbox
A `Vagrantfile` has been placed in this directory. You are now
ready to `vagrant up` your first virtual environment! Please read
the comments in the Vagrantfile as well as documentation on
`vagrantup.com` for more information on using Vagrant.
Bringing machine 'default' up with 'virtualbox' provider...
==> default: Importing base box 'ubuntu/trusty64'...
==> default: Matching MAC address for NAT networking...
==> default: Checking if box 'ubuntu/trusty64' is up to date...
==> default: Setting the name of the VM: ubuntu_default_1457794813049_39517
==> default: Clearing any previously set forwarded ports...
==> default: Clearing any previously set network interfaces...
==> default: Preparing network interfaces based on configuration...
    default: Adapter 1: nat
==> default: Forwarding ports...
    default: 22 => 2222 (adapter 1)
==> default: Booting VM...
==> default: Waiting for machine to boot. This may take a few minutes...
    default: SSH address: 127.0.0.1:2222
    default: SSH username: vagrant
    default: SSH auth method: private key
    default: Warning: Connection timeout. Retrying...
    default:
    default: Vagrant insecure key detected. Vagrant will automatically replace
    default: this with a newly generated keypair for better security.
    default:
    default: Inserting generated public key within guest...
    default: Removing insecure key from the guest if it's present...
    default: Key inserted! Disconnecting and reconnecting using new SSH key...
==> default: Machine booted and ready!
==> default: Checking for guest additions in VM...
    default: The guest additions on this VM do not match the installed version of
    default: VirtualBox! In most cases this is fine, but in rare cases it can
    default: prevent things such as shared folders from working properly. If you see
    default: shared folder errors, please make sure the guest additions within the
    default: virtual machine match the version of VirtualBox you have installed on
    default: your host and reload your VM.
    default:
    default: Guest Additions Version: 4.3.36
    default: VirtualBox Version: 5.0
==> default: Mounting shared folders...
    default: /vagrant => /Users/russ/Desktop/ubuntu
russ in ~/Desktop/ubuntu
⚡  vagrant status
Current machine states:

default                   running (virtualbox)

The VM is running. To stop this VM, you can run `vagrant halt` to
shut it down forcefully, or you can run `vagrant suspend` to simply
suspend the virtual machine. In either case, to restart it again,
simply run `vagrant up`.
russ in ~/Desktop/ubuntu
⚡  []
```

Now that we have our virtual server up and running, let's connect to it and install the Puppet agent:

```
vagrant ssh
```

```
sudo su -
```

```
curl -fsS https://raw.githubusercontent.com/russmckendrick/puppet-
install/master/ubuntu | bash
```

You should see something similar to the following terminal session:

```
● ● ●                    ⌂ root@vagrant-ubuntu-trusty-64: ~ — ssh ◦ vagrant ssh — 118×40
russ in ~/Desktop/ubuntu
∤ vagrant ssh
Welcome to Ubuntu 14.04.4 LTS (GNU/Linux 3.13.0-79-generic x86_64)

 * Documentation:  https://help.ubuntu.com/

  System information as of Sat Mar 12 15:00:33 UTC 2016

  System load:  0.22              Processes:           80
  Usage of /:   3.5% of 39.34GB   Users logged in:      0
  Memory usage: 25%               IP address for eth0: 10.0.2.15
  Swap usage:   0%

  Graph this data and manage this system at:
    https://landscape.canonical.com/

  Get cloud support with Ubuntu Advantage Cloud Guest:
    http://www.ubuntu.com/business/services/cloud

0 packages can be updated.
0 updates are security updates.


vagrant@vagrant-ubuntu-trusty-64:~$ sudo su -
root@vagrant-ubuntu-trusty-64:~# curl -fsS https://raw.githubusercontent.com/russmckendrick/puppet-install/master/ubun
tu | bash
Initial apt-get update...
Installing wget...
Configuring PuppetLabs repo...
Installing Puppet...
dpkg: warning: unable to delete old directory '/etc/ldap/schema': Directory not empty
Puppet installed!
Installing RubyGems...
Fetching: rubygems-update-2.6.1.gem (100%)
Successfully installed rubygems-update-2.6.1
1 gem installed
RubyGems installed!
root@vagrant-ubuntu-trusty-64:~# puppet --version
3.8.6
root@vagrant-ubuntu-trusty-64:~# []
```

Now that we have the Puppet agent installed, the final step is to install the Docker module from Puppet Forge:

```
puppet module install garethr-docker
```

You may see warnings such as the one in the following terminal session; don't worry about these, they are to just inform you of the upcoming changes to Puppet:

```
● ● ●                    ⌂ root@vagrant-ubuntu-trusty-64: ~ — ssh ◦ vagrant ssh — 118×12
root@vagrant-ubuntu-trusty-64:~# puppet module install garethr-docker
Warning: Setting templatedir is deprecated. See http://links.puppetlabs.com/env-settings-deprecations
   (at /usr/lib/ruby/vendor_ruby/puppet/settings.rb:1139:in `issue_deprecation_warning')
Notice: Preparing to install into /etc/puppet/modules ...
Notice: Downloading from https://forgeapi.puppetlabs.com ...
Notice: Installing -- do not interrupt ...
/etc/puppet/modules
└─┬ garethr-docker (v5.1.0)
  ├── puppetlabs-apt (v2.2.2)
  ├── puppetlabs-stdlib (v4.11.0)
  └── stahnma-epel (v1.2.2)
root@vagrant-ubuntu-trusty-64:~#
```

At this point, it's worth point out that we haven't actually installed Docker yet, so let's do that now by running our first puppet manifest. On your local machine, create a file called `docker.pp` in the `ubuntu` folder. The file should contain the following contents:

```
include 'docker'

docker::image { 'russmckendrick/base': }

docker::run { 'helloworld':
  image   => 'russmckendrick/base',
  command => '/bin/sh -c "while true; do echo hello world; sleep 1;
done"',
}
```

When we run this manifest using `puppet apply`, Puppet will know that we need Docker installed to be able download the `russmckendrick/base` image and then launch the `helloworld` container.

Back on our virtual machine, let's apply the manifest by running the following command:

puppet apply /vagrant/docker.pp

You will see a lot of output from the command, as shown in the following screenshot:

```
root@vagrant-ubuntu-trusty-64:~# puppet apply /vagrant/docker.pp
Warning: Setting templatedir is deprecated. See http://links.puppetlabs.com/env-settings-deprecations
   (at /usr/lib/ruby/vendor_ruby/puppet/settings.rb:1139:in `issue_deprecation_warning')
Warning: Could not retrieve fact fqdn
Warning: Config file /etc/puppet/hiera.yaml not found, using Hiera defaults
Warning: Scope(Apt::Source[docker]): $include_src is deprecated and will be removed in the next major release, please use $include => { '
Warning: Scope(Apt::Source[docker]): $required_packages is deprecated and will be removed in the next major release, please use package r
Warning: Scope(Apt::Source[docker]): $key_source is deprecated and will be removed in the next major release, please use $key => { 'sourc
Warning: Scope(Apt::Key[Add key: 5811BE89F3A912897C070ADBF76221572C52609D from Apt::Source docker]): $key_source is deprecated and will b
Notice: Compiled catalog for vagrant-ubuntu-trusty-64 in environment production in 0.45 seconds
Notice: /Stage[main]/Apt/Apt::Setting[conf-update-stamp]/File[/etc/apt/apt.conf.d/15update-stamp]/content: content changed '{md5}b9de0ac9
Notice: /Stage[main]/Apt/File[preferences]/ensure: created
Notice: /Stage[main]/Docker::Repos/Apt::Source[docker]/Apt::Key[Add key: 5811BE89F3A912897C070ADBF76221572C52609D from Apt::Source docker]
/ensure: created
Notice: /Stage[main]/Docker::Repos/Apt::Source[docker]/Apt::Pin[docker]/Apt::Setting[pref-docker]/File[/etc/apt/preferences.d/docker.pref
Notice: /Stage[main]/Docker::Repos/Apt::Source[docker]/Apt::Setting[list-docker]/File[/etc/apt/sources.list.d/docker.list]/ensure: create
Notice: /Stage[main]/Apt::Update/Exec[apt_update]: Triggered 'refresh' from 1 events
Notice: /Stage[main]/Docker::Repos/Package[cgroup-lite]/ensure: ensure changed 'purged' to 'present'
Notice: /Stage[main]/Docker::Install/Package[linux-image-extra-3.13.0-79-generic]/ensure: ensure changed 'purged' to 'present'
Notice: /Stage[main]/Docker::Install/Package[docker]/ensure: ensure changed 'purged' to 'present'
Notice: /Stage[main]/Docker::Service/File[/etc/default/docker]/content: content changed '{md5}df04972d0cf6aefc63ad37c69a26a8bb' to '{md5}
Notice: /Stage[main]/Docker::Service/File[/etc/init.d/docker]/ensure: ensure changed 'file' to 'link'
Notice: /Stage[main]/Docker::Service/Service[docker]: Triggered 'refresh' from 2 events
Notice: /Stage[main]/Main/Docker::Image[russmckendrick/base]/File[/usr/local/bin/update_docker_image.sh]/ensure: created
Notice: /Stage[main]/Main/Docker::Image[russmckendrick/base]/Exec[/usr/local/bin/update_docker_image.sh russmckendrick/base]/returns: exe
Notice: /Stage[main]/Main/Docker::Run[helloworld]/File[/etc/init.d/docker-helloworld]/ensure: created
Notice: /Stage[main]/Main/Docker::Run[helloworld]/Service[docker-helloworld]/ensure: ensure changed 'stopped' to 'running'
Notice: Finished catalog run in 177.94 seconds
root@vagrant-ubuntu-trusty-64:~#
```

The first thing that happens is that Puppet will compile a catalogue, this is essentially a list of all the tasks that it needs to complete in order to apply the configuration that we have defined in the manifest file. Puppet will then execute these tasks. You should be able to see Puppet:

- Add the official Docker APT repository
- Perform an `apt` update to initialize the new repository
- Install Docker and its prerequisites
- Download the `russmckendrick/base` image
- Launch the `helloworld` container

Let's check whether this happened by confirming the Docker version, look at the images that are downloaded, check which containers are running, and finally attach to the `helloworld` container:

```
docker --version
docker images
docker ps
docker attach helloworld
```

To detach from the container, press *Ctrl + C* on your keyboard. This will not only return your prompt to the virtual machine, but also stop the `helloworld` container:

```
docker ps -a
```

You can see the output I got when running the commands in the following terminal session:

So what happens if we apply the manifest again? Let's see it by running `puppet apply /vagrant/docker.pp` for a second time.

You should see a lot less output this time, in fact, the only output you should see other than the warnings is the confirmation that the `helloworld` container has started backing up:

```
root@vagrant-ubuntu-trusty-64:~# puppet apply /vagrant/docker.pp
Warning: Setting templatedir is deprecated. See http://links.puppetlabs.com/env-settings-deprecations
  (at /usr/lib/ruby/vendor_ruby/puppet/settings.rb:1139:in `issue_deprecation_warning')
Warning: Could not retrieve fact fqdn
Warning: Config file /etc/puppet/hiera.yaml not found, using Hiera defaults
Warning: Scope(Apt::Source[docker]): $include_src is deprecated and will be removed in the next major release, please use $include => { 's
rc' => false } instead
Warning: Scope(Apt::Source[docker]): $required_packages is deprecated and will be removed in the next major release, please use package re
sources instead.
Warning: Scope(Apt::Source[docker]): $key_source is deprecated and will be removed in the next major release, please use $key => { 'source
' => https://apt.dockerproject.org/gpg } instead.
Warning: Scope(Apt::Key[Add key: 58118E89F3A912897C070ADBF76221572C52609D from Apt::Source docker]): $key_source is deprecated and will be
 removed in the next major release. Please use $source instead.
Notice: Compiled catalog for vagrant-ubuntu-trusty-64 in environment production in 0.45 seconds
Notice: /Stage[main]/Main/Docker::Run[helloworld]/Service[docker-helloworld]/ensure: ensure changed 'stopped' to 'running'
Notice: Finished catalog run in 0.37 seconds
root@vagrant-ubuntu-trusty-64:~# docker ps
CONTAINER ID        IMAGE                 COMMAND                CREATED             STATUS              PORTS               NAMES
865ad5807d4b        russmckendrick/base   "/bin/sh -c 'while tr" 8 seconds ago       Up 7 seconds                            helloworld
root@vagrant-ubuntu-trusty-64:~#
```

Now that we have an idea of how to get something basic up and running, let's deploy our WordPress installation. First of all, by default, our virtual machine has quite a limited vagrant configuration, so let's remove the virtual machine and bring up a more complex configuration.

To remove the virtual machine, type exit in your terminal until you are back on your local PC; once there, type the following command:

vagrant destroy

Once you hit Enter, you will receive a prompt asking *Are you sure you want to destroy the 'default' VM?*, answer yes and the virtual machine will be powered down and removed.

Next, replace the entire content of the file called `Vagrantfile` that can be found in your `ubuntu` folder:

```ruby
# -*- mode: ruby -*-
# vi: set ft=ruby :

VAGRANTFILE_API_VERSION = "2"

Vagrant.configure(VAGRANTFILE_API_VERSION) do |config|
    config.vm.box = "ubuntu/trusty64"
    config.vm.network "private_network", ip: "192.168.33.10"
    HOSTNAME = 'docker'
    DOMAIN   = 'media-glass.es'
    Vagrant.require_version '>= 1.7.0'
```

```
      config.ssh.insert_key = false

  config.vm.host_name = HOSTNAME + '.' + DOMAIN

  config.vm.provider "VirtualBox" do |v|
    v.memory = 2024
    v.cpus = 2
  end

  config.vm.provider "vmware_fusion" do |v|
    v.vmx["memsize"] = "2024"
    v.vmx["numvcpus"] = "2"
  end

$script = <<SCRIPT
sudo sh -c 'curl -fsS https://raw.githubusercontent.com/
russmckendrick/puppet-install/master/ubuntu | bash'
sudo puppet module install garethr-docker
SCRIPT

config.vm.provision "shell",
    inline: $script
end
```

You can also find a copy of the file in the book's GitHub repository, which can be found at `https://github.com/russmckendrick/extending-docker/blob/master/chapter06/puppet-docker/Vagrantfile`.

Once you have `Vagrantfile` in place, run `vagrant up` again and the virtual machine will boot.

The differences between this virtual machine and the previous one that we launched is that it will have an IP address of `192.168.33.10`, which is only accessible from your local PC. The `Vagrantfile` also runs the commands to install Puppet and the Docker Puppet module.

While the machine is booting, put a copy of the following Puppet manifest in your `ubuntu` folder, call it `wordpress.pp`:

```
include 'docker'

docker::image { 'wordpress': }
docker::image { 'mysql': }

docker::run { 'wordpress':
```

```
     image            => 'wordpress',
     ports            => ['80:80'],
     links            => ['mysql:mysql'],
}

docker::run { 'mysql':
    image             => 'mysql',
    env               => ['MYSQL_ROOT_PASSWORD=password', 'FOO2=BAR2'],
}
```

As you can see, the format itself resembles the Docker Compose file we used to launch our WordPress installation back in *Chapter 2, Introducing First-party Tools*. Once the virtual machine has booted, connect to it, and apply the wordpress.pp manifest by running the following command:

vagrant ssh

sudo puppet apply /vagrant/wordpress.pp

As before, you will see quite a bit of output:

```
vagrant@docker:~$ sudo puppet apply /vagrant/wordpress.pp
Warning: Setting templatedir is deprecated. See http://links.puppetlabs.com/env-settings-deprecations
   (at /usr/lib/ruby/vendor_ruby/puppet/settings.rb:1139:in `issue_deprecation_warning')
Warning: Config file /etc/puppet/hiera.yaml not found, using Hiera defaults
Warning: Scope(Apt::Source[docker]): $include_src is deprecated and will be removed in the next major release, please use
Warning: Scope(Apt::Source[docker]): $required_packages is deprecated and will be removed in the next major release, pleas
Warning: Scope(Apt::Source[docker]): $key_source is deprecated and will be removed in the next major release, please use $
Warning: Scope(Apt::Key[Add key: 58118E89F3A912897C070ADBF76221572C52609D from Apt::Source docker]): $key_source is deprec
Notice: Compiled catalog for docker.media-glass.es in environment production in 0.50 seconds
Notice: /Stage[main]/Apt/Apt::Setting[conf-update-stamp]/File[/etc/apt/apt.conf.d/15update-stamp]/content: content changed
Notice: /Stage[main]/Apt/File[preferences]/ensure: created
Notice: /Stage[main]/Docker::Repos/Apt::Source[docker]/Apt::Key[Add key: 58118E89F3A912897C070ADBF76221572C52609D from Apt]
/ensure: created
Notice: /Stage[main]/Docker::Repos/Apt::Source[docker]/Apt::Pin[docker]/Apt::Setting[pref-docker]/File[/etc/apt/preference
Notice: /Stage[main]/Docker::Repos/Apt::Source[docker]/Apt::Setting[list-docker]/File[/etc/apt/sources.list.d/docker.list]
Notice: /Stage[main]/Apt::Update/Exec[apt_update]: Triggered 'refresh' from 1 events
Notice: /Stage[main]/Docker::Repos/Package[cgroup-lite]/ensure: ensure changed 'purged' to 'present'
Notice: /Stage[main]/Docker::Install/Package[linux-image-extra-3.13.0-79-generic]/ensure: ensure changed 'purged' to 'pres
Notice: /Stage[main]/Docker::Install/Package[docker]/ensure: ensure changed 'purged' to 'present'
Notice: /Stage[main]/Docker::Service/File[/etc/default/docker]/content: content changed '{md5}df04972d0cf6aefc63ad37c69a2f
Notice: /Stage[main]/Docker::Service/File[/etc/init.d/docker]/ensure: ensure changed 'file' to 'link'
Notice: /Stage[main]/Docker::Service/Service[docker]: Triggered 'refresh' from 2 events
Notice: /Stage[main]/Main/Docker::Image[wordpress]/File[/usr/local/bin/update_docker_image.sh]/ensure: created
Notice: /Stage[main]/Main/Docker::Image[mysql]/Exec[/usr/local/bin/update_docker_image.sh mysql]/returns: executed success
Notice: /Stage[main]/Main/Docker::Image[wordpress]/Exec[/usr/local/bin/update_docker_image.sh wordpress]/returns: executec
Notice: /Stage[main]/Main/Docker::Run[mysql]/File[/etc/init.d/docker-mysql]/ensure: created
Notice: /Stage[main]/Main/Docker::Run[mysql]/Service[docker-mysql]/ensure: ensure changed 'stopped' to 'running'
Notice: /Stage[main]/Main/Docker::Run[wordpress]/File[/etc/init.d/docker-wordpress]/ensure: created
Notice: /Stage[main]/Main/Docker::Run[wordpress]/Service[docker-wordpress]/ensure: ensure changed 'stopped' to 'running'
Notice: Finished catalog run in 103.94 seconds
```

Once the manifest has been applied, you should be able to point your browser to the IP address at http:// 192.168.33.10/ or use the following URL at http:// docker.media-glass.es/, this URL resolves to the IP address configured in Vagrantfile and will only be accessible once the virtual machine is running and then manifest applied.

From here, you can install WordPress as you have done in other chapters. Once you have finished, don't forget to destroy your virtual machine using the `vagrant destroy` command, as it will quite happily sit in the background using resources.

So, there you have it, a very basic practical introduction to running Puppet and Docker together.

A more advanced Puppet example

So far, we have been running Puppet on a single virtual machine, this isn't actually where its strengths lie.

Where Puppet comes into its own is when you deploy a Puppet Master server and have the Puppet Agents on your hosts talk to the Master. Here, you are able to define exactly how you want your hosts to look. For example, the following diagram shows a single Puppet Master server controlling four Docker nodes:

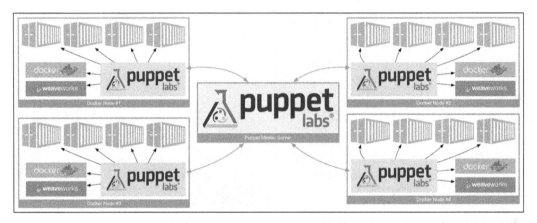

In this example, we could have a Puppet manifest on the Puppet Master for each of the hosts, along with a manifest for configuration this is common across all four of the nodes.

In the example, I have Weave installed on each of the nodes, check the Puppet Forge at `https://forge.puppetlabs.com/`, there is a module that allows you to manage Weave called `tayzlor/weave`, this module alongside `garethr/docker` will allow you to perform the following tasks:

- Install Docker on each node
- Install Weave on each node
- Create a Weave network across all four nodes

- Manage images on each node
- Launch containers on each node and configure them to use the Weave network

By default, the Puppet agent on each of the nodes will call back to the Puppet master server every 15 minutes; when it does this, it will work through the manifests that apply to the node. If there are any changes, these will be applied during the Puppet Agent run; if there are no changes to the manifests, then no action will be taken.

Add to this that the Puppet configuration, including the manifests, lends itself really well in order to being managed by a source control and you can create some really useful workflows.

The only downside of this configuration is that it does not replace Docker Swarm, as all of the logic as to where the containers are launched is defined manually within each of manifest files. That's not to say that you can't launch a Swarm cluster using Puppet, as you can, with a little more work.

We are not going to work through the example as we still have four more tools to work through in this chapter, there are plenty of resources available on the Puppetlabs website:

- **Learning VM**: `https://puppetlabs.com/download-learning-vm`
- **Puppet Open Source Docs**: `https://docs.puppetlabs.com/puppet/`

You can find more details on the two Puppet modules that I have mentioned:

- **Docker module**: `https://forge.puppetlabs.com/garethr/docker/`
- **Weave module**: `https://forge.puppetlabs.com/tayzlor/weave/`

A final note about Puppet

In the next part of this chapter, we are going to be looking at Ansible, which most people, I suspect, think that it does exactly the same job as Puppet. While its true that there is a lot of crossover between the two, I see Ansible's strengths as an orchestration tool and Puppet excels at being a configuration management tool.

As Puppet is a really great configuration management tool, there is the temptation to start bundling a Puppet Agent inside your containers, using it as part of your image build process, or even for real-time configuration, as the container launches.

Try to avoid this, as it may add unnecessary bloat to your containers as well as introduce additional processes. Remember in an ideal world, your containers should run a single process and be ready to work as soon as they are started.

Orchestration with Ansible

I suspect a lot of people will be expecting an Ansible versus Puppet opening to this section of the chapter. In fact, as mentioned at the end of the previous section, while the two tools have a lot of crossover, their strengths lie in doing two different jobs.

They also work in completely different ways. Rather than going into the details now, let's jump right in and install Ansible and then launch our WordPress containers using an Ansible playbook.

Preparation

 Note that if, for any reason, you are not able to work through this section of the chapter, I have recorded a screencast to show you what happens when you launch the Ansible playbook, which can be found at https://asciinema.org/a/39537.

Before launching our containers, we need to do a few things. The first thing is to install Ansible.

If you are running OS X, I would recommend installing Ansible using Homebrew. Homebrew is available at http://brew.sh/ and can be installed with the following single command:

```
/usr/bin/ruby -e "$(curl -fsSL https://raw.githubusercontent.com/
Homebrew/install/master/install)"
```

Once you have followed the on-screen prompts, you should be in a position to install Ansible using the following command:

```
brew install ansible
```

Now that Ansible is installed, we need to install a certain version of the DigitalOcean Python library. To do this, we need to use the `pip` command. If you don't have the `pip` command installed, then you need to run:

```
sudo easy_install pip
```

Now that `pip` is installed, run the following command to install the correct version of the Python library we need:

```
sudo pip install dopy==0.3.5
```

The final thing you will need is the name of your DigitalOcean key. The Ansible playbook we are going to run will create one for you and upload it if you don't have one already configured, so if that's the case, you can skip this part.

If you do happen to have one already associated with your DigitalOcean account, then you will name the name of it to launch the two instances and then connect to them.

To find this out, log in to the DigitalOcean control panel at `https://cloud.digitalocean.com/` and click on the `cog icon` on the top right-hand side of the screen and from the menu that pops up, click on the **Settings** button. Once the settings page loads, click on the **Security** button, you should then see a list of SSH keys, make a note of the name you want to use:

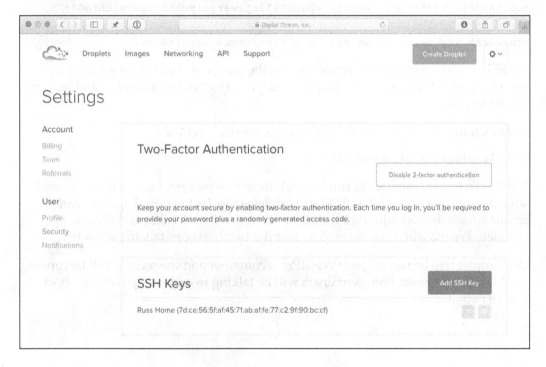

In the preceding example, my SSH key is creatively called `Russ Home`.

Time to get a copy of the Ansible playbook we are going to be running. The code for this can be found in the `chapter06/docker-ansible` folder on the GitHub repository for this book, the complete URL is as follows:

```
https://github.com/russmckendrick/extending-docker/tree/master/
chapter06/docker-ansible
```

Once you have the playbook downloaded, open your terminal and go to the `docker-ansible` folder. Once in there, run the following command, replacing the DigitalOcean API with your own:

```
echo 'do_api_token:
"sdnjkjdfgkjb345kjdgljknqwetkjwhgoih314rjkwergoiyu34rjkherglkhrg0"' >
group_vars/do.yml
echo 'ssh_key_name: "Your Key Name"' >> group_vars/do.yml
```

We are now in a position where we can run the playbook, but before we do, remember that this playbook will connect to your DigitalOcean account and launch two instances.

To launch the playbook, run the following command and wait:

```
ansible-playbook -i hosts site.yml
```

It will take several minutes to run through the entire process, but what you should have the end of it is two Ubuntu 14.04 Droplets launched in your DigitalOcean account. Each droplet will have the latest version of both Docker and Weave installed, Weave will be configured so that the two hosts can talk to each other.

One droplet will be running our WordPress container and the second will be running our MySQL container, both containers will be talking to each using the cross-host Weave network.

Once the task completes, you will should see something similar to the following screenshot:

As you can see, in my case, I can go to `http://46.101.4.247` in my browser to start the WordPress installation.

If, for any reason, parts of the installation fail, for example, sometimes droplets can take a little longer to start and won't be available for Ansible to connect to when it tries to SSH to them, then don't worry, you will be able to rerun the Ansible playbook using the following command:

```
ansible-playbook -i hosts site.yml
```

Ansible will also work through the entire playbook again, this time, skipping anything that has already been created or actioned.

If you are not working through this example, or have problems, I have recorded an entire run-through of launching the playbook and then rerunning it, you can view this at `https://asciinema.org/a/39537`.

The playbook

There are quite a few parts of the playbook, as you can see from the following list of folders and files:

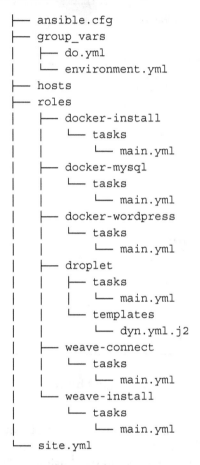

```
├── ansible.cfg
├── group_vars
│   ├── do.yml
│   └── environment.yml
├── hosts
├── roles
│   ├── docker-install
│   │   └── tasks
│   │       └── main.yml
│   ├── docker-mysql
│   │   └── tasks
│   │       └── main.yml
│   ├── docker-wordpress
│   │   └── tasks
│   │       └── main.yml
│   ├── droplet
│   │   ├── tasks
│   │   │   └── main.yml
│   │   └── templates
│   │       └── dyn.yml.j2
│   ├── weave-connect
│   │   └── tasks
│   │       └── main.yml
│   └── weave-install
│       └── tasks
│           └── main.yml
└── site.yml
```

The main file we called when launching the playbook was the `site.yml` file, this defines the order which tasks in defined in the roles folder are executed. Let's take a look at the content of this file and the roles that are being called.

Section one

The file itself is split into four sections, the following first section deals with connecting to DigitalOcean's API from your local machine and launching the two Droplets:

```
- name: "Provision two droplets in DigitalOcean"
  hosts: localhost
```

```
connection: local
gather_facts: True
vars_files:
  - group_vars/environment.yml
  - group_vars/do.yml
roles:
  - droplet
```

It loads the both the main `environment.yml` variables file, this is where we define things such as which region the droplet is being launched in, name of the droplets, size to use, and also which image should be launched.

It also loads the `do.yml` file which contains your DigitalOcean API key and SSH keyname. If you look into the role task file in the `droplet` folder, you will see that along with launching the two droplets, it also creates the following three host groups:

- `dockerhosts`: This group contains both droplets
- `dockerhost01`: This contains our first droplet
- `dockerhost02`: This group contains the second droplet

The final action that is taken at this stage is that a file is written to the `group_vars` folder, which contains the public IP addresses of our two droplets.

Section Two

The next section of the `site.yml` file deals with the installation of some basic prerequisites, Docker, and Weave on the droplets within the `dockerhosts` group:

```
- name: "Install Docker & Weave on our two DigitalOcean hosts"
  hosts: dockerhosts
  remote_user: root
  gather_facts: False
  vars_files:
    - group_vars/environment.yml
  roles:
    - docker-install
    - weave-install
```

The first role deals with the installation of Docker, let's take a look at what's going within the task file for this role.

First of all, we will install curl using the `apt` package manager as we will need this later:

```
- name: install curl
  apt: pkg=curl update_cache=yes
```

Once curl has been installed, we will start configuring the official Docker APT repository by first adding the keys for the repo:

```
- name: add docker apt keys
  apt_key: keyserver=p80.pool.sks-keyservers.net id=58118E89F3A912897C
070ADBF76221572C52609D
```

Then, we'll add the actual repository:

```
- name: update apt
  apt_repository: repo='deb https://apt.dockerproject.org/repo ubuntu-
trusty main' state=present
```

Once the repository has been added, we can do the actual installation of Docker, making sure that we update the cached repository list before the package is installed:

```
- name: install Docker
  apt: pkg=docker-engine update_cache=yes
```

Now that Docker is installed, we need to ensure that the Docker daemon has started:

```
- name: start Docker
  service: name=docker state=started
```

Now we need to install the tools that Ansible will use to interact with the Docker daemon on our hosts, like Ansible, this is a Python program. To make sure that we can install it, we need to ensure that `pip`, the Python package manager, is installed:

```
- name: install pip
  apt:
    pkg: "{{ item }}"
    state: installed
  with_items:
    - python-dev
    - python-pip
```

Now that we know that pip is installed, we can install the `docker-py` package:

```
- name: install docker-py
  pip:
    name: docker-py
```

This package is a Docker client written in Python and supplied by Docker itself. More details on the client can be found at `https://github.com/docker/docker-py`.

This ends the first role that is called in the second section of the `site.yml` file. Now that Docker is installed, it's time to install Weave, this is handled by the `weave-install` task.

First of all, we download the weave binary from the URL defined in the `environment.yml` file to the filesystem path that is also defined in the `environment.yml` file:

```
- name: download and install weave binary
  get_url: url={{ weave_url }} dest={{ weave_bin }}
```

Once we have the binary downloaded, we need to see the correct read, write, and execute permissions on the file so that it can be executed:

```
- name: setup permissions on weave binary
  file: path={{ weave_bin }} mode="u+rx,g+rx,o+rwx"
```

Finally, we need to start weave and also pass it a password to enable encryption, the password is also defined in the `environment.yml` file:

```
- name: download weave containers and launch with password
  command: weave launch --password {{ weave_password}}
  ignore_errors: true
```

As you can see, at the end of this part of the task, we are telling Ansible to ignore any errors generated here. This is because, if the playbook was to be launched for a second time and weave was already running, it would complain saying that the weave router was already active. This will stop playbook from progressing any further, as Ansible interprets this message as a critical error.

Due to this, we have to tell Ansible to ignore what it thinks is a critical error here for the playbook to progress pass this stage.

Section three

The next section of the `site.yml` file performs one last piece of configuration before launching the containers that go to make up our WordPress installation. All of these roles are run on our first droplet:

```
- name: "Connect the two Weave hosts and start MySQL container"
  hosts: dockerhost01
  remote_user: root
  gather_facts: False
```

```
    vars_files:
      - group_vars/environment.yml
    roles:
      - weave-connect
      - docker-mysql
```

The first role, which is called, connects the two weave networks on the two hosts together:

```
    - include_vars: group_vars/dyn.yml
    - name: download weave containers and launch with password
      command: weave connect {{ docker_host_02 }}
```

As you can see, the variable file that contains the IP address of our two droplets is loaded for the first time here and is used to get the IP address of the second droplet; this file, called `dyn.yml`, was created by the role that originally launched the two droplets.

Once we have the IP address of the second droplet, the `weave connect` command is executed and the configuration of the weave network is completed. We can now launch the containers.

The first container that we need to launch is the database container:

```
    - name: start mysql container
      docker:
        name: my-wordpress-database
        image: mysql
        state: started
        net: weave
        dns: ["172.17.0.1"]
        hostname: mysql.weave.local
        env:
          MYSQL_ROOT_PASSWORD: password
        volumes:
          - "database:/var/lib/mysql/"
```

As you can see, this is quite a similar syntax to Docker Compose files; however, there may be slight differences, so double-check the Docker pages on the Ansible core module documentation site to ensure that you are using the right syntax.

Once the `my-wordpress-database` container has been started, it means that all the tasks we need to execute on `dockerhost01` are completed.

Section four

The final section of the `site.yml` file connects to our second droplet and then launches the WordPress container:

```
- name: "Start the Wordpress container"
  hosts: dockerhost02
  remote_user: root
  gather_facts: False
  roles:
    - docker-wordpress
```

All this role does is launch the WordPress container, again the file has close resemblance to the Docker Compose file:

```
- include_vars: group_vars/dyn.yml
- name: start wordpress container
  docker:
    name: my-wordpress-app
    image: wordpress
    state: started
    net: weave
    dns: ["172.17.0.1"]
    hostname: wordpress.weave.local
    ports:
      - "80:80"
    env:
      WORDPRESS_DB_HOST: mysql.weave.local:3306
      WORDPRESS_DB_PASSWORD: password
    volumes:
      - "uploads:/var/www/html/wp-content/uploads/"
- debug: msg="You should be able to see a WordPress installation
  screen by going to http://{{ docker_host_02 }}"
```

The final debug line prints the message at the end of the playbook run that contains the IP address of the second droplet.

Ansible and Puppet

Like Puppet, Ansible, when used with a playbook like the one we have discussed, can be used as a replacement for Docker Machine and Docker Compose.

However, one thing you may have noticed is that unlike Puppet, we did not install an agent in the target machine.

When you run an Ansible playbook, it is compiled locally, and then the compiled script is pushed to your target servers using SSH and then executed.

This is one of the reasons why, during our playbook run, we have to install the Docker Python library on our two droplets, without which the compiled playbook would not have been able to launch the two containers.

Another important difference between the two tools is that Ansible executes the tasks in the order you define in the playbook.

The Puppet example we worked through wasn't complex enough to really demonstrate why this can be an issue when it comes to running Puppet manifests, but Puppet works using an eventual consistency concept, meaning that it may take a few manifest runs for your configuration to be applied.

It is possible to add requirements to Puppet manifests, for example, requiring XYZ to be executed after ABC has run. However, this can start to cause performance issues if your manifest is quite large; also, you could find yourself in a position where the manifest stops working altogether as Puppet is not able to successfully execute the manifest in the order you are defining.

This is why, in my opinion, Ansible is a lot better when it comes to orchestration than Puppet.

It's situations like this where it really matters that the tasks you have defined are executed in the exact order you need them to run in rather than leaving it up to the tool you are using to figure out the most efficient way of applying the tasks.

To me, this is the reason you should not approach any task with an attitude of "I need to choose one tool and only use that for everything," you should always choose the tool that works for the job you want to do.

This can probably be said for a lot of the tools we are looking at in this chapter; rather than assessing a tool in a "this versus that" manner, we should be asking "this or that" or even "this and that" and not limit ourselves.

Vagrant (again)

As we have already discovered earlier in this chapter, Vagrant can be used as a virtual machine manager. We have already used it to bring up a local Ubuntu 14.04 instance using VirtualBox on our local machine; however, if we wanted to, we could have done this using VMware Fusion, Amazon Web Services, DigitalOcean, or even OpenStack.

Like Puppet and Ansible, when Docker was first released, there were a lot of articles published around Vagrant versus Docker. In fact, when the question was asked on Stack Overflow, the authors of both Vagrant and Docker weighed in on the question. You can read the full discussion at `http://stackoverflow.com/questions/16647069/should-i-use-vagrant-or-docker-for-creating-an-isolated-environment`

So, in what ways can Vagrant support Docker? There are two main ones we are going to be looking at. The first is the provisioner.

Provisioning using Vagrant

When we worked out way through Puppet, we used Vagrant to launch Ubuntu 14.04 locally using VirtualBox; as part of that, we used the Shell provisioner to install Puppet and deploy the Docker Puppet module. Vagrant has the following provisioners available:

- **File**: This copies files in place onto the Vagrant host
- **Shell**: This compiles/copies bash scripts to the host and executes them
- **Ansible**: This runs an Ansible playbook either on or against the host
- **Chef and Puppet**: There are around dozen different ways you can use Chef or Puppet to provision your Vagrant host
- **Docker**: This is what we will be using to provision our containers on the Vagrant host

The `Vagrantfile` looks really close to the one we used to deploy our Puppet WordPress example:

```ruby
# -*- mode: ruby -*-
# vi: set ft=ruby :

VAGRANTFILE_API_VERSION = "2"

Vagrant.configure(VAGRANTFILE_API_VERSION) do |config|

  config.vm.box = "ubuntu/trusty64"
  config.vm.network "private_network", ip: "192.168.33.10"
  HOSTNAME = 'docker'
  DOMAIN   = 'media-glass.es'
  Vagrant.require_version '>= 1.7.0'
  config.ssh.insert_key = false
```

```
    config.vm.host_name = HOSTNAME + '.' + DOMAIN

    config.vm.provider "VirtualBox" do |v|
      v.memory = 2024
      v.cpus = 2
    end

    config.vm.provider "vmware_fusion" do |v|
      v.vmx["memsize"] = "2024"
      v.vmx["numvcpus"] = "2"
    end

    config.vm.provision "docker" do |d|
      d.run "mysql",
        image: "mysql",
        args: "-e 'MYSQL_ROOT_PASSWORD=password'"
      d.run "wordpress",
        image: "wordpress",
        args: "-p 80:80 --link mysql:mysql -e WORDPRESS_DB_
PASSWORD=password"
    end

  end
```

As you can see, this will download (if you don't have it already) and launch an
Ubuntu 14.04 server and then provision two containers, one WordPress and one
MySQL.

To launch the host, run the following command:

```
vagrant up --provider VirtualBox
```

You should see something similar to the following terminal output:

```
● ● ●                              provisioner — -bash — 125×45
↯
russ in ~/Documents/Code/extending-docker/chapter06/vagrant-docker/provisioner on master◦
↯ vagrant up --provider virtualbox
Bringing machine 'default' up with 'virtualbox' provider...
==> default: Importing base box 'ubuntu/trusty64'...
==> default: Matching MAC address for NAT networking...
==> default: Checking if box 'ubuntu/trusty64' is up to date...
==> default: Setting the name of the VM: provisioner_default_1458482876983_39440
==> default: Clearing any previously set forwarded ports...
==> default: Clearing any previously set network interfaces...
==> default: Preparing network interfaces based on configuration...
    default: Adapter 1: nat
    default: Adapter 2: hostonly
==> default: Forwarding ports...
    default: 22 => 2222 (adapter 1)
==> default: Running 'pre-boot' VM customizations...
==> default: Booting VM...
==> default: Waiting for machine to boot. This may take a few minutes...
    default: SSH address: 127.0.0.1:2222
    default: SSH username: vagrant
    default: SSH auth method: private key
    default: Warning: Connection timeout. Retrying...
==> default: Machine booted and ready!
==> default: Checking for guest additions in VM...
    default: The guest additions on this VM do not match the installed version of
    default: VirtualBox! In most cases this is fine, but in rare cases it can
    default: prevent things such as shared folders from working properly. If you see
    default: shared folder errors, please make sure the guest additions within the
    default: virtual machine match the version of VirtualBox you have installed on
    default: your host and reload your VM.
    default:
    default: Guest Additions Version: 4.3.36
    default: VirtualBox Version: 5.0
==> default: Setting hostname...
==> default: Configuring and enabling network interfaces...
==> default: Mounting shared folders...
    default: /vagrant => /Users/russ/Documents/Code/extending-docker/chapter06/vagrant-docker/provisioner
==> default: Running provisioner: docker...
    default: Installing Docker (latest) onto machine...
==> default: Starting Docker containers...
==> default: -- Container: mysql
==> default: -- Container: wordpress
russ in ~/Documents/Code/extending-docker/chapter06/vagrant-docker/provisioner on master◦
↯ open http://docker.media-glass.es/
russ in ~/Documents/Code/extending-docker/chapter06/vagrant-docker/provisioner on master◦
```

You can also run the following command to open your browser and get to your WordPress installation screen (remember: we have launched the Vagrant host with a fixed local IP address, which means the following URL should resolve to your local installation):

open http://docker.media-glass.es/

You may have already noticed one thing that happened when we launched the Vagrant host: we didn't have to provide Vagrant any commands to install Docker; it took care of that for us.

Also, we had to launch our MySQL container before we launched our WordPress one. This is because we have linked our WordPress container to the MySQL one. If we tried to launch the WordPress container first, we would have received an error telling us that we are trying to reach a link that does not exist.

As you can see from the following terminal output, you can connect to your Vagrant host using the `vagrant  ssh` command:

```
russ in ~/...................................................... on master
✗ vagrant ssh
Welcome to Ubuntu 14.04.4 LTS (GNU/Linux 3.13.0-83-generic x86_64)

 * Documentation:  https://help.ubuntu.com/

  System information as of Sun Mar 20 14:08:13 UTC 2016

  System load:  0.89             Processes:           90
  Usage of /:   3.5% of 39.34GB  Users logged in:     0
  Memory usage: 6%               IP address for eth0: 10.0.2.15
  Swap usage:   0%

  Graph this data and manage this system at:
    https://landscape.canonical.com/

  Get cloud support with Ubuntu Advantage Cloud Guest:
    http://www.ubuntu.com/business/services/cloud

0 packages can be updated.
0 updates are security updates.


vagrant@docker:~$ docker ps
CONTAINER ID      IMAGE          COMMAND               CREATED         STATUS          PORTS                   NAMES
c1dfb578aa98      wordpress      "/entrypoint.sh apach" 2 minutes ago   Up 2 minutes    0.0.0.0:80->80/tcp      wordpress
fb45d6cd806b      mysql          "/entrypoint.sh mysql" 3 minutes ago   Up 3 minutes    3306/tcp                mysql
vagrant@docker:~$ docker --version
Docker version 1.9.1, build a34a1d5
vagrant@docker:~$ []
```

The other thing you may notice is that the Docker version installed isn't the most up-to-date one; this is because Vagrant installs the version that is available in the operating system's default repository rather than the latest version provided by Docker in their repository.

The Vagrant Docker provider

As I mentioned, there are two ways in which you can use Docker with Vagrant: the one we just looked at is a provisioner, and the second way is to use a provider.

So, what's a provider? We have already used a provider twice in this chapter when we launched our Docker hosts. A provider is a virtual machine process, manager, or API that Vagrant can make a connection to and then launch a virtual machine from.

Vagrant has the following providers built in:

- VirtualBox
- Docker
- Hyper-V

There is also a commercial plugin provided by the authors, which adds the following provider:

• VMware Fusion and Workstation

Finally, Vagrant supports custom providers, such as ones for Amazon Web Services, libvirt, and even LXC, for example. A full list of custom providers and other Vagrant plugins can be found at `http://vagrant-lists.github.io/`.

Obviously, if you are using OS X, then you won't be able to use the Docker provider natively; however, Vagrant takes care of this you. Let's look at launching an NGINX container using the Docker provider rather than a provisioner.

The `Vagrantfile` looks a little different to the ones we have been using:

```
VAGRANTFILE_API_VERSION = "2"
Vagrant.configure(VAGRANTFILE_API_VERSION) do |config|
  config.vm.define "boot2docker", autostart: false do |dockerhost|
    dockerhost.vm.box = "russmckendrick/boot2docker"
    dockerhost.nfs.functional = false
    dockerhost.vm.network :forwarded_port, guest: 80, host: 9999
    dockerhost.ssh.shell = "sh"
    dockerhost.ssh.username = "docker"
    dockerhost.ssh.password = "tcuser"
    dockerhost.ssh.insert_key = false
  end
  config.vm.define "nginx", primary: true do |v|
    v.vm.provider "docker" do |d|
      d.vagrant_vagrantfile = "./Vagrantfile"
      d.vagrant_machine = "boot2docker"
      d.image = "russmckendrick/nginx"
      d.name  = "nginx"
      d.ports = ["80:80"]
    end
  end
end
```

As you can see, it is split into two parts: one for a Boot2Docker virtual machine and the second part for the container itself. If you were to run `vagrant up`, you would see something like the following terminal output:

```
                                        provider — -bash — 155×60
russ in                                              on master
↯ vagrant up
Bringing machine 'nginx' up with 'docker' provider...
==> nginx: Docker host is required. One will be created if necessary...
    nginx: Vagrant will now create or start a local VM to act as the Docker
    nginx: host. You'll see the output of the `vagrant up` for this VM below.
    nginx:
    nginx: Box 'russmckendrick/boot2docker' could not be found. Attempting to find and install...
    nginx: Box Provider: virtualbox
    nginx: Box Version: >= 0
    nginx: Loading metadata for box 'russmckendrick/boot2docker'
    nginx: URL: https://atlas.hashicorp.com/russmckendrick/boot2docker
    nginx: Adding box 'russmckendrick/boot2docker' (v1.1.10.3) for provider: virtualbox
    nginx: Downloading: https://atlas.hashicorp.com/russmckendrick/boxes/boot2docker/versions/1.1.10.3/providers/virtualbox.box
    nginx: Successfully added box 'russmckendrick/boot2docker' (v1.1.10.3) for 'virtualbox'!
    nginx: Importing base box 'russmckendrick/boot2docker'...
    nginx: Matching MAC address for NAT networking...
    nginx: Checking if box 'russmckendrick/boot2docker' is up to date...
    nginx: Setting the name of the VM: provider_boot2docker_1458819694393_65134
    nginx: Clearing any previously set network interfaces...
    nginx: Preparing network interfaces based on configuration...
    nginx: Adapter 1: nat
    nginx: Forwarding ports...
    nginx: 2375 => 2375 (adapter 1)
    nginx: 80 => 9999 (adapter 1)
    nginx: 22 => 2222 (adapter 1)
    nginx: Running 'pre-boot' VM customizations...
    nginx: Booting VM...
    nginx: Waiting for machine to boot. This may take a few minutes...
    nginx: SSH address: 127.0.0.1:2222
    nginx: SSH username: docker
    nginx: SSH auth method: password
    nginx: Warning: Connection timeout. Retrying...
    nginx: Machine booted and ready!
==> nginx: Syncing folders to the host VM...
    nginx: The machine you're rsyncing folders to is configured to use
    nginx: password-based authentication. Vagrant can't script rsync to automatically
    nginx: enter this password, so you'll likely be prompted for a password
    nginx: shortly.
    nginx:
    nginx: If you don't want to have to do this, please enable automatic
    nginx: key insertion using `config.ssh.insert_key`.
    nginx: Rsyncing folder: /Users/russ/Documents/Code/extending-docker/chapter06/vagrant-docker/provider/ => /var/lib/docker/docker_1458819717_37066
docker@127.0.0.1's password:
==> nginx: Warning: When using a remote Docker host, forwarded ports will NOT be
==> nginx: immediately available on your machine. They will still be forwarded on
==> nginx: the remote machine, however, so if you have a way to access the remote
==> nginx: machine, then you should be able to access those ports there. This is
==> nginx: not an error, it is only an informational message.
==> nginx: Creating the container...
    nginx:    Name: nginx
    nginx:   Image: russmckendrick/nginx
    nginx:  Volume: /var/lib/docker/docker_1458819717_37066:/vagrant
    nginx:    Port: 80:80
    nginx:
    nginx: Container created: ed7ef7abcdde4c4e
==> nginx: Starting container...
==> nginx: Provisioners will not be run since container doesn't support SSH.
russ in                                              on master
↯ ☐
```

As you can see, as I am using OS X, Vagrant knows that I can run Docker natively, so it takes the first section of `Vagrantfile` and launches a Boot2Docker instance. Boot2Docker is the tiny Linux distribution that powers Docker Machine's default driver.

Once it has downloaded the Boot2Docker Vagrant Box, it launches the virtual machine and maps port `22` on the virtual machine to port `2222` on our local PC so that we can get SSH access. Also, as defined in `Vagrantfile`, port `80` from the virtual machine is mapped to port `9999` on the local PC.

Its worth noting that if I were running this on a Linux PC that had Docker installed, then this step would have been skipped and Vagrant would have made use of my local Docker installation.

Now that Boot2Docker has been started, the second part of the `Vagrantfile` can be run. If, like in my case, Vagrant has downloaded and launched the Boot2Docker Vagrant Box, then you will be asked for a password; this is because we have not exchanged keys with the Boot2Docker virtual machine. The password is `tcuser`.

Once you have entered the password, Vagrant will download the NGINX image from `https://hub.docker.com/r/russmckendrick/nginx/` and launch the container, opening port `80`.

Once the container has been launched, you should be able to go to the NGINX welcome page at `http://localhost:9999/`.

If you like, you can SSH into the Boot2Docker virtual machine, as Vagrant is primarily managing the container and not the Boot2Docker virtual machine. You will have to use the following command:

```
ssh docker@localhost -p2222
```

Again, because we have not exchanged keys, you will need to enter the password, `tcuser`. You should then see this:

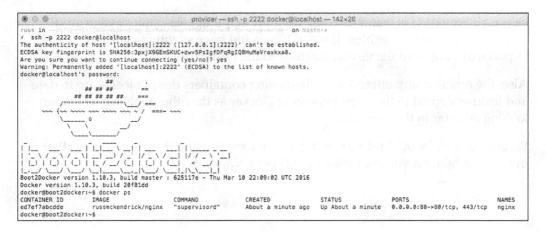

Once SSHed in, you will be able to run Docker commands locally. Finally, to terminate both the container and virtual machine, run the following command from within the same folder as your `Vagrantfile` and you will see something as following:

vagrant destroy

```
                                          provider — -bash — 143×11
russ in                                                           on master*
ƒ  vagrant destroy
    nginx: Are you sure you want to destroy the 'nginx' VM? [y/N] y
==> nginx: Stopping container...
==> nginx: Deleting the container...
==> nginx: Removing synced folders...
    boot2docker: Are you sure you want to destroy the 'boot2docker' VM? [y/N] y
==> boot2docker: Forcing shutdown of VM...
==> boot2docker: Destroying VM and associated drives...
russ in                                                           on master*
ƒ
```

This will prompt you, asking whether you are sure you would like to remove the container and then the virtual machine; answer yes to both questions.

You must have noticed that we didn't cover our WordPress example while walking through the Docker provider. The reason for this is that the Docker provider functionality, in my opinion, is pretty much redundant now, especially as it has quite a few limitations that can all be easily overcome by using the provisioner or other tools.

One such limitation is that it can only use port mapping; we cannot assign an IP address to the virtual machine. If we did, it would have silently failed and reverted to port mapping from the virtual machine to the host PC.

Also, the functionality offered when launching containers doesn't feel as up to date and feature aligned to the latest version of Docker as the other tools we have been looking at so far in the chapter.

Because of this, I would recommend that you look at using the provisioner rather than the provider if you are looking at utilizing Vagrant.

Packaging images

So far, we have been quite happily downloading prebuilt images from the Docker Hub to test with. Next up, we are going to be looking at creating our own images. Before we dive into creating images using third-party tools, we should have a quick look at how to go about building them in Docker.

An application

Before we start building our own images, we should really have an application to "bake" into it. I suspect you are probably getting bored of doing the same WordPress installation over and over again. We are going to be looking at something completely different.

So, we are going to build an image that has Moby Counter installed. Moby counter is an application written by Kai Davenport, who describes it as follows:

> *"A small app to demonstrate keeping state inside a docker-compose application."*

The application runs in a browser and will add a Docker logo to the page wherever you click, the idea being that it uses a Redis or Postgres backend to store the number of Docker logos and their positions, which demonstrates how data can persist on volumes such as the ones we looked at in *Chapter 3, Volume Plugins*. You can find the GitHub repository for the application at `https://github.com/binocarlos/moby-counter/`.

The Docker way

Now that we know a little about the application we are going to be launching, let's take a look at how the image would be built using Docker itself.

The code for this part of the chapter is available from the GitHub repository that accompanies this book; you can find it at `https://github.com/russmckendrick/extending-docker/tree/master/chapter06/images/docker`.

The `Dockerfile` for the basic build is quite simple:

```
FROM russmckendrick/nodejs
ADD . /srv/app
WORKDIR /srv/app
RUN npm install
EXPOSE 80
ENTRYPOINT ["node", "index.js"]
```

When we run the build, it will download the russmckendrick/nodejs image from the Docker Hub; this, as you may have guessed, has NodeJS installed.

Once that image has been downloaded, Docker will launch the container and add the content of the current working directory, which contains the Moby Counter code. It will then change the working directory to where the the code was uploaded to /srv/app.

It will then install the prerequisites required to run the application by issuing the npm install command; as we have set the working directory, all of the commands will be run from that location, meaning that the package.json file will be used.

Accompanying the Dockerfile is a Docker Compose file, this kicks off the build of the Moby Counter image, downloads the official Redis image, and then launches the two containers, linking them together.

Before we do that, we need to bring up a machine to run the build on; to do this, run the following command to launch a local VirtualBox-based Docker host:

```
docker-machine create --driver "VirtualBox" chapter06
```

Now that the Docker host has been launched, run the following to configure your local Docker client to talk directly to it:

```
eval $(docker-machine env chapter06)
```

Now that you have the host ready and client configured, run the following to build the image and launch the application:

```
docker-compose up -d
```

When you run the command, you should see something like the following output in your terminal:

```
● ● ●                          docker — -bash — 111×88
russ in ~/Documents/Code/extending-docker/chapter06/images/docker on master
⚡  docker-compose up -d
Creating docker_redis_1
Building web
Step 1 : FROM russmckendrick/nodejs
latest: Pulling from russmckendrick/nodejs
4d06f2521e4f: Pull complete
49227cc4fd73: Pull complete
66b206691caf: Pull complete
5dca16fe8956: Pull complete
Digest: sha256:797eabd75d57ec30846ee3e49fd69dd1116f5715378b8582714f55deddc12a50
Status: Downloaded newer image for russmckendrick/nodejs:latest
 ---> f5f284d2c5d4
Step 2 : ADD . /srv/app
 ---> 79eb028973c1
Removing intermediate container 9975dfce4a20
Step 3 : WORKDIR /srv/app
 ---> Running in ea38c87c04ba
 ---> fad4dab033e8
Removing intermediate container ea38c87c04ba
Step 4 : RUN npm install
 ---> Running in 14d8adbcefa1
moby-counter@1.0.0 /srv/app
+-- concat-stream@1.5.1
| +-- inherits@2.0.1
| +-- readable-stream@2.0.6
| | +-- core-util-is@1.0.2
|   +-- body@0.1.0
|   `-- content-types@0.1.0
|     `-- iterators@0.1.0
|       `-- ap@0.1.0
+-- httperr@0.5.0
+-- routes@2.1.0
+-- send-data@3.3.4
| +-- json-stringify-safe@5.0.1
| `-- xtend@3.0.0
`-- xtend@2.1.2
  `-- object-keys@0.4.0

 ---> 2bb43fdefc8c
Removing intermediate container 14d8adbcefa1
Step 5 : EXPOSE 80
 ---> Running in a187da1650f9
 ---> 3b86f0e54b7f
Removing intermediate container a187da1650f9
Step 6 : ENTRYPOINT node index.js
 ---> Running in 6804f7c8ccee
 ---> af7d95e81f35
Removing intermediate container 6804f7c8ccee
Successfully built af7d95e81f35
Creating docker_web_1
russ in ~/Documents/Code/extending-docker/chapter06/images/docker on master
⚡ 
```

Now that the application has been launched, you should be able to open your browser by running this:

```
open http://$(docker-machine ip chapter06)/
```

You will see a page that says Click to add logos, if you were to click around the page, Docker logos would start appearing. If you were to click on refresh, the logos you added would remain as the number of the logos, their position being stored in the Redis database.

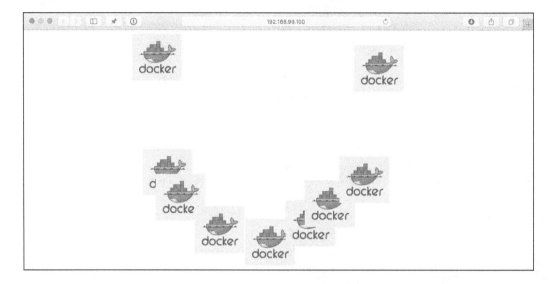

To stop the containers and remove them, run the following commands:

```
docker-compose stop
docker-compose rm
```

Before we look into the pros and cons of using the Docker approach to building container images, let's look at a third-party alternative.

Building with Packer

Packer is written by *Mitchell Hashimoto* from *Hashicorp*, the same author as Vagrant's. Because of this, there are quite a lot of similarities in the terms we will be using.

The Packer website has probably the best description of the tool:

> *"Packer is an open source tool for creating identical machine images for multiple platforms from a single source configuration. Packer is lightweight, runs on every major operating system, and is highly performant, creating machine images for multiple platforms in parallel. Packer does not replace configuration management like Chef or Puppet. In fact, when building images, Packer is able to use tools like Chef or Puppet to install software onto the image."*

I have been using Packer since its first release to build images for both Vagrant and public clouds.

You can download Packer from `https://www.packer.io/downloads.html` or, if you installed Homebrew, you can run the following command:

```
brew install packer
```

Now that you have Packer installed, let's take a look at a configuration file. Packer configuration files are all defined in JSON.

 JavaScript Object Notation (JSON) is a lightweight data-interchange format. It is easy for humans to read and write and for machines to parse and generate.

The following file does almost exactly what our `Dockerfile` did:

```
{
  "builders":[{
    "type": "docker",
    "image": "russmckendrick/nodejs",
    "export_path": "mobycounter.tar"
  }],
  "provisioners":[
    {
      "type": "file",
      "source": "app",
      "destination": "/srv"
    },
    {
      "type": "file",
      "source": "npmrc",
      "destination": "/etc/npmrc"
    },
    {
      "type": "shell",
      "inline": [
        "cd /srv/app",
        "npm install"
      ]
    }
  ]
}
```

Again, all of the files required to build the image, along with the Docker Compose file to run it, are in the GitHub repository at `https://github.com/russmckendrick/extending-docker/tree/master/chapter06/images/packer`.

Rather than using the Docker Compose file to build the image, we are going to have to run **packer** and then import the image file. To start the build, run the following command:

```
packer build docker.json
```

You should see the following in your terminal:

```
● ● ●                        packer — -bash — 111×88
russ in                                                      on master*
✗  packer build docker.json
docker output will be in this color.

==> docker: Creating a temporary directory for sharing data...
==> docker: Pulling Docker image: russmckendrick/nodejs
    docker: Using default tag: latest
    docker: latest: Pulling from russmckendrick/nodejs
    docker: 4d06f2521e4f: Already exists
    docker: 49227cc4fd73: Already exists
    docker: 66b286691caf: Already exists
    docker: 5dca16fe8956: Already exists
    docker: Digest: sha256:797eabd75d57ec30846ee3e49fd69dd1116f5715378b8582714f55deddc12a50
    docker: Status: Image is up to date for russmckendrick/nodejs:latest
==> docker: Starting docker container...
    docker: Run command: docker run -v /Users/russ/.packer.d/tmp/packer-docker056189653:/packer-files -d -i -t
russmckendrick/nodejs /bin/bash
    docker: Container ID: db938cefd19a360ba6afca5ad623977e07ccb5cbb5f3711dae3ab30d9bf78433
==> docker: Uploading . => /srv/app
==> docker: Provisioning with shell script: /var/folders/3z/wd1dszzx5xx_l8mbtcjgnhn88800gn/T/packer-shell988836
138
    docker: moby-counter@1.0.0 /srv/app
    docker: +-- concat-stream@1.5.1
    docker: | +-- inherits@2.0.1
    docker: | +-- readable-stream@2.0.6
    docker: | | +-- core-util-is@1.0.2
    docker: | | +-- isarray@1.0.0
    docker: | | +-- process-nextick-args@1.0.6
    docker: +-- error@3.0.0
    docker: | +-- string-template@0.1.3
    docker: | `-- xtend@2.1.2
    docker: +-- hammock@0.1.10
    docker: | +-- cookies@0.3.8
    docker: | `-- lodash@2.4.2
    docker: +-- http-methods@0.1.0
    docker: | +-- body@0.1.0
    docker: | `-- content-types@0.1.0
    docker: |     `-- iterators@0.1.0
    docker: |         `-- ap@0.1.0
    docker: +-- httperr@0.5.0
    docker: +-- routes@2.1.0
    docker: +-- send-data@3.3.4
    docker: | +-- json-stringify-safe@5.0.1
    docker: | `-- xtend@3.0.0
    docker: `-- xtend@2.1.2
    docker: `-- object-keys@0.4.0
    docker:
==> docker: Exporting the container
==> docker: Killing the container: db938cefd19a360ba6afca5ad623977e07ccb5cbb5f3711dae3ab30d9bf78433
Build 'docker' finished.

==> Builds finished. The artifacts of successful builds are:
--> docker: Exported Docker file: mobycounter.tar
russ in                                                      on master*
✗  ☐
```

Once Packer has built the image, it will save a copy to the folder you initiated the Packer build command from; in our case, the image file is called `mobycounter.tar`.

To import the image so that we can use it, run the following command:

`docker import mobycounter.tar mobycounter`

This will import the image and name it `mobycounter`; you can check whether the image is available by running this:

`docker images`

You should see something like this:

```
● ● ●                          packer — -bash — 111×15
russ in ~/Documents/Code/extending-docker/chapter06/images/packer on master*
⚡  ls -lhat mobycounter.tar
-rw-r--r--  1 russ  staff    52M 26 Mar 18:56 mobycounter.tar
russ in ~/Documents/Code/extending-docker/chapter06/images/packer on master*
⚡  docker import mobycounter.tar mobycounter
sha256:2a68ff362dbba140bb283668abf4008465c95d9ae4408bb483998cdc2a05922a
russ in ~/Documents/Code/extending-docker/chapter06/images/packer on master*
⚡  docker images
REPOSITORY              TAG            IMAGE ID        CREATED            SIZE
mobycounter             latest         2a68ff362dbb    4 seconds ago      47.07 MB
docker_web              latest         af7d95e81f35    About an hour ago  47.9 MB
russmckendrick/nodejs   latest         f5f284d2c5d4    2 days ago         42.96 MB
redis                   latest         4f5f397d4b7c    3 weeks ago        177.6 MB
russ in ~/Documents/Code/extending-docker/chapter06/images/packer on master*
⚡  ▯
```

Once you have confirmed the image has been imported and is called `mobycounter`, you can launch a container by running this:

`docker-compose up -d`

Again, you will be able to open your browser and start clicking around to place logos by running this:

`open http://$(docker-machine ip chapter06)/`

While there may not seem to be much difference, let's take a look at what's going on under the hood.

Packer versus Docker Build

Before we go into detail about the difference between the two methods of building images, let's try running Packer again.

This time though, let's to try and reduce the image size: rather than using the `russmckendrick/nodejs` image, which has nodejs preinstalled, let's use the base image that this was built on, `russmckendrick/base`.

This image just has bash installed; install NodeJS and the application using Packer:

```json
{
  "builders":[{
    "type": "docker",
    "image": "russmckendrick/base",
    "export_path": "mobycounter-small.tar"
  }],
  "provisioners":[
    {
      "type": "file",
      "source": "app",
      "destination": "/srv"
    },
    {
      "type": "file",
      "source": "npmrc",
      "destination": "/etc/npmrc"
    },
    {
      "type": "shell",
      "inline": [
        "apk update",
        "apk add --update nodejs",
        "npm -g install npm",
        "cd /srv/app",
        "npm install",
        "rm -rf /var/cache/apk/**/",
        "npm cache clean"
      ]
    }
  ]
}
```

As you can see, we have added a few more commands to the shell provisioner; these use Alpine Linux's package manager to perform an update, install nodejs, configure the application, and finally, clean both the apk and npm caches.

If you like, you can build the image using the following command:

```
packer build docker-small.json
```

This will leave us with two image files. I also exported a copy of the container we built using the `Dockerfile` using the following command while the container was running:

```
docker export docker_web_1 > docker_web.tar
```

I now have three image files, and all three are running the same application, with the same software stack installed, using as close to the same commands as possible. As you can see from the following list of file sizes, there is a difference in the image size:

- **Dockerfile** (using `russmckendrick/nodejs`) = 52 MB
- **Packer** (using `russmckendrick/nodejs`) = 47 MB
- **Packer** (installing the full stack using packer) = 40 MB

12 MB may not seem like a lot, but when you are dealing with an image that is only 52 MB big, that's quite a decent saving.

So why is there a difference? Let's start by discussing the way in which Docker images work.

They are essentially made up of layers of changes on top of a base. When we built our first image using the `Dockerfile`, you may have noticed that each line of the `Dockerfile` generated a different step in the build process.

Each step is actually Docker starting a new filesystem layer to store the changes for that step of the build. So, for example, when our `Dockerfile` ran, we had six filesystem layers:

```
FROM russmckendrick/nodejs
ADD . /srv/app
WORKDIR /srv/app
RUN npm install
EXPOSE 80
ENTRYPOINT ["node", "index.js"]
```

The first layer contains the base operating system along with the layers on which NodeJS is installed, and the second layer contains the files for the application itself.

The third layer just contains the metadata for setting the `workdir` variable; next up, we have the layer that contains the NodeJS dependencies for the application. The fifth and sixth layers just contain the metadata needed to configure which ports are exposed and what the "entry point" is.

As each of these layers is effectively a separate archive within the image file, we also have the additional overhead of these archives within our image file.

A better example of how the layers work is to look at some of the most popular images from the Docker Hub in the ImageLayers website, which can be found at `https://imagelayers.io/`.

This site is a tool provided by Century Link Labs (`https://labs.ctl.io/`) to visualize Docker images that have been built from a `Dockerfile`.

As you can see from the following screenshot, some of the official images are quite complex and also quite large:

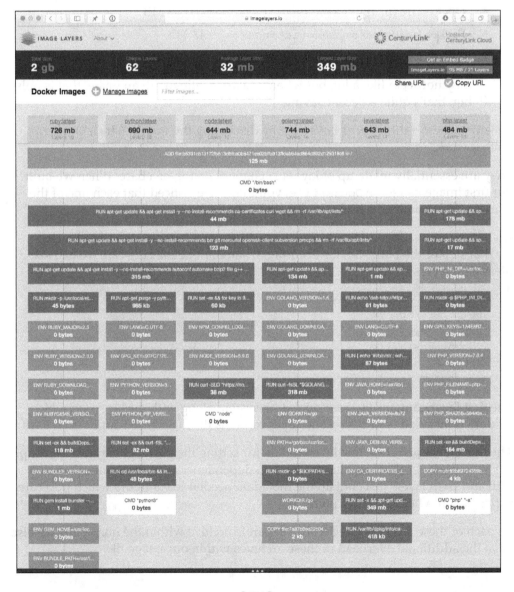

You can view the previous page at the following URL:

`https://imagelayers.io/?images=java:latest,golang:latest,node:latest,`
`python:latest,php:latest,ruby:latest`.

Even while the official images should be getting smaller thanks to Docker hiring the creator of Alpine Linux and moving the official images over to the smaller base operating system (check out the following hacker news post for more information `https://news.ycombinator.com/item?id=11000827`), it does not change the amount of layers required for each image. It's also worth pointing out that each image can have a maximum of 127 layers.

So what does Packer do differently? Rather than creating a separate filesystem layer for each step, it produces only two: the first layer is the base image you define, and the second one is everything else — this is where our space savings come in.

The other advantage of using Packer over Dockfiles is that you can reuse your scripts. Imagine you were doing your local development work using Docker but when you launched into production, you for one reason or another had to launch on one of the containerized virtual machines. Using Packer, you can do exactly that knowing that you could actually use the same set of build scripts to bootstrap your virtual machines as you did for your development containers.

As I have already mentioned, I have been using Packer for a while and it helps to no end to have a single tool that you can use to target different platforms with the same set of build scripts. The consistency this approach brings is well worth the initial effort of learning a tool such as Packer as you will end up saving a lot of time in the long run; it also helps with eliminating the whole "worked in development" meme we discussed at the start of *Chapter 1, Introduction to Extending Docker*.

There are some downsides to using this approach, which may put some people off.

The biggest one in my opinion is that while you are able to push the final image automatically to the Docker Hub, you will not be able to add it as an automated build.

This means that while it may be available for people to download, it might not be considered trusted as people cannot see exactly what has been added to the image.

Next up is the lack of support for metadata — functions that configure runtime options such as exposing ports and the command executed by default when the container launches are not currently supported.

While this can be seen as a drawback, it is easily overcome by defining what you would have defined in your `Dockerfile` in a Docker Compose file or passing the information directly using the `docker run` command.

Image summary

So, to summarize, if you need to build not only container images but also target different platforms, then Packer is exactly the tool you are after. If it's just container images you need to build, then you may be better off sticking with the `Dockerfile` build.

Some of the other tools we have looked at in this chapter, such as Ansible and Puppet, also support building images by issuing a `docker build` command against a `Dockerfile`, so there are plenty of ways to build that into your workflow, which leads us to the next tool we are going be looking at: Jenkins.

Before we move on, let's quickly just double-check that you are not running any Docker hosts. To do this, run the following commands to check for any Docker hosts and then remove them:

```
docker-machine ls
docker-machine rm <name-of-host>
```

Don't forget to only remove hosts that you are using for following along with this book; don't remove any you are using for you own projects!

Serving up Docker with Jenkins

Jenkins is quite a big topic to cover in a small section of a single chapter, so the walkthrough is going to be really basic and will only deal with building and launching containers.

The other thing to note is that I am going to be covering Jenkins 2.0; at the time of writing this, the first beta has just been released, which means that while things may change slightly as themes and such are refined, all of the features and basic functionality are locked in.

The reason for covering Jenkins 2.0 rather than the Jenkins 1.x branch is that as far as Jenkins is concerned, Docker is now a first-class citizen, meaning that it fully supports and embraces the Docker way of working. A full overview of the current status of Jenkins 2.0 can be found at `https://jenkins.io/2.0/`.

So what is Jenkins? Jenkins is an open source continuous integration tool written in Java, and it has a lot of uses.

Personally, I am really late to the Jenkins party; being from an operations background, I have always just shrugged it off a tool used for running unit tests on code; however, as I have moved more into orchestration and automation, I am finding the need for a tool that can run tasks based on the results of unit tests.

As I have already mentioned, I am not going to go into much detail about the testing side of Jenkins; there are plenty of resources that cover this functionality, such as the following:

- *Mastering Jenkins* by Jonathan McAllister
- *Jenkins Continuous Integration Cookbook* by Alan Mark Berg

These are both available from `https://www.packtpub.com/`.

Preparing the environment

Rather than running it locally, let's launch a DigitalOcean droplet and install Jenkins there. First off, we need to use Docker Machine to launch the droplet:

```
docker-machine create \
    --driver digitalocean \
    --digitalocean-access-token
sdnjkjdfgkjb345kjdgljknqwetkjwhgoih314rjkwergoiyu34rjkherglkhrg0 \
    --digitalocean-region lon1 \
    --digitalocean-size 1gb \
    jenkins
```

Once the droplet has been launched, we don't need to bother configuring our local Docker client to talk on the droplet by running the Docker engine as Jenkins will be handling everything to do with Docker.

Because we need Jenkins to run Docker, we will need to install it directly on our droplet rather than run it as a container; first of all, we will need to SSH onto the droplet. To do this, run the following command:

```
docker-machine ssh jenkins
```

Now, on the droplet, we need to install Docker Compose, Jenkins, and all of its prerequisites. Let's start by installing Docker Compose. I have written a quick script to do this, which can be executed by running the following command:

```
curl -fsS https://raw.githubusercontent.com/russmckendrick/docker-install/master/install-compose | bash
```

Now that we have Docker Compose installed, it's time to install Jenkins. As version 2 is currently in beta, it is not in any of the main repositories yet; however, there is a DEB package for it.

To install it, we need to download a local copy and run the following commands:

```
apt-get install gdebi-core
```

This will install the `gdebi` tool, which we will then use to install Jenkins and its dependencies:

```
wget http://pkg.jenkins-ci.org/debian-rc/binary/jenkins_2.0_all.deb
gdebi jenkins_2.0_all.deb
```

Now that Jenkins is installed, we need to add the Jenkins user to the Docker group so that the user has permissions to interact with Docker:

```
usermod -aG docker jenkins
```

Finally, to ensure that Jenkins picks up that it has been added to the group, we need to restart it using this command:

```
/etc/init.d/jenkins restart
```

You can now open your browser to complete the installation:

```
open http://$(docker-machine ip jenkins):8080/
```

When your browser opens, you should be greeted with a screen that looks like the following:

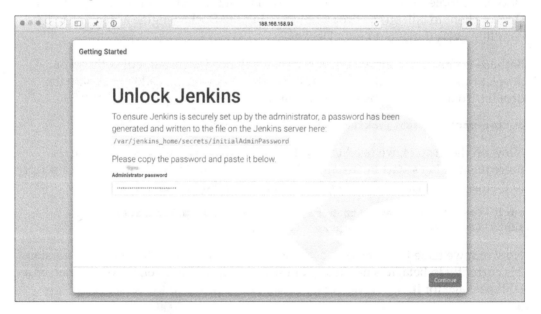

For security reasons, when the Jenkins container was launched, a random string was generated; before you can proceed with the installation, Jenkins requires you to confirm what this string is. You can find it out by running this command:

```
less /var/lib/jenkins/secrets/initialAdminPassword
```

You can quit `less` by pressing the *Q* key.

This feature is a most welcome one as not securing your Jenkins installation correctly from the start can have quite bad implications, as I found out when a third party hijacked a test Jenkins 1.x installation I had up running and forgotten about—whoops!

Once you have entered the initial admin password, click on the **Continue** button.

The next page you come to will ask you which plugins you would like to install:

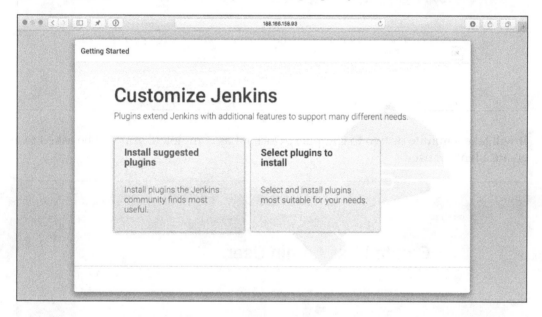

For our purposes, just click on **Install suggested Plugins**, which is highlighted. The next page will show you the progress of the suggested plugins:

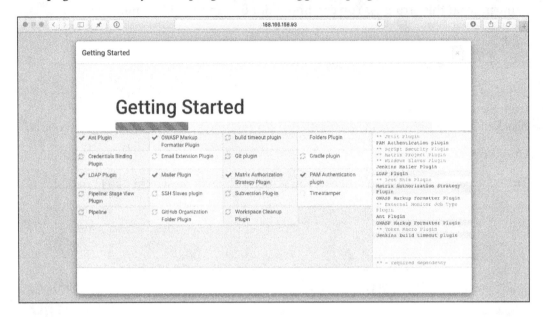

It will take a minute or two to complete. Once it has completed, you will be asked to create a Jenkins user:

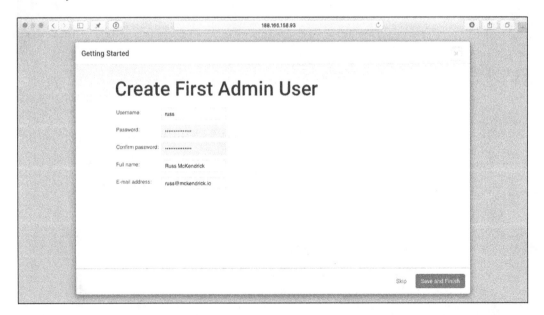

As I have already mentioned, it's important to secure your Jenkins installation from the start, so I recommend you don't skip this step. Once you have filled in the requested information, click on the **Save and Finish** button. If all has gone well, you will be presented with the following screen:

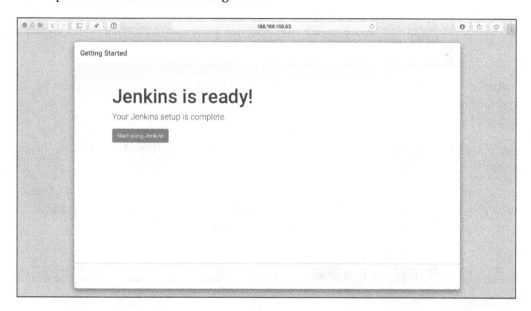

All you have to do now is click on **Start using Jenkins** and you will be logged in and taken to the start screen, which looks like this:

This installation process is one of the many improvements that Jenkins 2 brings to the table; earlier, you would have had to install Jenkins and then manually work through several wizards and procedures to both secure and configure the software, which as I have already mentioned can have bad consequences if you don't get it right.

The final step of the setup is to install the CloudBees Docker Pipeline plugin; to do this, click on the **Manage Jenkins** button from the left-hand side menu, and then click on **Manage Plugins** button.

As this is a new installation, you will probably see a message about plugins being updated at some point. Ignore the request to restart Jenkins; we will be doing this as part of the installation.

There are four tabs on the main screen; click on **Available** button and you will be presented with a list of all of the Jenkins plugins.

In the top right-hand portion of the main screen, there is a search box labelled **Filter**. Type in `Docker Pipeline` here, and you should receive one result. Tick the install box and then click on the **Download now and install after restart** button.

It will take a minute or two to restart Jenkins; after it has started back up, you will be prompted to log back in using the credentials you provided during the installation.

Now that you have Jenkins installed and configured, it's time to add our pipeline. To do this, we need an application to add.

Creating an application

There is a sample application based on Moby Counter available at the following GitHub repository: `https://github.com/russmckendrick/jenkins-docker-example/tree/master`. The main page looks like this:

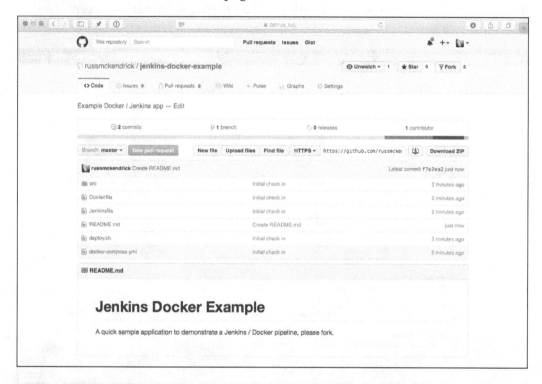

Before we add the application, it is best that you fork the code, as we will be making changes to the codebase later on. To do this, click on the **Fork** button in the top right of the screen. You will be asked where you want to fork the repository. Once you have forked it, make a note of the URL.

As I own the repository, I was not able to fork it. Because of this, I have created a copy called `jenkins-pipeline`, so you will see references to this in the following section.

Creating a pipeline

Now that Jenkins is configured and we have a GitHub repository that contains the application, we would like to deploy. It's time to roll our sleeves up and configure the pipeline within Jenkins.

To start, click on the **create new jobs** button on the main page, you will be taken to a screen that has several options on it, enter the name of the pipeline in the top box.

I am calling mine `Docker Pipeline`, and then click on **Pipeline** button. You should see a small box that says **OK** button at the bottom of the screen, click on the **OK** button to create the pipeline, which will take you to the configuration screen:

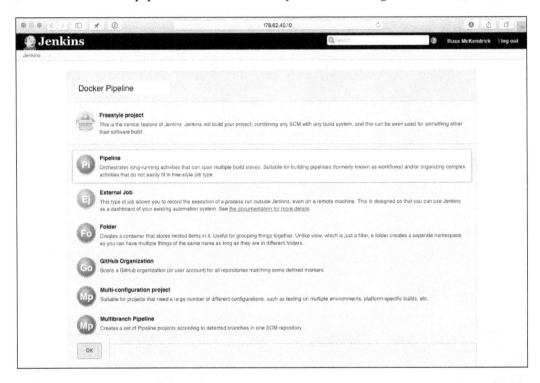

You will now be on the pipeline configuration screen, as you can see, there are a lot of options. We are going to be keeping things really simple and will be just adding a pipeline script. The script looks similar to the following code:

```
node {
    stage 'Checkout'
    git url: 'https://github.com/russmckendrick/jenkins-pipeline.git'

    stage 'build'
    docker.build('mobycounter')

    stage 'deploy'
    sh './deploy.sh'
}
```

Before you add the script to the Pipeline section of the configuration page, replace the Git URL with the one of your own repository. Leave all the other options as they are and click on the **Save** button:

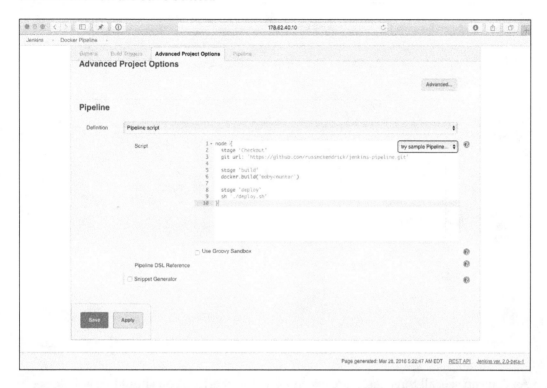

That's it, our pipeline is now configured. We have told Jenkins to perform the following three tasks each time a build is triggered:

- **Checkout**: This downloads the latest code for our application from your GitHub repository.

- **Build**: This uses `Dockerfile` that is in the GitHub repository to build the `Mobycounter` image.

- **Deploy**: This runs a script that clears down any currently running containers and then uses the included Docker Compose file to relaunch the application. When launching Redis, the Docker Compose file uses the built-in volume driver for `/data`, meaning that the position of the Docker logos will persist between the containers being relaunched.

To trigger a build, click on the **Build Now** button option on the left-hand side menu. If everything goes well, you should see something similar to the following screenshot:

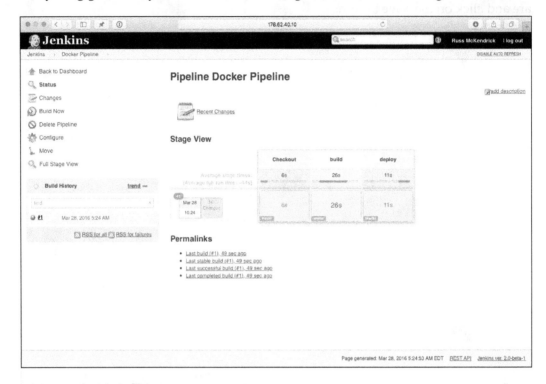

As you can see, all three tasks are executed without error. You should be able to see the application by opening your browser using the following command:

```
open http://$(docker-machine ip jenkins)/
```

Place some logos to test that everything is working as expected, and that's it, you have deployed your application using Jenkins:

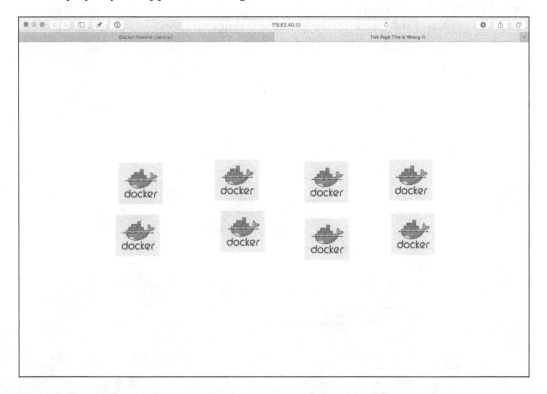

Hold on a minute—there is a problem! As you may have already noticed, the page title is wrong.

Let's go ahead and fix that. To do so, navigate to the following page in your GitHub repository: `your-github-repo | src | client | index.html`. From here, click on the **Edit** button. Once in the editing screen, update the title between the `<title>` and `</title>` tags, and then click on the **Commit changes** button.

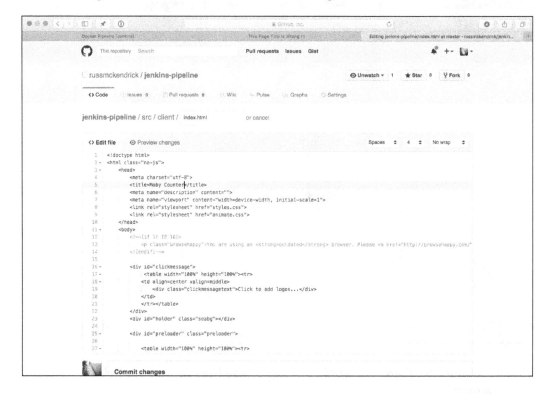

Now that you have updated your application code, go back to Jenkins and click on **Build Now** again. This will trigger a second build, which will deploy the changes we made in GitHub.

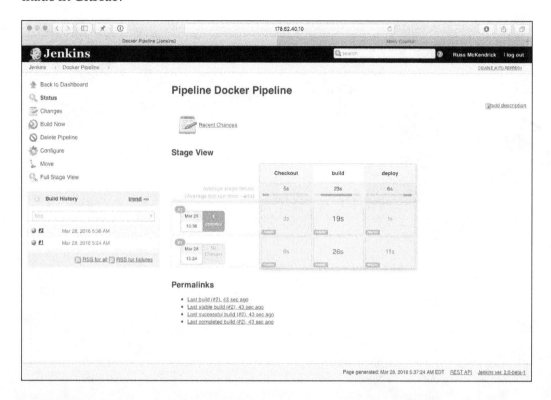

As you can see from the second browser tag in the previous screenshot, the title of our application has changed and the second build was successful. If you refresh your application window, you should see that your title has been updated and the Docker logos are where you left them.

A few other things to note are that that the second build confirms that there is one commit difference between our initial build and the current one. Also, the build itself took less time than our original build; this is because Docker didn't have to download the base image for a second time.

You can view logs for each task by hovering your mouse over the stage you want to see the logs for and clicking on the **Logs** link. This will make a dialog pop up with the logs for the task:

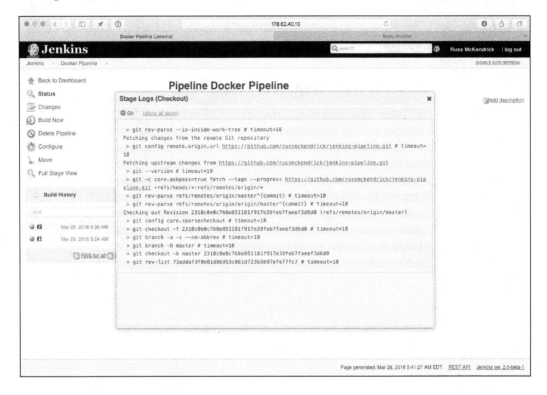

You can also look at the full console output for each build by clicking on the build number, say #2, in the left-hand side menu and then clicking on the **Console Output** button:

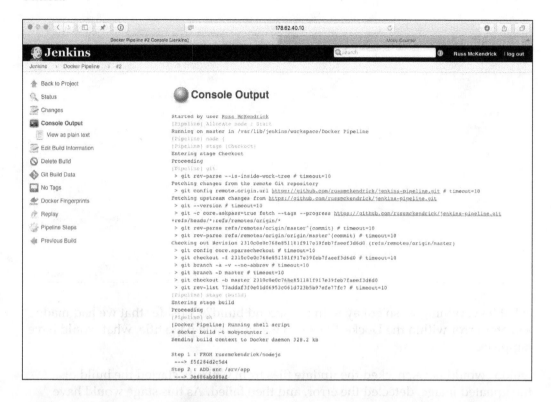

This is useful if your build has errors. Try clicking on some of the options, such as **Docker Fingerprints** and **Changes**, to look at the other information that is recorded during each build.

Going back to the main Jenkins page, you should see a quick summary of your builds. You should also see a sun icon next to your pipeline, meaning that everything is OK.

What if everything wasn't okay with the second build? Consider that we had made a syntax error within the Dockerfile when we edited the page title, what would have happened?

Jenkins would have checked the update files from GitHub, started the build of the updated image, detected the error, and then failed. As this stage would have given an error, the deploy stage would not have been executed, meaning that our application would still be running in its current state, wrong title and all.

This is where Jenkins' strength lies, if you configure enough tests with both your code and deployment pipelines, you can stop any potential service affecting changes being deployed, it also records enough information to be an extremely valuable resource when it comes to tracking down errors.

Summing up Jenkins

As you may have noticed, we have only touched the tip of the iceberg when it comes to Jenkins, there is a lot of functionality we haven't covered as it is out of scope of this book.

However, from the little we have discussed, I hope you can see the value of using a continuous integration and deployment platform such as Jenkins to help build and deploy your containers and code. Don't be late to the party like I was, if you deploy any type of code, then consider using Jenkins to assist you, don't wait until you have deployed a serious application-breaking bug.

Summary

A common thread among all the tools we have looked at in this chapter is that they all quickly evolved to offer support for Docker, filling in gaps in functionality, which was missing from the core Docker toolset.

Over the past 12 months, the rapid development of Docker has meant that some of these tools may not necessarily be required any more.

However, as they all provide a wide range of functionality outside of Docker, it means that they can still be a valuable part of your day-to-day workflow should Docker only be one of the technologies you are working with.

There is one thing using that the tools in this chapter does not provide and that's some intelligence around where your containers are launched, you still have to instruct the tools to *place container A on Docker host Z*.

In our next chapter, we will be looking at schedulers that make the decision as to where a container should be launched for you, based on host availability, utilization, and other rules such as *don't place Container A on the same host as Container B*, meaning that you are no longer confined to a fixed infrastructure.

7
Looking at Schedulers

In this chapter, we will look at a few different schedulers that are capable of launching containers on both your own infrastructures as well as public cloud-based infrastructures. To start with, we will look at two different schedulers, both of which we will use to launch clusters on Amazon Web Services. The two schedulers are as follows:

- **Kubernetes**: http://kubernetes.io/
- **Amazon ECS**: https://aws.amazon.com/ecs/

We will then take a look at a tool that offers its own scheduler as well as supports others:

- **Rancher**: http://rancher.com/

Let's dive straight in by looking at Kubernetes.

Getting started with Kubernetes

Kubernetes is an open source tool, originally developed by Google. It is described as:

> "A tool for automating deployment, operations, and scaling of containerized applications. It groups containers that make up an application into logical units for easy management and discovery. Kubernetes builds upon a decade and a half of experience of running production workloads at Google, combined with best-of-breed ideas and practices from the community." http://www.kubernetes.io

While it is not the exact tool that Google uses to deploy their containers internally, it has been built from the ground up to offer the same functionality. Google is also slowly transitioning to internally use Kubernetes themselves. It is designed around the following three principles:

- **Planet scale**: Designed on the same principles that allow Google to run billions of containers a week, Kubernetes can scale without increasing your ops team

- **Never outgrow**: Whether testing locally or running a global enterprise, Kubernetes' flexibility grows with you in order to deliver your applications consistently and easily no matter how complex your need is

- **Run anywhere**: Kubernetes is open source, giving you the freedom to take advantage of on-premise, hybrid, or public cloud infrastructure, letting you effortlessly move workloads to where it matters to you

Out of the box, it comes with quite a mature feature set:

- **Automatic bin packing**: This is the core of the tool, a powerful scheduler that makes decisions on where to launch your containers based on the resources currently being consumed on your cluster nodes

- **Horizontal scaling**: This allows you to scale up your application, either manually or based on CPU utilization

- **Self-healing**: You can configure status checks; if your container fails a check, then it will be relaunched where the resource is available

- **Load balancing & service discovery**: Kubernetes allows you to attach your containers to services, these can expose your container either locally or externally

- **Storage orchestration**: Kubernetes supports a number of backend storage modules out of the box, including Google Cloud Platform, AWS, and services such as NFS, iSCSI, Gluster, or Flocker to name a few

- **Secret and configuration management**: This allows you to deploy and update secrets such as API keys to your containers, without exposing them or rebuilding your container images

There are a lot more features that we could talk about; rather than covering these features, let's dive right in and install a Kubernetes cluster.

Installing Kubernetes

As hinted by the Kubernetes website, there are a lot of ways you can install Kubernetes. A lot of the documentation refers to Google's own public cloud; however, rather than introducing a third public cloud into the mix, we are going to be looking at deploying our Kubernetes cluster onto Amazon Web Services.

Before we start the Kubernetes installation, we need to ensure that you have the AWS Command Line Interface installed and configured.

> The AWS **Command Line Interface** (**CLI**) is a unified tool to manage your AWS services. With just one tool to download and configure, you can control multiple AWS services from the command line and automate them through scripts:
>
> https://aws.amazon.com/cli/

As we have already used Homebrew several times during the previous chapters, we will use that to install the tools. To do this, simply run the following command:

```
brew install awscli
```

Once the tools have been installed, you will be able to configure the tools by running the following command:

```
aws configure
```

This will ask for the following four pieces of information:

- AWS Access Key ID
- AWS Secret Access Key
- Default region name
- Default output format

You should have your AWS Access and Secret keys from the when we launched a Docker Machine in Amazon Web Services in *Chapter 2, Introducing First-party Tools*. For the `Default region name`, I used `eu-west-1` (which is the closest region to me) and I left the `Default output format` as None:

```
● ● ●                                    russ — -bash — 111×34
russ in
⚡ brew install awscli
==> Downloading https://homebrew.bintray.com/bottles/awscli-1.10.16.el_capitan.bottle.tar.gz
###################################################################### 100.0%
==> Pouring awscli-1.10.16.el_capitan.bottle.tar.gz
==> Caveats
The "examples" directory has been installed to:
  /usr/local/share/awscli/examples

Add the following to ~/.bashrc to enable bash completion:
  complete -C aws_completer aws

Add the following to ~/.zshrc to enable zsh completion:
  source /usr/local/share/zsh/site-functions/_aws

Before using awscli, you need to tell it about your AWS credentials.
The easiest way to do this is to run:
  aws configure

More information:
  https://docs.aws.amazon.com/cli/latest/userguide/cli-chap-getting-started.html

zsh completion has been installed to:
  /usr/local/share/zsh/site-functions
==> Summary
🍺 /usr/local/Cellar/awscli/1.10.16: 2,650 files, 19M
russ in
⚡ aws configure
AWS Access Key ID [None]: JHFDIGJKBDS8639FJHDS
AWS Secret Access Key [None]: sfvjbkdsvBKHDJBDFjbfsdvlkb+JLN873JKFLSJH
Default region name [None]: eu-west-1
Default output format [None]:
russ in
⚡ ▯
```

Now that we have the AWS Command Line Tools installed and configured, we can install the Kubernetes Command Line Tools. This is a binary that will allow you to interact with your Kubernetes' cluster in the same way that the local Docker client connects to a remote Docker Engine. This can be installed using Homebrew, just run the following command:

brew install kubernetes-cli

```
● ● ●                                    russ — -bash — 111×12
russ in
⚡ brew install kubernetes-cli
==> Downloading https://homebrew.bintray.com/bottles/kubernetes-cli-1.2.0.el_capitan.bottle.tar.gz
###################################################################### 100.0%
==> Pouring kubernetes-cli-1.2.0.el_capitan.bottle.tar.gz
==> Caveats
Bash completion has been installed to:
  /usr/local/etc/bash_completion.d
==> Summary
🍺 /usr/local/Cellar/kubernetes-cli/1.2.0: 6 files, 40.5M
russ in
⚡
```

We don't need to configure the tool once installed as this will be taken care of by the main Kubernetes deployment script that we will be running next.

Now that we have the tools needed to launch and interact with our AWS Kubernetes cluster, we can make a start deploying the cluster itself.

Before we kick off the installation, we need to let the installation script know a little bit of information about where we want our cluster to launch and also how big we would like it, this information is passed on to the installation script as environment variables.

First of all, I would like it launched in Europe:

```
export KUBE_AWS_ZONE=eu-west-1c
export AWS_S3_REGION=eu-west-1
```

Also, I would like two nodes:

```
export NUM_NODES=2
```

Finally, we need to instruct the installation script that we would like to launch the Kubernetes in Amazon Web Services:

```
export KUBERNETES_PROVIDER=aws
```

Now that we have told the installer where we would like our Kubernetes cluster to be launched, it's time to actually launch it. To do this, run the following command:

```
curl -sS https://get.k8s.io | bash
```

This will download the installer and the latest Kubernetes codebase, and then launch our cluster. The process itself can take anywhere between eight and fifteen minutes, depending on your network connection.

If you prefer not to run this installation yourself, you can view a recording of a Kubernetes cluster being deployed in Amazon Web Services at the following URL:

```
https://asciinema.org/a/41161
```

Once the installation script has completed, you will be given information on where to access your Kubernetes cluster, you should also be able to run the following command to get a list of the nodes within your Kubernetes cluster:

```
kubectl get nodes
```

This should return something similar to the following screenshot:

```
● ● ●                                       .aws — -bash — 111×7
russ in ~/.aws
⚡ kubectl get nodes
NAME                                          STATUS    AGE
ip-172-20-0-134.eu-west-1.compute.internal    Ready     42m
ip-172-20-0-135.eu-west-1.compute.internal    Ready     42m
russ in ~/.aws
⚡ ▯
```

Also, if you have the AWS Console open, you should see that a new VPC dedicated to Kubernetes has been created:

You will also see that three EC2 instances have been launched into the Kubernetes VPC:

The last thing to make a note of before we start to launch applications into our Kubernetes cluster is the username and password credentials for the cluster.

As you may have seen during the installation, these are stored in the Kubernetes CLI configuration, as they are right at the bottom of the file, you can get these by running the following command:

```
tail -3 ~/.kube/config
```

```
russ — -bash — 111×7
russ in
⚡  tail -3 ~/.kube/config
   user:
     password: fmn9w4SAzV6JPnJ7
     username: admin
russ in
⚡  
```

Now that our Kubernetes cluster has been launched, and we have access to it using the command-line tools, we can start launching an application.

Launching our first Kubernetes application

To start off with, we are going to be launching a really basic cluster of NGINX containers, each container within the cluster will be serving a simple graphic and also print its host name on the page. You can find the image for container on the Docker Hub at `https://hub.docker.com/r/russmckendrick/cluster/`.

Like a lot of the tools we have looked at in the previous chapters, Kubernetes uses the YAML format for its definition file. The file we are going to launch into our cluster is the following file:

```
apiVersion: v1
kind: ReplicationController
metadata:
  name: nginxcluster
spec:
  replicas: 5
  selector:
    app: nginxcluster
  template:
    metadata:
      name: nginxcluster
      labels:
        app: nginxcluster
```

```
spec:
  containers:
  - name: nginxcluster
    image: russmckendrick/cluster
    ports:
    - containerPort: 80
```

Let's call the file `nginxcluster.yaml`. To launch it, run the following command:

`kubectl create -f nginxcluster.yaml`

Once launched, you will be able to see the active pods by running the following command:

`kubectl get pods`

You may find that you need to run the `kubectl get pods` command a few times to ensure that everything is running as expected:

```
● ● ●                              nginx — -bash — 111×21
russ in ~/Documents/Code/extending-docker/chapter07/kubernetes/nginx on master*
⚡ kubectl create -f nginxcluster.yaml
replicationcontroller "nginxcluster" created
russ in ~/Documents/Code/extending-docker/chapter07/kubernetes/nginx on master*
⚡ kubectl get pods
NAME                  READY    STATUS            RESTARTS    AGE
nginxcluster-12lyl    0/1      ContainerCreating  0          8s
nginxcluster-b6dz0    0/1      ContainerCreating  0          8s
nginxcluster-lrbux    0/1      ContainerCreating  0          8s
nginxcluster-tygwk    0/1      ContainerCreating  0          8s
nginxcluster-z2pb1    0/1      ContainerCreating  0          8s
russ in ~/Documents/Code/extending-docker/chapter07/kubernetes/nginx on master*
⚡ kubectl get pods
NAME                  READY    STATUS    RESTARTS   AGE
nginxcluster-12lyl    1/1      Running   0          41s
nginxcluster-b6dz0    1/1      Running   0          41s
nginxcluster-lrbux    1/1      Running   0          41s
nginxcluster-tygwk    1/1      Running   0          41s
nginxcluster-z2pb1    1/1      Running   0          41s
russ in ~/Documents/Code/extending-docker/chapter07/kubernetes/nginx on master*
⚡ []
```

Now that you have your pods up and running, we need to expose them so that we can access the cluster using a browser. To do this, we need to create a service. To view the current services, type the following:

`kubectl get services`

You should see just the main Kubernetes service. When we launched our pods, we defined a replication controller, this is the process that manages the number of pods. To view the replication controllers, run the following command:

`kubectl get rc`

You should see the nginxcluster controller with five pods in the desired and current column. Now that we have confirmed that our replication controller is active with the expected number of pods registered with it, let's create the service and expose the pods to the outside world by running the following command:

```
kubectl expose rc nginxcluster --port=80 --type=LoadBalancer
```

Now, if you run the get services command again, you should see our new service:

```
kubectl get services
```

Your terminal session should look something similar to the following screenshot:

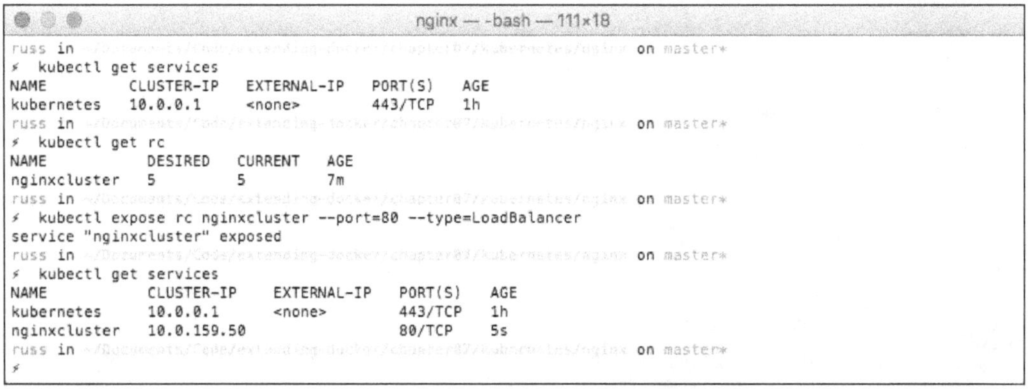

Great, you now have your pods exposed to the Internet. However, you may have noticed that the cluster IP address is an internal one, so how do you access your cluster?

As we are running our Kubernetes cluster in Amazon Web Services, when you exposed the service, Kubernetes made an API call to AWS and launched an Elastic Load Balancer. You can get the URL of the load balancer by running the following command:

```
kubectl describe service nginxcluster
```

As you can see, in my case, my load balancer can be accessed at `http://af92913bcf98a11e5841c0a7f321c3b2-1182773033.eu-west-1.elb.amazonaws.com/`.

Opening the load balancer URL in a browser shows our container page:

nginxcluster-b6dz0

Finally, if you open the AWS console, you should be able to see the elastic load balancer created by Kubernetes:

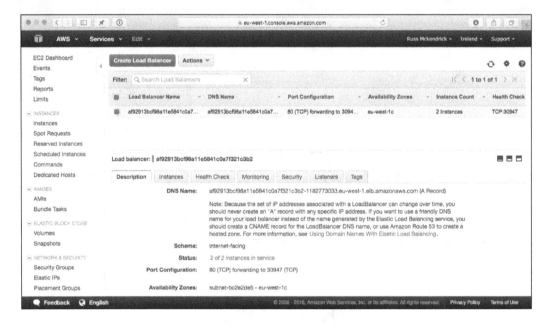

An advanced example

Let's try something more advanced than launching a few of the same instances and load balancing them.

For the following example, we are going to launch our WordPress stack. This time we are going to mount Elastic Block Storage volumes to store both our MySQL database and WordPress files on:

> "*Amazon Elastic Block Store (Amazon EBS) provides persistent block level storage volumes for use with Amazon EC2 instances in the AWS Cloud. Each Amazon EBS volume is automatically replicated within its Availability Zone to protect you from component failure, offering high availability and durability. Amazon EBS volumes offer the consistent and low-latency performance needed to run your workloads. With Amazon EBS, you can scale your usage up or down within minutes – all while paying a low price for only what you provision.*" - https://aws.amazon.com/ebs/

Creating the volumes

Before we launch our pods and services, we need to create the two EBS volumes that we will be attaching to our pods. As we already have the AWS Command Line Interface installed and configured, we will be using that to create the volume rather than logging into the console and creating it using the GUI.

To create the two volumes, simply run the following command twice, making sure that you update the availability zone to match where your Kubernetes cluster was configured to launch:

```
aws ec2 create-volume --availability-zone eu-west-1c --size 10
--volume-type gp2
```

Each time you run the command, you will get a blob of JSON returned, this will contain all of the metadata generated when the volume was created:

```
● ● ●                              wordpress — -bash — 111×28
russ in ~/Documents/Code/extending-docker/chapter07/kubernetes/wordpress on master*
↯  aws ec2 create-volume --availability-zone eu-west-1c --size 10 --volume-type gp2
{
    "AvailabilityZone": "eu-west-1c",
    "Encrypted": false,
    "VolumeType": "gp2",
    "VolumeId": "vol-10f792ae",
    "State": "creating",
    "Iops": 30,
    "SnapshotId": "",
    "CreateTime": "2016-04-03T14:27:30.640Z",
    "Size": 10
}
russ in ~/Documents/Code/extending-docker/chapter07/kubernetes/wordpress on master*
↯  aws ec2 create-volume --availability-zone eu-west-1c --size 10 --volume-type gp2
{
    "AvailabilityZone": "eu-west-1c",
    "Encrypted": false,
    "VolumeType": "gp2",
    "VolumeId": "vol-3cf79282",
    "State": "creating",
    "Iops": 30,
    "SnapshotId": "",
    "CreateTime": "2016-04-03T14:27:32.397Z",
    "Size": 10
}
russ in ~/Documents/Code/extending-docker/chapter07/kubernetes/wordpress on master*
↯  ⬚
```

Make a note of VolumeId for each of the two volumes, you will need to know these when we create our MySQL and WordPress pods.

Launching MySQL

Now that we have the volumes created, we are now able to launch our MySQL Pod and Service. First of all, let's start with the Pod definition, make sure that you add one of the volumeIDs at the where promoted towards the bottom of the file:

```
apiVersion: v1
kind: Pod
metadata:
  name: mysql
  labels:
    name: mysql
spec:
  containers:
    - resources:
      image: russmckendrick/mariadb
      name: mysql
      env:
        - name: MYSQL_ROOT_PASSWORD
          value: yourpassword
      ports:
        - containerPort: 3306
          name: mysql
      volumeMounts:
        - name: mysql-persistent-storage
          mountPath: /var/lib/mysql
  volumes:
    - name: mysql-persistent-storage
      awsElasticBlockStore:
        volumeID:<insert your volume id here>
        fsType: ext4
```

As you can see, this follows pretty closely to our first Kubernetes application, except this time, we are only creating a single Pod rather than one with a Replication Controller.

Also, as you can see, I have added my volumeID to the bottom of the file; you will need to add your own volumeID when you come to launch the Pod.

I call the file `mysql.yaml`, so to launch it, we need to run the following command:

```
kubectl create -f mysql.yaml
```

Kubernetes will validate the `mysql.yaml` file before it tries to launch the Pod; if you get any errors, please check whether the indentation is correct:

```
                                   wordpress — -bash — 111×14
russ in ~/Documents/Code/extending-docker/chapter07/kubernetes/wordpress  on master*
↯ kubectl create -f mysql.yaml
pod "mysql" created
russ in ~/Documents/Code/extending-docker/chapter07/kubernetes/wordpress  on master*
↯ kubectl get pods
NAME                 READY     STATUS     RESTARTS    AGE
mysql                0/1       Pending    0           11s
nginxcluster-3j5q7   1/1       Running    0           3m
nginxcluster-c28zw   1/1       Running    0           3m
nginxcluster-dylkm   1/1       Running    0           3m
nginxcluster-hikeb   1/1       Running    0           3m
nginxcluster-z4mkl   1/1       Running    0           3m
russ in ~/Documents/Code/extending-docker/chapter07/kubernetes/wordpress  on master*
↯ 
```

You should now have the Pod launched; however, you should probably check if it's there. Run the following command to view the status of your Pods:

```
kubectl get pods
```

If you see that the Pod has a status of `Pending`, like I did, you will probably be wondering *what's going on?* Luckily, you can easily find that out by getting more information on the Pod we are trying to launch by using the `describe` command:

```
kubectl describe pod mysql
```

This will print out everything you will ever want know about the Pod, as you can see from the following terminal output, we did not have enough capacity within our cluster to launch the Pod:

```
● ● ●                                    wordpress — ~bash — 161×45
russ in                                              on master
↗ kubectl describe pod mysql
Name:          mysql
Namespace:     default
Node:          /
Labels:        name=mysql
Status:        Pending
IP:
Controllers:   <none>
Containers:
  mysql:
    Image:     russmckendrick/mariadb
    Port:      3306/TCP
    QoS Tier:
      cpu:     Burstable
      memory:  BestEffort
    Requests:
      cpu:     100m
    Environment Variables:
      MYSQL_ROOT_PASSWORD:       yourpassword
Volumes:
  mysql-persistent-storage:
    Type:       AWSElasticBlockStore (a Persistent Disk resource in AWS)
    VolumeID:   vol-10f792ae
    FSType:     ext4
    Partition:  0
    ReadOnly:   false
  default-token-clb8g:
    Type:       Secret (a volume populated by a Secret)
    SecretName: default-token-clb8g
Events:
  FirstSeen     LastSeen        Count   From                    SubobjectPath   Type      Reason            Message
  ---------     --------        -----   ----                    -------------   --------  ------            -------
  1m            54s             5       {default-scheduler }                    Warning   FailedScheduling  pod (mysql) failed to fit in any node
  fit failure on node (ip-172-20-0-135.eu-west-1.compute.internal): Node didn't have enough resource: CPU, requested: 100, used: 930, capacity: 1000
  fit failure on node (ip-172-20-0-134.eu-west-1.compute.internal): Node didn't have enough resource: CPU, requested: 100, used: 920, capacity: 1000

  1m            22s             2       {default-scheduler }                    Warning FailedScheduling   pod (mysql) failed to fit in any node
  fit failure on node (ip-172-20-0-134.eu-west-1.compute.internal): Node didn't have enough resource: CPU, requested: 100, used: 920, capacity: 1000
  fit failure on node (ip-172-20-0-135.eu-west-1.compute.internal): Node didn't have enough resource: CPU, requested: 100, used: 930, capacity: 1000


russ in                                              on master
↗ []
```

We can free up some resources by removing our previous Pods and Services by running the following command:

```
kubectl delete rc nginxcluster
kubectl delete service nginxcluster
```

Once you run the commands to remove `nginxcluster`, your mysql Pod should automatically launch after a few seconds:

```
● ● ●                          wordpress — -bash — 111×18
russ in ~/Documents/Code/extending-docker/chapter07/kubernetes/wordpress on master*
⚡ kubectl delete rc nginxcluster
replicationcontroller "nginxcluster" deleted
russ in ~/Documents/Code/extending-docker/chapter07/kubernetes/wordpress on master*
⚡ kubectl get pods
NAME                 READY     STATUS        RESTARTS   AGE
mysql                0/1       Pending       0          3m
nginxcluster-3j5q7   1/1       Terminating   0          6m
nginxcluster-c28zw   1/1       Terminating   0          6m
nginxcluster-dylkm   1/1       Terminating   0          6m
nginxcluster-hikeb   1/1       Terminating   0          6m
nginxcluster-z4mkl   1/1       Terminating   0          6m
russ in ~/Documents/Code/extending-docker/chapter07/kubernetes/wordpress on master*
⚡ kubectl get pods
NAME      READY    STATUS    RESTARTS   AGE
mysql     1/1      Running   0          4m
russ in ~/Documents/Code/extending-docker/chapter07/kubernetes/wordpress on master*
⚡
```

Now that the Pod has been launched, we need to attach a service so that port 3306 is exposed, rather than doing this using the `kubectl` command like we did before, we will use a second file called `mysql-service.yaml`:

```
apiVersion: v1
kind: Service
metadata:
  labels:
    name: mysql
  name: mysql
spec:
  ports:
    - port: 3306
  selector:
    name: mysql
```

To launch the service, simply run the following command:

```
kubectl create -f mysql-service.yaml
```

So now that we have the MySQL Pod and Service launched, it's time to launch the actual WordPress container.

Launching WordPress

Like the MySQL Pod and Service, we will be launching our WordPress container using two files. The first file is for the Pod:

```yaml
apiVersion: v1
kind: Pod
metadata:
  name: wordpress
  labels:
    name: wordpress
spec:
  containers:
    - image: wordpress
      name: wordpress
      env:
        - name: WORDPRESS_DB_PASSWORD
          value: yourpassword
      ports:
        - containerPort: 80
          name: wordpress
      volumeMounts:
        - name: wordpress-persistent-storage
          mountPath: /var/www/html
  volumes:
    - name: wordpress-persistent-storage
      awsElasticBlockStore:
        volumeID: <insert your volume id here>
        fsType: ext4
```

As an EBS volume cannot be attached to more than one device at a time, remember to use the second EBS volume you created here. Call the `wordpress.yaml` file and launch it using the following command:

```
kubectl create -f wordpress.yaml
```

Then wait for the Pod to launch:

```
● ● ●                          wordpress — -bash — 111×15
russ in ~/Documents/Code/extending-docker/chapter07/kubernetes/wordpress on master*
⚡ kubectl create -f wordpress.yaml
pod "wordpress" created
russ in ~/Documents/Code/extending-docker/chapter07/kubernetes/wordpress on master*
⚡ kubectl get pods
NAME          READY     STATUS              RESTARTS   AGE
mysql         1/1       Running             0          14m
wordpress     0/1       ContainerCreating   0          3s
russ in ~/Documents/Code/extending-docker/chapter07/kubernetes/wordpress on master*
⚡ kubectl get pods
NAME          READY     STATUS     RESTARTS   AGE
mysql         1/1       Running    0          14m
wordpress     1/1       Running    0          37s
russ in ~/Documents/Code/extending-docker/chapter07/kubernetes/wordpress on master*
⚡ ▯
```

As we have already removed `nginxcluster`, there should be enough resources to launch the Pod straightaway, meaning that you should not get any errors.

Although the Pod should be running, it's best to check whether the container launched without any problems. To do this, run the following command:

kubectl logs wordpress

This should print out the container logs, you will see something similar to the following screenshot:

```
● ● ●                          wordpress — -bash — 111×17
russ in ~/Documents/Code/extending-docker/chapter07/kubernetes/wordpress on master*
⚡ kubectl logs wordpress
WordPress not found in /var/www/html - copying now...
WARNING: /var/www/html is not empty - press Ctrl+C now if this is an error!
+ ls -A
lost+found
+ sleep 10
Complete! WordPress has been successfully copied to /var/www/html
AH00558: apache2: Could not reliably determine the server's fully qualified domain name, using 10.244.1.8. Set
the 'ServerName' directive globally to suppress this message
AH00558: apache2: Could not reliably determine the server's fully qualified domain name, using 10.244.1.8. Set
the 'ServerName' directive globally to suppress this message
[Sun Apr 03 14:44:31.599524 2016] [mpm_prefork:notice] [pid 1] AH00163: Apache/2.4.10 (Debian) PHP/5.6.19 confi
gured -- resuming normal operations
[Sun Apr 03 14:44:31.603270 2016] [core:notice] [pid 1] AH00094: Command line: 'apache2 -D FOREGROUND'
russ in ~/Documents/Code/extending-docker/chapter07/kubernetes/wordpress on master*
⚡ ▯
```

Now that the Pod has launched and WordPress appears to have bootstrapped itself as expected, we should launch the service. Like `nginxcluster`, this will create an Elastic Load Balancer. The service definition file looks similar to the following code:

```
apiVersion: v1
kind: Service
metadata:
  labels:
```

```
          name: wpfrontend
      name: wpfrontend
    spec:
      ports:
        - port: 80
      selector:
        name: wordpress
      type: LoadBalancer
```

To launch it, run the following command:

```
kubectl create -f wordpress-service.yaml
```

Once launched, check whether the service has been created and get the details of the Elastic Load Balancer by running the following command:

```
kubectl get services
```

```
kubectl describe service wpfrontend
```

When I ran the commands, I got the following output:

```
● ● ●                                              wordpress — -bash — 146×28
russ in                                                    on master*
↯ kubectl get services
NAME            CLUSTER-IP      EXTERNAL-IP    PORT(S)    AGE
kubernetes      10.0.0.1        <none>         443/TCP    5h
mysql           10.0.228.86     <none>         3306/TCP   14m
wpfrontend      10.0.32.125                    80/TCP     35s
russ in                                                    on master*
↯ kubectl describe service wpfrontend
Name:                   wpfrontend
Namespace:              default
Labels:                 name=wpfrontend
Selector:               name=wordpress
Type:                   LoadBalancer
IP:                     10.0.32.125
LoadBalancer Ingress:   a6baa8ac5f9ab11e5841c0a7f321c3b2-1989472125.eu-west-1.elb.amazonaws.com
Port:                   <unset> 80/TCP
NodePort:               <unset> 31206/TCP
Endpoints:              10.244.1.8:80
Session Affinity:       None
Events:
  FirstSeen   LastSeen    Count   From                    SubobjectPath   Type       Reason                 Message
  ---------   --------    -----   ----                    -------------   --------   ------                 -------
  45s         45s         1       {service-controller }                   Normal     CreatingLoadBalancer   Creating load balancer
  43s         43s         1       {service-controller }                   Normal     CreatedLoadBalancer    Created load balancer

russ in                                                    on master*
↯
```

After a few minutes, you should be able to access the URL for Elastic Load Balancer, and as expected, you will be presented with a WordPress installation screen:

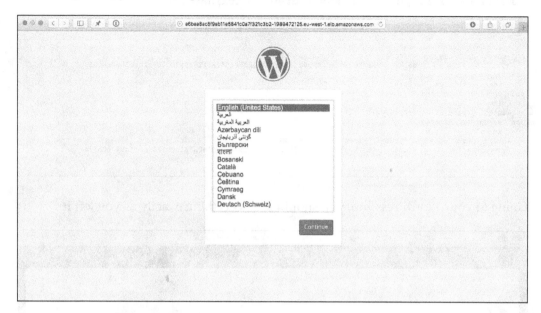

As we did in *Chapter 3*, *Volume Plugins* when we were looking at storage plugins, complete the installation, log in, and attach an image to the Hello World post.

Now that we have the WordPress site up and running, let's try removing the wordpress Pod and relaunching it, first of let's make a note of the Container ID:

```
kubectl describe pod wordpress | grep "Container ID"
```

Then delete the Pod and relaunch it:

```
kubectl delete pod wordpress
kubectl create -f wordpress.yaml
```

Check the Container ID again to make sure that we have a different one:

```
kubectl describe pod wordpress | grep "Container ID"
```

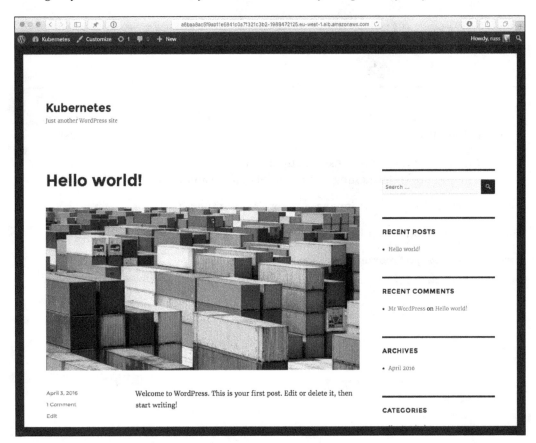

Going to your WordPress site, you should see everything exactly as you left it:

If we wanted to, we could perform the same action for the MySQL pod and our data would be exactly as we left it, as it is stored in the EBS volume.

Let's remove the Pod and Service for the WordPress application by running the following command:

```
kubectl delete pod wordpress
kubectl delete pod mysql
kubectl delete service wpfrontend
kubectl delete service mysql
```

This should leave us with a nice clean Kubernetes cluster for the next section of the chapter.

Supporting tools

You may be wondering to yourself why we bothered grabbing the username and password when we first deployed our Kubernetes cluster as we have not had to use it yet. Let's take a look at some of the supporting tools that are deployed as part of our Kubernetes cluster.

When you first deployed your Kubernetes cluster, there was a list of URLs printed on the screen, we will be using these for this section. Don't worry if you didn't make a note of them as you can get all the URLs for the supporting tools by running the following command:

```
kubectl cluster-info
```

This will print out a list of URLs for the various parts of your Kubernetes cluster:

```
russ in
↯ kubectl cluster-info
Kubernetes master is running at https://52.49.188.233
Elasticsearch is running at https://52.49.188.233/api/v1/proxy/namespaces/kube-system/services/elasticsearch-logging
Heapster is running at https://52.49.188.233/api/v1/proxy/namespaces/kube-system/services/heapster
Kibana is running at https://52.49.188.233/api/v1/proxy/namespaces/kube-system/services/kibana-logging
KubeDNS is running at https://52.49.188.233/api/v1/proxy/namespaces/kube-system/services/kube-dns
kubernetes-dashboard is running at https://52.49.188.233/api/v1/proxy/namespaces/kube-system/services/kubernetes-dashboard
Grafana is running at https://52.49.188.233/api/v1/proxy/namespaces/kube-system/services/monitoring-grafana
InfluxDB is running at https://52.49.188.233/api/v1/proxy/namespaces/kube-system/services/monitoring-influxdb
russ in
↯ ▯
```

You will need the username and password to view some of these tools, again if you don't have these to hand, you can get them by running the following command:

```
tail -3 ~/.kube/config
```

Kubernetes Dashboard

First of all, let's take a look at the Kubernetes Dashboard. You can get this by putting the URL for the Kubernetes-dashboard in your browser. When you enter it, depending on your browser, you will get warnings about the certificates, accept the warnings and you will be given a login prompt. Enter the username and password here. Once logged in, you will see the following screen:

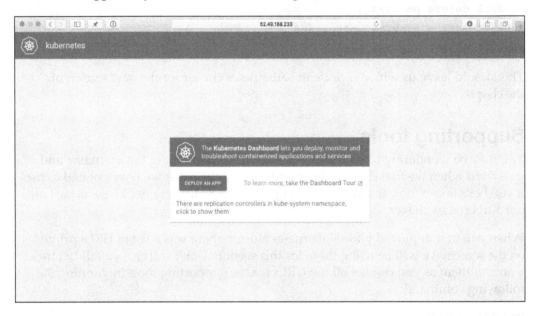

Let's deploy the NGINX Cluster application using the UI. To do this, click on **Deploy An App** and enter the following:

- **App name** = nginx-cluster
- **Container image** = russmckendrick/cluster
- **Number of pods** = 5
- **Port** = Leave blank
- **Port** = 80
- **Target port** = 80
- Tick the box for **Expose service externally**

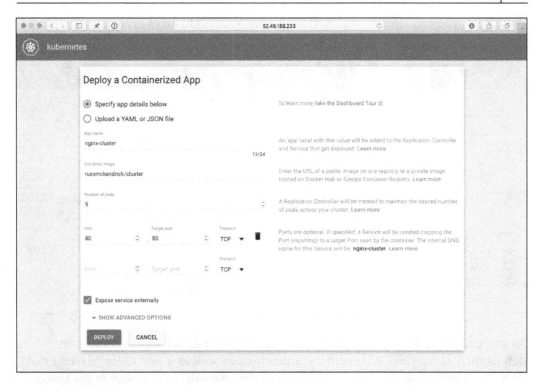

Once you click on **Deploy**, you will be taken back to the overview screen:

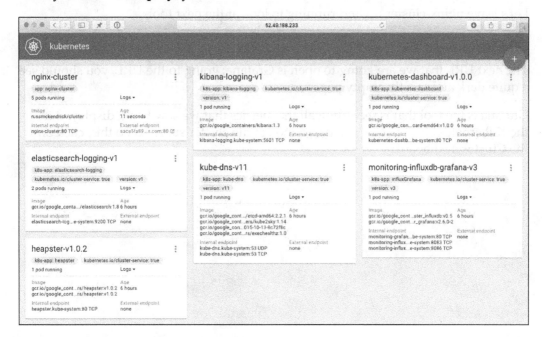

From here, you can click on **nginx-cluster** and be taken to an overview screen:

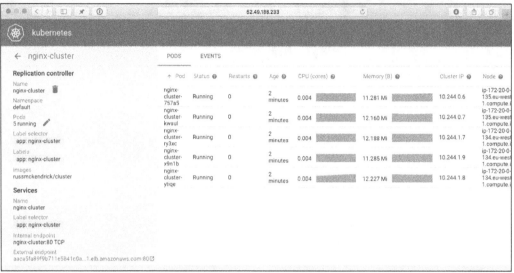

As you can see, this gives you all the details on both the Pod and Service, with details such as the CPU and memory utilization, as well as a link to the Elastic Load Balancer. Clicking the link should take you to the default cluster page of the image and the container's hostname.

Let's leave nginx-cluster up and running to look at the next tool.

Grafana

The next URL that we are going to open is Grafana; going to the URL, you should see a quite dark and mostly empty page.

Grafana is the tool that is recording all the metrics that we saw being displayed in the Kubernetes dashboard. Let's take a look at the cluster stats. To do this, click on the **Cluster** dashboard:

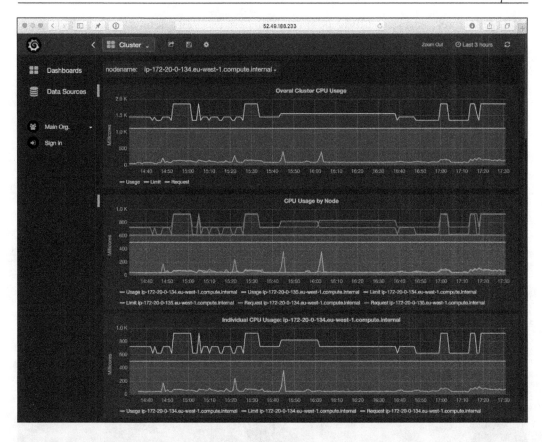

As you can see, this gives us a breakdown of all of the metrics that you would expect to see from a system-monitoring tool. Scrolling down, you can see:

- CPU Usage
- Memory Usage
- Network Usage
- Filesystem Usage

Both collectively and per individual node. You can also view details on Pods by clicking on the **Pods** dashboard. As Grafana gets its data from the InfluxDB pod, which has been running since we first launched our Kubernetes cluster, you can view metrics for every Pod that you have launched, even if it is not currently running. The following is the Pod metrics for the `mysql` pod we launched when installing WordPress:

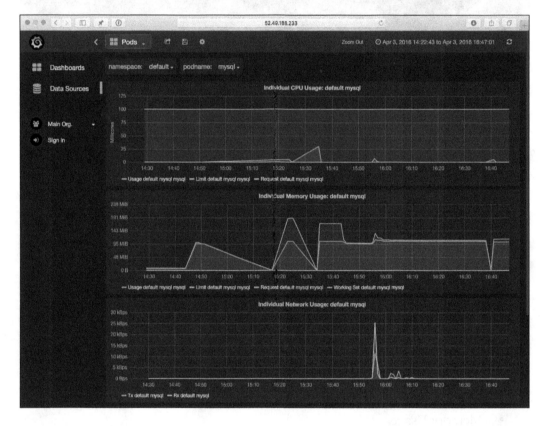

I would recommend you to look around to view some of the other Pod metrics.

ELK

The final tool we are going to look at is the ELK stack that has been running in the background since we first launch our Kubernetes cluster. An ELK stack is a collection of the following three different tools:

- **Elasticsearch**: `https://www.elastic.co/products/elasticsearch`
- **Logstash**: `https://www.elastic.co/products/logstash`
- **Kibana**: `https://www.elastic.co/products/kibana`

Together they form a powerful central logging platform.

When we ran the following command earlier in this section of the chapter (please note you will not be able to run it again as we removed the WordPress pod):

```
kubectl logs wordpress
```

The logs displayed for our `wordpress` pod the log file entries were actually read from the Elasticsearch pod. Elasticsearch comes with its own dashboard called Kibana. Let's open the Kibana URL.

When you first open Kibana, you will be asked to configure an index pattern. To do this, just select Time-field name from the drop-down box and click on **Create** button:

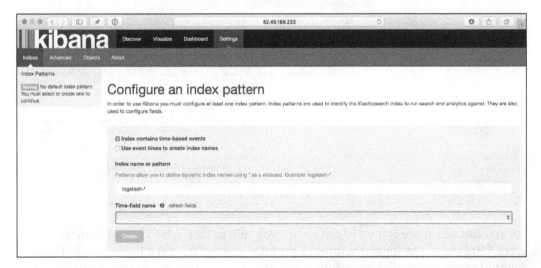

Once the index pattern has been created, click on the **Discover** link in the top menu. You will then be taken to an overview of all of the log data that has been sent to Elasticsearch by the Logstash installations that are running on each of the nodes:

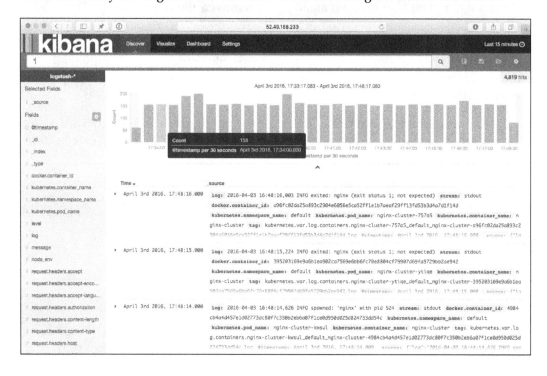

As you can see, there is a lot of data being logged; in fact, when I looked, there were 4,918 messages logged within 15 minutes alone. There is a lot of data in here, I would recommend clicking around and trying some searches to get an idea of what is being logged.

To give you an idea of what each log entry looks like, here is one for one of my
nginx-cluser pods:

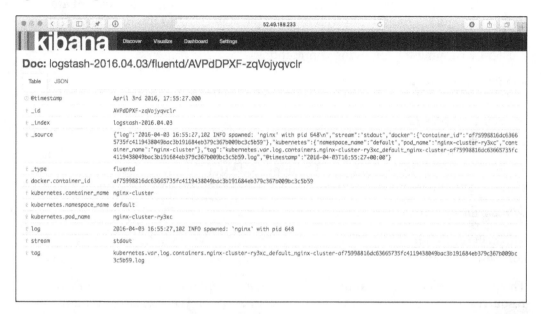

Remaining cluster tools

The remaining cluster tools that we are yet to open in the browser are as follows:

- **Kubernetes**
- **Heapster**
- **KubeDNS**
- **InfluxDB**

These all are API endpoints, so you will not see anything other than an API
response, they are using by Kubernetes internally to both manage and schedule
within the cluster.

Destroying the cluster

As the cluster is sat in your Amazon Web Services account on instances that are pay-as-you-go, we should look at removing the cluster; to do this, let's re-enter the original configuration that we entered when we first deployed the Kubernetes cluster by running the following command:

```
export KUBE_AWS_ZONE=eu-west-1c

export AWS_S3_REGION=eu-west-1

export NUM_NODES=2

export KUBERNETES_PROVIDER=aws
```

Then, from the same location you first deployed your Kubernetes cluster, run the following command:

```
./kubernetes/cluster/kube-down.sh
```

This will connect to the AWS API and start to tear down all of the instances, configuration, and any other resources that have been launched with Kubernetes.

The process will take several minutes, do not interrupt it or you maybe left with resources that incur costs running within your Amazon Web Services account:

```
russ in
⚡  export KUBE_AWS_ZONE=eu-west-1c
russ in
⚡  export AWS_S3_REGION=eu-west-1
russ in
⚡  export NUM_NODES=2
russ in
⚡  export KUBERNETES_PROVIDER=aws
russ in
⚡  ./kubernetes/cluster/kube-down.sh
Bringing down cluster using provider: aws
Deleting ELBs in: vpc-b9475cdc
Waiting for ELBs to be deleted
All ELBs deleted
Deleting instances in VPC: vpc-b9475cdc
Deleting auto-scaling group: kubernetes-minion-group-eu-west-1c
Deleting auto-scaling launch configuration: kubernetes-minion-group-eu-west-1c
Deleting auto-scaling group: kubernetes-minion-group-eu-west-1c
Waiting for instances to be deleted
Waiting for instance i-06e4308a to be terminated (currently shutting-down)
Sleeping for 3 seconds...
Waiting for instance i-06e4308a to be terminated (currently shutting-down)
Sleeping for 3 seconds...
Waiting for instance i-06e4308a to be terminated (currently shutting-down)
Sleeping for 3 seconds...
All instances deleted
Releasing Elastic IP: 52.49.188.233
Deleting volume vol-d3abce6d
Cleaning up resources in VPC: vpc-b9475cdc
Cleaning up security group: sg-9d7290fa
Cleaning up security group: sg-eb3bd98c
Cleaning up security group: sg-ec3bd98b
Deleting security group: sg-9d7290fa
Deleting security group: sg-eb3bd98c
Deleting security group: sg-ec3bd98b
Deleting VPC: vpc-b9475cdc
Done
russ in
⚡  
```

I would also recommend logging into your Amazon Web Services console and remove the unattached EBS volumes that we created for the WordPress installation and also any Kubernetes labelled S3 buckets as these will be incurring costs as well.

Recap

Kubernetes, like Docker, has matured a lot since its first public release. It has become easier to deploy and manage with each release without having a negative impact on the feature set.

As a solution that offers scheduling for your containers, it is second to none, and as it is not tied to any particular provider, you can easily deploy it to providers other than Amazon Web Services, such as Google's own Cloud Platform, where it is considered a first class citizen. It is also possible to deploy it on premise on your own bare metal of virtual servers, making sure that it keeps itself inline with the build once and deploy anywhere philosophy that Docker has.

Also, it adapts to work with the technologies available in every platform you deploy it onto; for example, if you need persistent storage, then as already mentioned, there are multiple options available to you.

Finally, just like Docker has been over the past 18 months, Kubernetes has quite a unifying platform, with multiple vendors such as Google, Microsoft, and Red Hat. They all support and use it as part of their products.

Amazon EC2 Container Service (ECS)

The next tool that we are going to be looking at is the Elastic Container Service from Amazon. The description that Amazon gives is as follows:

> *"Amazon EC2 Container Service (ECS) is a highly scalable, high performance container management service that supports Docker containers and allows you to easily run applications on a managed cluster of Amazon EC2 instances. Amazon ECS eliminates the need for you to install, operate, and scale your own cluster management infrastructure. With simple API calls, you can launch and stop Docker-enabled applications, query the complete state of your cluster, and access many familiar features like security groups, Elastic Load Balancing, EBS volumes, and IAM roles. You can use Amazon ECS to schedule the placement of containers across your cluster based on your resource needs and availability requirements. You can also integrate your own scheduler or third-party schedulers to meet business or application specific requirements."* - https://aws.amazon.com/ecs/

It wasn't a surprise that Amazon would offer their own container-based service.

After all, if you are following Amazon's best practices, then you will already be treating each of your EC2 instances in the same way you are treating your containers.

When I deploy applications into Amazon Web Services, I always try to ensure that I build and deploy production-ready images, along with ensuring that all the data written by the application is sent to a shared source as the instances could be terminated any time due to scaling events.

To help support this approach, Amazon offers a wide range of services such as:

- **Elastic Load Balancing** (**ELB**): This is a highly available and scalable load balancer
- **Amazon Elastic Block Store** (**EBS**): This provides persistent block-level storage volumes for your compute resources
- **Auto Scaling**: This scales EC2 resources up and down, allowing you to manage both, peaks in traffic and failures within the application
- **Amazon Relational Database Service** (**RDS**): This is a highly available database as a service supporting MySQL, Postgres, and Microsoft SQL

All of these are designed to help you remove all single points of failure within your Amazon-hosted application.

Also, as all of Amazon's services are API-driven, it wasn't too much of a jump for them to extend support to Docker containers.

Launching ECS in the console

I am going to be using the the AWS Console to launch my ECS cluster. As my AWS account is quite old, a few of the steps may differ. To try and account for this, I will be launching my cluster in one of the newer AWS regions.

Once you have logged into the AWS Console at `http://console.aws.amazon.com/`, make sure that you are in the region you would like to launch your ECS cluster in, and then click on the **EC2 Container Service** link from the **Services** drop-down menu.

As this is your first time launching an ECS cluster, you will be greeted with an overview video of the service.

Click on **Get started** to be taken to the Wizard that will help us launch our first cluster.

First of all, you will be prompted to create a task definition. This is the equivalent of creating a Docker Compose file. Here you will define the container image that you would like to run and the resources it is allowed to consume, such as RAM and CPU. You will also map the ports from the host to container here.

For now, we will use the defaults and look at launching our own containers once the cluster is up and running. Fill in the details as per the following screenshot and click on **Next step**:

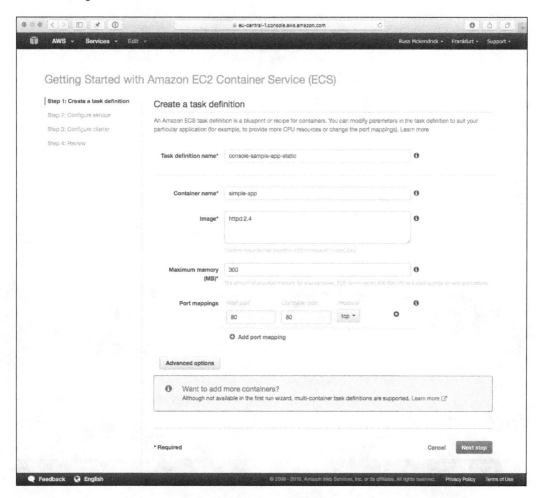

Now that the task has been defined, we need to attach it to a service. This allows us to create a group of tasks, which initially will be three copies of the `console-sample-app-static` task, and register them with an Elastic Load Balancer.
Fill in the details as per the following screenshot and click on **Next step** button:

Now that we have the service defined, we need a location to launch it. This is where EC2 instances come into play, and also where you still to be charged. While the Amazon EC2 Container Service is free of charge to set up, you will be charged for the resources used to deliver the compute side of the cluster. These will be your standard EC2 instance charges. Fill in the details as per the following screenshot and click on **Review & launch**:

Before anything is launched, you will get the opportunity to double-check everything that is configured within your AWS account, this is your last chance to back out of launching the ECS cluster. If you are happy with everything, click on **Launch instance & run service** button:

What you will see now is an overview of what is happening. Typically, it will take about 10 minutes to run through these tasks. In the background, it is doing the following:

- Creating an IAM role that accesses the ECS service
- Creating a VPC for your cluster to be launched in
- Creating a Launch Configuration to run an Amazon ECS-optimized Amazon Linux AMI with the ECS IAM role
- Attaching the newly created Launch Configuration to an Auto Scaling Group and configuring it with the number of instances you defined
- Creating the ECS Cluster, Task, and Service within the Console
- Waiting for the EC2 instances that have been launched by the Auto Scaling Group to launch and register themselves with the ECS service
- Running the Service on your newly created ECS cluster
- Creating an Elastic Load Balancer and registering your Service with it

You can find more information on the Amazon ECS-Optimized Amazon Linux AMI on its AWS Marketplace page at `https://aws.amazon.com/marketplace/pp/B00U6QTYI2/ref=srh_res_product_title?ie=UTF8&sr=0-2&qid=1460291696921`. This image is a cut-down version of Amazon Linux that only runs on Docker.

Once everything is completed, you will be given the option to go to your newly created Service. You should see something similar to the following screenshot:

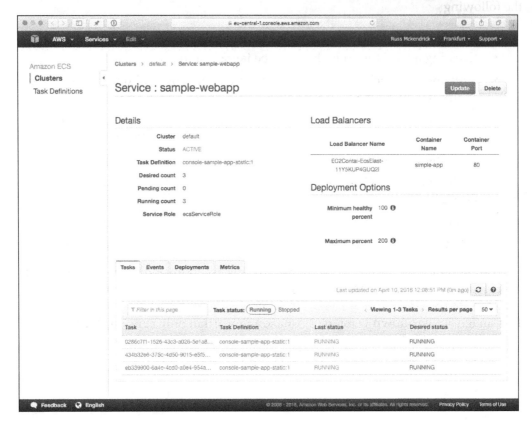

As you can see, we have three running tasks and a load balancer.

Now let's create our own task and service. From the preceding Service view, click on **Update** button and change the desired count from three to zero, this will stop the tasks and allow us to remove the Service. To do this, click on **default** button to go to the cluster view and then remove the Service.

Now that the `sample-webapp` Service has been removed, click on the **Task Definitions** button and then the **Create new task definition** button. On the page that opens, click on the **Add container** button and fill in the following details:

- **Container name**: `cluster`
- **Image**: `russmckendrick/cluster`
- **Maximum memory (MB)**: `32`
- **Port mappings**: `80` (**Host port**) `80` (**Container port**) `tcp` (**Protocol**)

Everything else can be left at the default values:

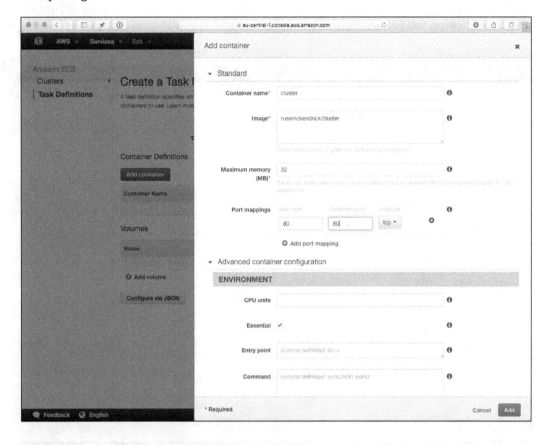

Once filled in, click on the **Add** button. This will take you back to the **Create a Task Definition** screen, fill in the Task Definition Name, let's call it `our-awesome-cluster` and then click on the **Create** button:

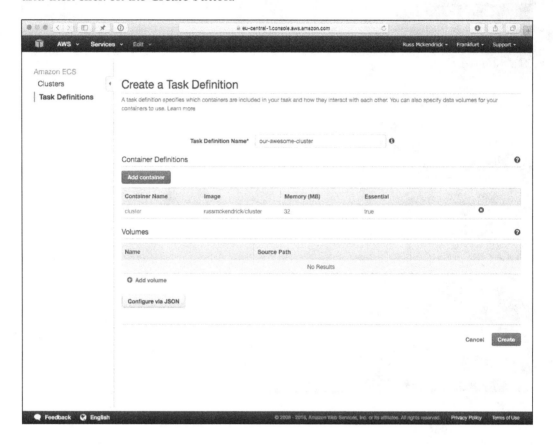

Now that we have our new Task defined, we need to create a Service to attach it to. Click on the **Clusters** tab, then click on the **default** cluster, you should see something similar to the following image:

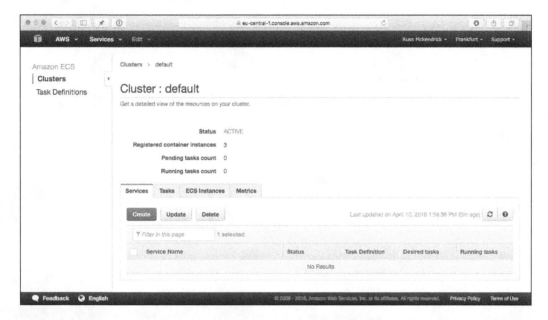

Click on the **Create** button in the **Services** tab. From this screen, fill in the following information:

- **Task Definition**: our-awesome-cluster:1
- **Cluster**: default
- **Service name**: Our-Awesome-Cluster
- **Number of tasks**: 3
- **Minimum healthy percent**: 50
- **Maximum percent**: 200

Also, in the **Optional configurations** section, click on **Configure ELB** button and use the Elastic Load Balancer that was originally configured for the `sample-webapp` service:

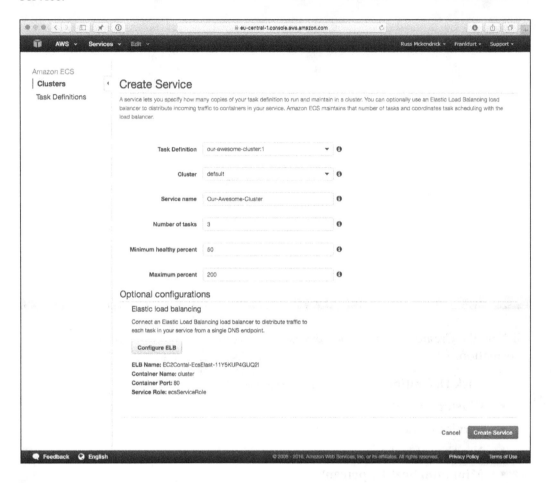

Once you have filled in the information, click on the **Create Service** button. If all goes well, you should see something similar to the following page:

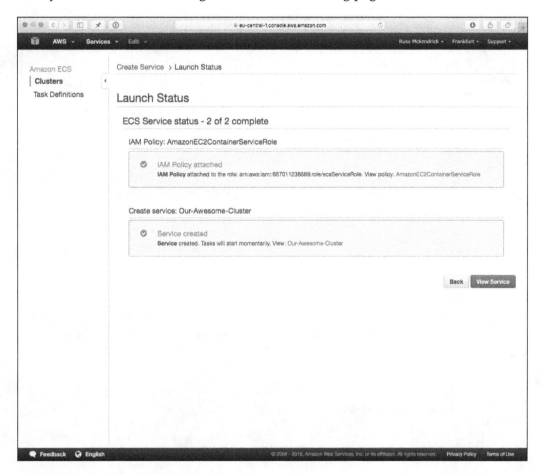

Clicking on **View Service** will give you an overview similar to the one we first saw for the `Sample-Webapp` Service:

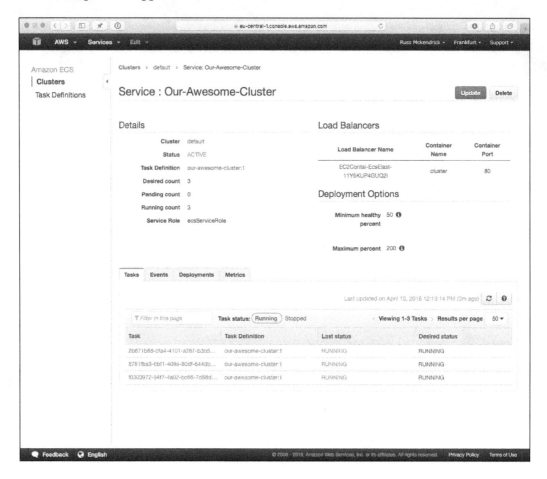

All that's left to do now is to click on **Load Balancer Name** to be taken to the ELB overview page; from here, you will be able to get the URL for the ELB, putting this into a browser should show you our clustered application:

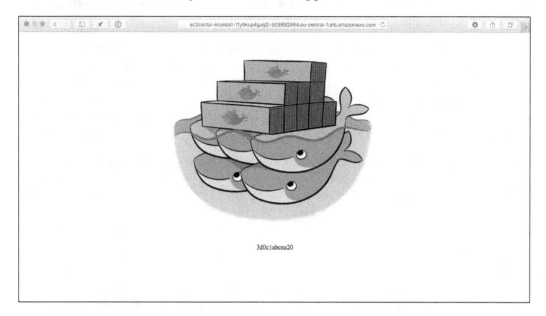

Click refresh a few times and you should see the container's hostname change, indicating that we are being load balanced between different containers.

Rather than launching any more instances, let's terminate our cluster. To do this, go to the **EC2** service in the **Services** menu at the top of the AWS Console.

From here, scroll down to **Auto Scaling Groups** that can be found at the bottom of the left-hand side menu. From here, remove the auto scaling group and then the launch configuration. This will terminate the three EC2 instances that formed our ECS cluster.

Once the instances have been terminated, click on **Load Balancer** and terminate the Elastic Load Balancer.

Finally, go back to the **EC2 Container Service** and delete the default cluster by clicking on the **x**. This will remove the remainder of the resources that were created by us launching the ECS cluster.

Recap

As you can see, Amazon's EC2 Container Service can be run from the web-based AWS Console. There are command tools available, but I won't be covering them here. Why, you might ask?

Well, although the service offering Amazon has built is complete, it feels very much like a product that is in an early alpha stage. The versions of Docker that ship on the Amazon ECS-Optimized Amazon Linux AMI are quite old. The process of having to launch instances outside of the default stack feels very clunky. Its integration with some of the supporting services provided by Amazon is also a very manual process, making it feel incomplete. There is also the feeling that you don't have much control.

Personally, I think the service has a lot of potential; however, in the last 12 months, a lot of alternatives have launched and are being developed at a more rapid pace, meaning that Amazon's ECS service is left feeling old and quite outdated compared to the other services we are looking at.

Rancher

Rancher is a relatively new player, at the time of writing this book, it has only just hit its 1.0 release. Rancher Labs (the developers) describe Rancher (the platform) as:

> *"An open source software platform that implements a purpose-built infrastructure for running containers in production. Docker containers, as an increasingly popular application workload, create new requirements in infrastructure services such as networking, storage, load balancer, security, service discovery, and resource management.*
>
> *Rancher takes in raw computing resources from any public or private cloud in the form of Linux hosts. Each Linux host can be a virtual machine or a physical machine. Rancher does not expect more from each host than CPU, memory, local disk storage, and network connectivity. From Rancher's perspective, a VM instance from a cloud provider and a bare metal server hosted at a colo facility are indistinguishable."* - `http://docs.rancher.com/rancher/`

Rancher Labs also provide RancherOS — a tiny Linux distribution that runs the entire operating system as Docker containers. We will look at that in the next chapter.

Installing Rancher

Rancher needs a host to run on, so let's launch a server in DigitalOcean using Docker Machine:

```
docker-machine create \
    --driver digitalocean \
    --digitalocean-access-token
sdnjkjdfgkjb345kjdgljknqwetkjwhgoih314rjkwergoiyu34rjkherglkhrg0 \
    --digitalocean-region lon1 \
    --digitalocean-size 1gb \
    rancher
```

Rancher runs as a container, so rather than using SSH to connect to the newly launched Docker host, let's configure our local client to connect to the host and then we can launch Rancher:

```
eval $(docker-machine env rancher)
docker run -d --restart=always -p 8080:8080 rancher/server
```

That's it, Rancher will be up and running shortly. You can watch the logs to keep an eye on when Rancher is ready.

First of all, check what the Rancher container is called by running the following command:

```
docker ps
```

In my case, it was `jolly_hodgkin`, so now run the following command:

```
docker logs -f <name of your container>
```

```
russ in
⚡ docker ps
CONTAINER ID        IMAGE             COMMAND              CREATED         STATUS         PORTS                           NAMES
85e42e11d044        rancher/server    "/usr/bin/s6-svscan /"  53 minutes ago  Up 53 minutes  3306/tcp, 0.0.0.0:8080->8080/tcp  jolly_hodgkin
russ in
⚡ docker logs jolly_hodgkin
160410 15:25:36 [Note] /usr/sbin/mysqld (mysqld 5.5.47-0ubuntu0.14.04.1-log) starting as process 29 ...
Uptime: 2  Threads: 1  Questions: 2  Slow queries: 0  Opens: 33  Flush tables: 1  Open tables: 26  Queries per second avg: 1.000
Setting up database
Importing schema
CATTLE_AGENT_PACKAGE_AGENT_BINARIES_URL=/usr/share/cattle/artifacts/agent-binaries.tar.gz
CATTLE_AGENT_PACKAGE_CADVISOR_URL=/usr/share/cattle/artifacts/cadvisor.tar.gz
CATTLE_AGENT_PACKAGE_HOST_API_URL=/usr/share/cattle/artifacts/host-api.tar.gz
CATTLE_AGENT_PACKAGE_NODE_AGENT_URL=/usr/share/cattle/artifacts/node-agent.tar.gz
CATTLE_AGENT_PACKAGE_PYTHON_AGENT_URL=/usr/share/cattle/artifacts/python-agent.tar.gz
CATTLE_AGENT_PACKAGE_RANCHER_DNS_URL=/usr/share/cattle/artifacts/rancher-dns.tar.gz
CATTLE_AGENT_PACKAGE_RANCHER_METADATA_URL=/usr/share/cattle/artifacts/rancher-metadata.tar.gz
CATTLE_AGENT_PACKAGE_RANCHER_NET_URL=/usr/share/cattle/artifacts/rancher-net.tar.gz
CATTLE_CATTLE_VERSION=v0.159.2
CATTLE_DB_CATTLE_DATABASE=mysql
CATTLE_DB_CATTLE_MYSQL_HOST=localhost
CATTLE_DB_CATTLE_MYSQL_NAME=cattle
CATTLE_DB_CATTLE_MYSQL_PORT=3306
```

You should see a lot of log file entries scroll pass, after a while, logs will stop being written. This is a sign that Rancher is ready and you can log in to the web interface. To do this, run the following command to open your browser:

```
open http://$(docker-machine ip rancher):8080/
```

Once open, you should see something similar to the following screenshot:

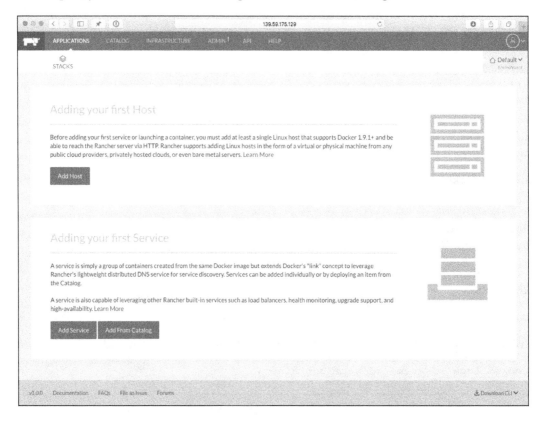

As you can see, we have logged in straight. As this is available on a public IP address, we have better lock the installation down. This is why the red warning icon is next to **Admin** in the top menu is there.

Securing your Rancher installation

As I don't have an Active Directory server configured, I am going to use GitHub to authenticate against my Rancher installation. Just like the installation itself, Rancher Labs have made this a really easy process. First of all, click on **Admin** in the top menu and then **Access Control** in the secondary menu, you will be taken to a screen that allows you to know everything you need in order to configure Rancher to use GitHub as its authentication backend.

For me, this screen looked similar to the following image:

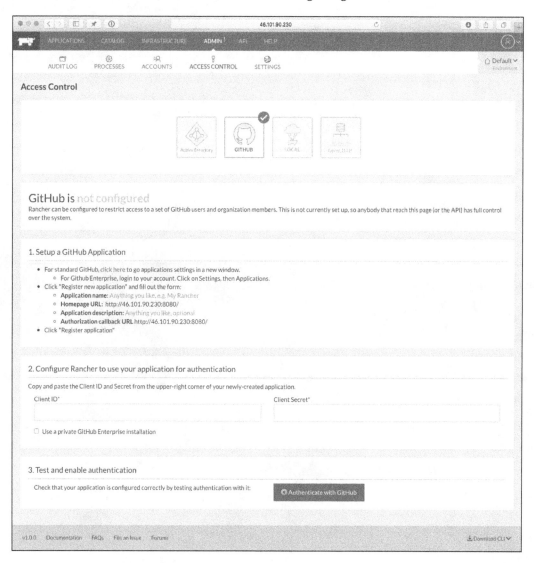

As I have a standard GitHub account rather than the Enterprise installation, all I had to do was click on the link, this took me to a page where I could register my Rancher installation.

This asked for several pieces of information, all of which are provided on the following screen:

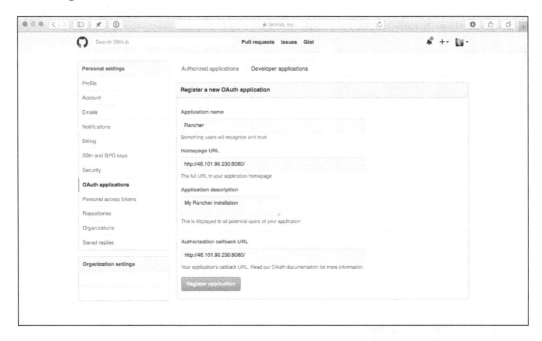

Once I filled in the information, I clicked on **Register application** button. Once the application had been registered, I was taken a page that gave me a Client ID and Client Secret:

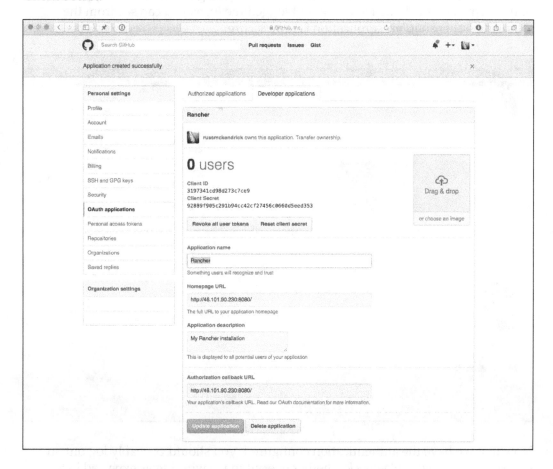

I entered these parameters into appropriate boxes on my Rancher page and then clicked on **Authenticate with GitHub**. This prompted a pop-up window from GitHub asking me to authorize the application. Clicking the **Authorize application** button refreshed the Rancher screen and logged me in, as you can see from the following screenshot, my application is now secure:

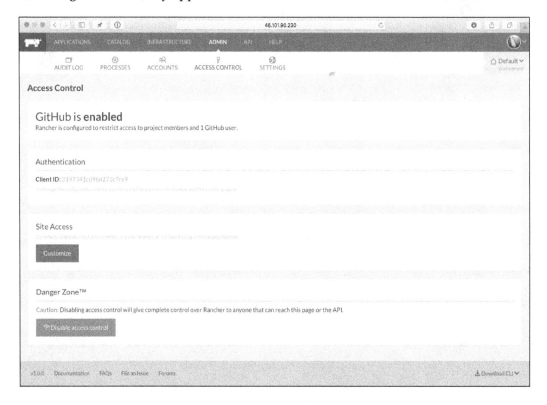

Now that we have the authentication configured, you should probably log out and log back in just to double-check whether everything is working as expected before we move onto the next step. To do this, click on your avatar at the right-hand top of the page and click on **Log Out**.

You will be instantly taken to the following page:

Click on **Authenticate with GitHub** to log back in.

So, why did we log out and then logged back in? Well, next up, we are going to be giving our Rancher installation our DigitalOcean API key so that it can launch hosts, if we hadn't secured our installation before adding this API key, it would mean that anyone could stumble upon our Rancher installation and start launching hosts as they see fit. This, as I am sure you could imagine, could get very expensive.

Cattle cluster

Rancher supports three different schedulers, we have already looked at two of them in both this and the previous chapters. From our Rancher installation, we will be able to launch a Docker Swarm Cluster, Kubernetes cluster, and also Rancher cluster.

For this part of the chapter, we are going to be looking at a Rancher cluster. The scheduler that will be used here is called Cattle. It is also the default scheduler, so we do not need to configure it, all we need to do is add some hosts.

As mentioned in the previous section, we are going to launch our hosts in DigitalOcean; to do this, click on **Add Host** in the **Adding your first Host** section of the front page.

You will be taken to a page with several hosting providers listed at the top, click on DigitalOcean and then enter the following details:

- **Quantity**: I wanted to launch three hosts, so I dragged the slider to 3.
- **Name**: This is how the hosts will appear in my DigitalOcean control panel.
- **Description**: A quick description to be attached to each host.

- **Access Token**: This is my API token, you should have yours from *Chapter 2, The First-party Tools*.

- **Image**: At the moment, only Ubuntu 14.04x64 is supported.

- **Size**: This is the size of the host you would like to launch. Don't forget, the bigger the host, the more money you will pay while the host is online.

- **Region**: Which DigitalOcean data center would you like to launch the hosts in?

I left the remainder of the options at their defaults:

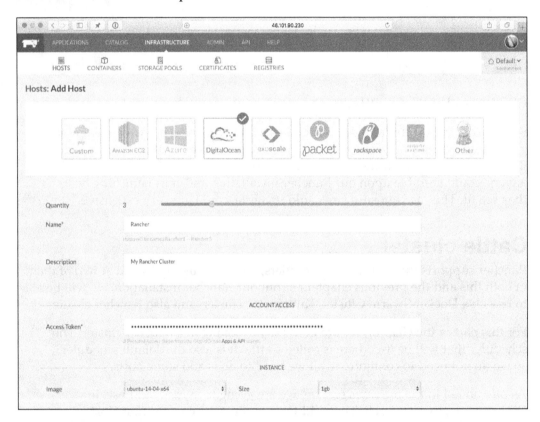

Once I was happy with what I had entered, I clicked on **Create** button. Rancher then, using the DigitalOcean API, went ahead and launched my hosts.

To check the status of the hosts, you should click on **Infrastructure** in the top menu and then **Hosts** in the secondary menu.

Here, you should see the hosts you are deploying, along with their status, which is updating in real time. You should see messages saying the following:

- The host has been launched
- Docker is being installed and configured
- The Rancher agent is being installed and configured

Finally, all three of your hosts are shown as active:

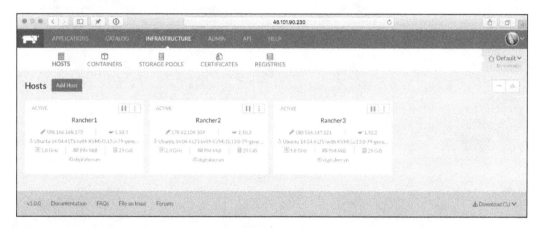

There you have it, your first Cattle cluster. As you can see, so far it has been incredibly easy to install, secure, and configure our first cluster in Rancher. Next up, we need to deploy our containers.

Deploying the Cluster application

As per the previous two schedulers, let's look at deploying our basic cluster application. To do this, click on the **Applications** tab in the top menu, and then click on **Add Service**. There is an option to **Add From Catalog**, we will be looking at this option when we have launched our own application.

On the **Add Service** page, enter the following information:

- **Scale**: `Always run one instance of this container on every host`
- **Name**: `MyClusterApp`
- **Description**: `My really awesome clustered application`
- **Select Image**: `russmckendrick/cluster`

- **Port map**: Add a port map for port 80 just in the **Private port** box

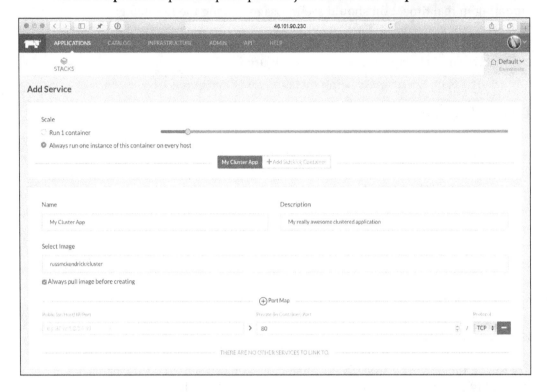

For now, leave the rest of the forms at their default values and click on the **Create** button.

After a few minutes, you should see that your service is active, clicking on the service name will take you a screen that gives you the details on all of the containers running within the service:

So, now that we have our containers running, we really need to be able to access them. To configure a load balancer, click on **Stacks** and then on the downward arrow on our default service:

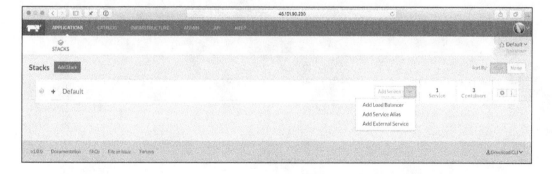

Selecting **Add Load Balancer** from the drop-down menu will take you to a screen that looks similar to the one where we added our cluster application.

Fill in the following details:

- **Scale**: Run 1 container
- **Name**: ClusterLoadBalancer
- **Description**: The Load Balancer for my clustered application
- **Listening Ports**: Source IP/Port 80 Default Target Post 80
- **Target Service**: MyClusterApp

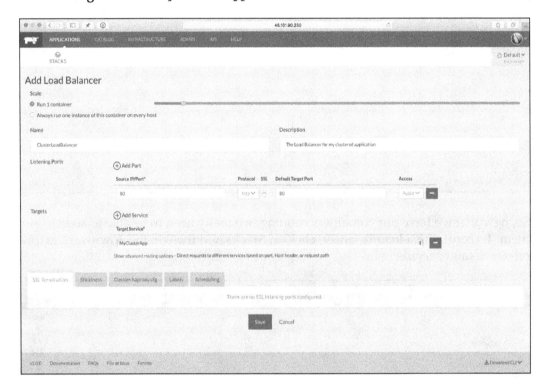

Click on the **Save** button and wait for the service to launch. You will be taken back to the list of services that you have launched, clicking on the information sign next to name of the load balancer will open an information pane at the bottom of the screen. From here, click on the IP address listed in the Ports section:

Your browser should open the now-familiar cluster application page.

Clicking on refresh a few times should change the host name of the container you are being connected to.

What's going on in the background?

One of Rancher's strengths is that there are a lot of tasks, configuration, and process running in the background, which are all hidden by an intuitive and easy-to-use web interface.

To get an idea of what's going on, let's have a look around the interface. To start off with, click on **Infrastructure** in the top menu, and then click on **Hosts**.

As you can see, the running containers are now listed; alongside the containers for our Default stack, there is a network agent container running on each host:

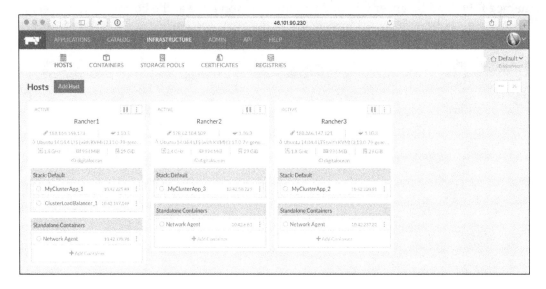

These containers form a network between all three of our hosts using iptables, allowing cross-host connectivity for our containers.

 iptables is a user-space application program that allows a system administrator to configure the tables provided by the Linux kernel firewall (implemented as different Netfilter modules) and the chains and rules it stores:

https://en.wikipedia.org/wiki/Iptables

To confirm this, click on **Containers** button in the secondary menu. You will see a list of the currently running containers, this list should include three containers running our cluster application.

Make a note of the IP address for **Default_MyClusterApp_2** (in my case, it's 10.42.220.91) and then click on **Default_MyClusterApp_1**.

You will be taken to a page that gives you real-time information about the CPU, memory, network, and storage utilization of the container:

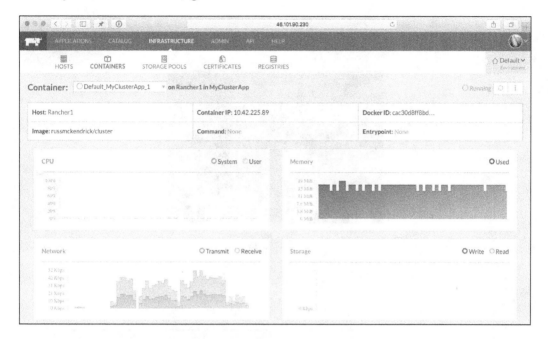

As you can see, the container is currently active on my first Rancher host. Let's get a little more information about the container by connecting to it. At the top right-hand side of the page, where it says **Running**, there is an icon with three dots, click on that, and then select **Execute Shell** from the drop-down menu.

This will open a terminal within your browser to the running container. Try entering some commands such as the following:

```
ps aux
```

```
hostname
```

```
cat /etc/*release
```

Also, while we have the shell open, let's ping our second container that is hosted on another one of our hosts (make sure that you replace the IP address with the one made a note of):

```
ping -c 2 10.42.220.91
```

As you can see, although it is on a different host within our cluster, we are able to ping it without any problems:

Another feature that is useful is Health Check. Let's configure Health Check for our service and then simulate an error.

Click on **Applications** in the top menu, then on the **+** next to our Default stack, this will bring up a list of services that make up the stack. Click on the **MyClusterApp** service to be taken to the overview page.

From here, as we did to access the container shell, click on the icon with the three dots in the top right-hand side, next to where it says **Active**. From the drop-down menu, select **Upgrade**, this will take us to a stripped-down version of the page we filled in to create the initial service.

At the bottom of this page there are several tabs, click on **Health Check** and fill out the following information:

- **Health Check**: HTTP Responds 2xx/3xx
- **HTTP Request**: /index.html
- **Port**: 80
- **When Unhealthy**: Re-create

Leave the rest of the settings as they are and then click on the **Upgrade** button. You will be taken back to the list of services that are in the Default stack, and next to the **MyClusterApp** service, it will say **Upgrading**.

During the upgrade process, Rancher has relaunched our containers with the new configuration. It did this one at a time, meaning that there would have been no downtime as far as people browsing our application would have been concerned.

You may also notice that it says there are six containers, and also that the stack is degraded; to resolve this, click on the **MyClusterApp** service in order to be taken to the list of containers.

As you can see, three of them have a state of Stopped. To remove them, click on the **Finish Upgrade** button, next to where it says **Degraded**, this will remove the stopped containers and return us to a stopped state.

So now that we have a health checking, make sure that each of our containers is serving a web page, let's stop NGINX from running and see what happens.

To do this, click on any of our three containers and then open a console by selecting **Execute Shell** from the drop-down menu.

As our container is running supervised to manage the processes within the container, all we need to do is run the following command to stop NGINX:

```
supervisorctl stop nginx
```

Then we need to kill the NGINX processes; to do this, find out the process IDs by running the following code:

```
ps aux
```

In my case, the PIDs were 12 and 13, so to kill them, I will run the following command:

```
kill 12 13
```

This will stop NGINX, but keep the container up and running. After a few seconds, you will notice that the stats in the background disappear:

Then your console will close, leaving you with something that looks similar to the following screenshot:

Going back to the list of containers for the MyClusterApp service, you will notice that there is a new **Default_MyClusterApp_2** container running under a different IP address:

Rancher has done exactly as we instructed it to, if port 80 on any of our containers stops responding for more than six seconds, it has to fail three checks that are made every 2,000 ms, then remove the container, and replace it with a new one.

The catalog

I am pretty sure that you would have clicked on the **Catalog** item in the top menu, this lists all the pre-built stacks that you can launch within Rancher. Let's look at launching WordPress using the catalog item. To do this, click on **Catalog** and scroll down to the bottom where you will see an entry for WordPress.

WordPress

Click on **View Details** to be taken to a screen where you are able to add a WordPress stack. All it asks is for you to provide a **Name** and **Description** for the stack, fill these in, and click on **Launch**.

This will launch two containers, one running MariaDB and the other running the WordPress container. These containers use the same images from the Docker Hub that we have been launching throughout the book.

If you click on **Stacks** in the secondary menu and then expand the two stacks. Once the WordPress stack is active, you will be able to click on the information icon next to where it says **wordpress**. Like before, this will give the IP address where you can access your WordPress installation:

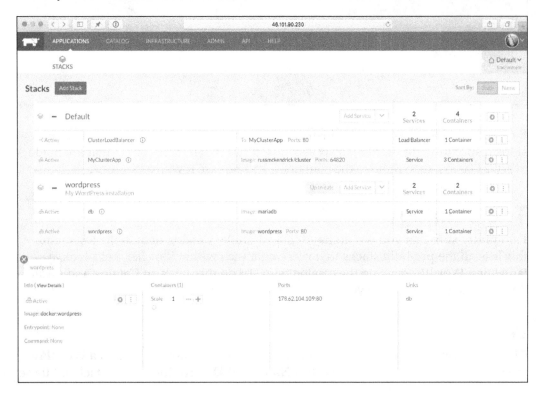

Clicking on it will open a new browser window and you will see a very familiar WordPress installation screen.

Again, Rancher did something interesting here. Remember that we have three hosts in total. One of these hosts is running a container that is acting as a load balancer for our **ClusterApp**, this is bound to port 80 on one of these hosts.

By default, the WordPress catalog stack launches the WordPress container and maps port 80 from the host to port 80 on the container. With no prompting from us, Rancher realized that one of our hosts already has a service bound to port 80, so it didn't even attempt to launch the WordPress container here, instead it chose the next available host without a service mapped to port 80 and launched our WordPress container there.

This is another example of Rancher doing tasks in the background to make the best use of the resources you have launched.

Storage

So far so good with Rancher, let's take a look at how we can add some shared storage to our installation. One of the things that DigitalOcean doesn't provide is block storage, because of which we will need to use a clustered filesystem, as we do not want to introduce a single point of failure within our application.

 Gluster FS is a scalable network filesystem. Using common off-the-shelf hardware, you can create large distributed storage solutions for media streaming, data analysis, and other data and bandwidth-intensive tasks: https://www.gluster.org

As you may have noticed when browsing the catalog, there are several storage items in there that we are going to be looking at GlusterFS to provide our distributed storage:

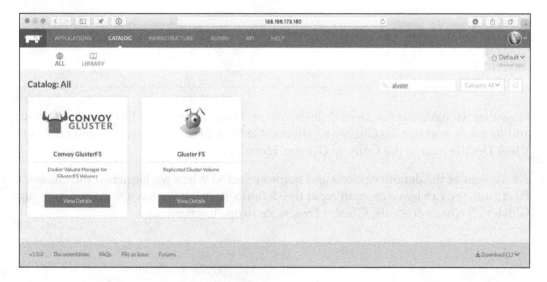

Once we have our Gluster cluster up and running, we will then use Convoy to expose it to our containers. Before we do this, we need to start GlusterFS. To do this, click on **View Details** on the **Gluster FS** catalog item.

You will be taken to a form that details exactly what is going to be configured and how. For our purpose, we can leave all the settings as they are and click on the **Launch** button at the bottom of the page.

It will take a few minutes to launch. When it has completed, you will see that a total of 12 containers have been created. Of these, six of them will be running and the other six will be marked as started. This is not anything to worry about, as they are acting as the volumes for the running containers:

Now that we have our Gluster FS cluster up and running, we need to launch Convoy and let it know about the Gluster FS cluster. Go back to the catalog page and click on **View Details** next to the **Convoy Gluster FS** entry.

As we kept of the default options and names selected when we launched the Gluster FS cluster, we can leave everything at the defaults here, all we have to do is select our Gluster FS cluster from the Gluster FS service drop-down menu.

Once you have made the selection and clicked on **Launch**, it won't take long to download and launch the `convoy-gluster` containers. Once completed, you should have four containers running. As you may have noticed, a new icon for **System** has appeared next to **Stacks** on the secondary menu, this is where you will find your `Convoy Gluster` stack:

So, we now have our distributed storage ready. Before we put it to use, let's look at one more catalog item.

Clustered database

We don't really want to store our database on a shared or distrusted filesystem, one of the other items in the catalog launches a MariaDB Galera Cluster.

Galera Cluster for MySQL is a true Multimaster Cluster based on synchronous replication. Galera Cluster is an easy-to-use, high-availability solution that provides high-system uptime, no data loss, and scalability for future growth:

`http://galeracluster.com/products/`

The cluster will sit behind a load balancer, meaning that your database requests will always be directed to an active master database server. As earlier, click on **View Details** on the **Galera Cluster** item and then fill in the database credentials you wish the cluster to be configured with. These credentials are as follows:

- MySQL Root Password
- MySQL Database Name
- MySQL DB User
- MySQL DB Password

Once filled in, click on the **Launch** button. The cluster will take a few minutes to launch. Once launched, it will contain 13 containers, these make up the cluster and load balancer.

Looking at WordPress again

Now that we have our clustered filesystem configured, and also our clustered database, let's look at launching WordPress again.

To do this, click on **Applications** from the top menu, and then make sure that you are on the **Stacks** page, click on **New Stack**.

From here, give it the name WordPress and then click on **Create**, and now click on **Add Service**. You will need to fill in the following information:

- **Scale**: Run 1 container (we will scale up later)
- **Name**: WordPress
- **Description**: My WordPress cluster
- **Select Image**: wordpress
- **Port Map**: Leave the public port blank and add 80 in the private port
- **Service Links**: **Destination Service** should your galera-lb and the **As Name** galera-lb

We then need to enter the following details on the tabbed options along the bottom:

Command:

- Enviroment Vars: Add the following variables:
    - **Variable** = WORDPRESS_DB_HOST
    - **Value** = galera-lb
    - **Variable** = WORDPRESS_DB_NAME

- ◦ **Value** = The name of the DB you created when setting up Galera
- ◦ **Variable** = WORDPRESS_DB_USER
- ◦ **Value** = The user you created when setting up Galera
- ◦ **Variable** = WORDPRESS_DB_PASSWORD
- ◦ **Value** = The password of the user you created when setting up Galera

Volumes:

- Add a volume as wpcontent:/var/www/html/wp-content/
- Volume Driver: convoy-gluster

Then click on the **Launch** button. It will take a minute to download and start the container, once it has started, you should see the status change to Active. Once you have a healthy service, click on the drop-down menu next to Add Service and add a Load Balancer:

- **Name**: WordPressLB
- **Description**: My WordPress Load Balancer
- **Source IP/Port**: 80
- **Default Target Port**: 80
- **Target Service**: WordPress

Once you have added the Load Balancer, click on the information icon next to the Load Balancer service to get the IP address, open this in your browser and then perform the WordPress installation, and add the featured image as we have done in other chapters.

Now we have a WordPress container up and running with a highly available database backend, which we can move between hosts maintaining the same IP address and content thanks to the load balancer and Gluster FS storage.

DNS

The last catalog item I thought I would cover is one of the DNS managers. What these items do is automatically connect with your DNS provider's API and create DNS records for each of the stacks and services you launch. As I use Route53 to manage my DNS records, I clicked on **View Details** on the **Route53 DNS Stack** on the catalog screen.

In the *Configuration Options* section, I entered the following information:

- **AWS access key**: My access key, the user must have permission to access Route53
- **AWS secret key**: The secret key that accompanies the preceding access key
- **AWS region**: The region I want to use
- **Hosted zone**: The zone I wanted to use was `mckendrick.io`, so I entered that here
- **TTL**: I left this as the default `299 seconds`, if you want a quicker update to your DNS, you should set this to `60 seconds`

Then I clicked on the **Launch** button. After a few minutes, I checked the hosted zone in the Route53 control panel and the service had connected automatically and created the following records for stacks and services I already had running.

The DNS entries are formatted in the following way:

```
<service>.<stack>.<environment>.<hosted zone>
```

So in my case, I had entries for the following:

- `clusterloadbalancer.default.default.mckendrick.io`
- `myclusterapp.default.default.mckendrick.io`

As `myclusterapp` contained three containers, three IP addresses were added to the entry so that round robin DNS would direct traffic to each container:

Another good thing about the DNS catalog items is that they are automatically updated, meaning that if we were to move a container to a different host, the DNS for the container would automatically be updated to reflect the new IP address.

Docker & Rancher Compose

Another thing that you may have noticed is that when you go to add a stack, Rancher gives you two boxes where you can enter the content of a Docker and Rancher Compose file.

So far, we have been creating services manually using the web interface, for each of the stacks we have built up with way you have the option of viewing it as a configuration files.

In the following screenshot, we are looking at the Docker and Rancher compose files for our Clustered Application stack. To get this view, click on the icon to the left of where it says **Active**:

This feature allows you to ship your stacks to other Rancher users. The contents of the preceding files are given in the following so that you can try it on your own Rachner installation.

Docker Compose

This is a standard version one Docker Compose file, there are Rancher settings passed as labels:

```
ClusterLoadBalancer:
  ports:
  - 80:80
  tty: true
  image: rancher/load-balancer-service
  links:
  - MyClusterApp:MyClusterApp
  stdin_open: true
MyClusterApp:
  ports:
  - 60036:80/tcp
  log_driver: ''
  labels:
    io.rancher.scheduler.global: 'true'
    io.rancher.container.pull_image: always
  tty: true
  log_opt: {}
  image: russmckendrick/cluster
  stdin_open: true
```

Rancher Compose

The Rancher Compose file wraps the containers defined in the Docker Compose file in Rancher services, as you can see where we are defining the health checks for both the Load Balancer and Cluster containers:

```
ClusterLoadBalancer:
  scale: 1
  load_balancer_config:
    haproxy_config: {}
  health_check:
    port: 42
    interval: 2000
    unhealthy_threshold: 3
    healthy_threshold: 2
    response_timeout: 2000
MyClusterApp:
  health_check:
    port: 80
    interval: 2000
```

```
initializing_timeout: 60000
unhealthy_threshold: 3
strategy: recreate
request_line: GET "/index.html" "HTTP/1.0"
healthy_threshold: 2
response_timeout: 2000
```

Rancher Compose is also the name of the command-line tool that can locally install to interact with your Rancher installation. As the command line duplicates the functionality, we have already covered, I won't be going into any detail about it here; however, if you would like give it a go, complete details about it can be found in the official Rancher documentation at `http://docs.rancher.com/rancher/rancher-compose/`.

Back to where we started

The last task we are going to do using Rancher is to launch a Kubernetes cluster in DigitalOcean. As mentioned at the start of the chapter, Rancher not only manages its own Cattle clusters, but also Kubernetes and Swarm ones.

To create a Kubernetes cluster, click on the drop-down menu where it says **Environment**, underneath your avatar and click on **Add Environment**:

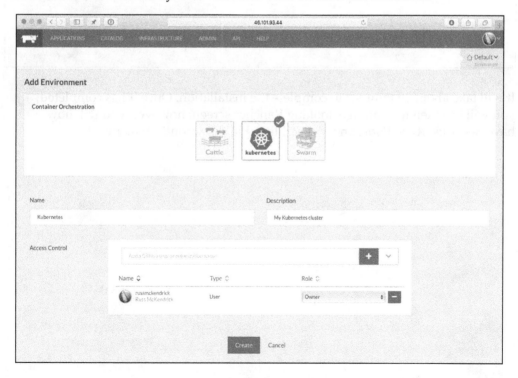

On the page, you will be asked which container-orchestration tool would you like to use for the environment, what it should be called, and finally who should be able to access it.

Select Kubernetes, fill in the remaining information, and click on the **Create** button. Once you have your second environment, you will be able to check between them on the **Environment** drop-down menu.

Similar to when we first launched Rancher, we will need to add some hosts that will make up our Kubernetes cluster. To do this, click on **Add Host** and then enter the details as done earlier, apart from this, time call them Kubernetes rather than Rancher.

You will then be taken to a screen that looks like the following screenshot:

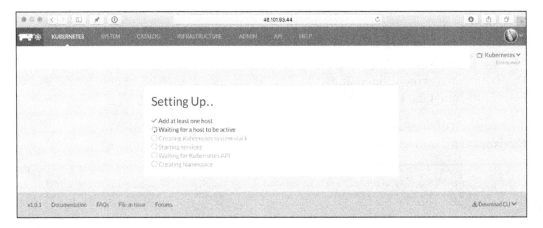

It will take about 10 minutes to complete the installation. Once it has completed, you will be taken to a familiar-looking Rancher screen; however, you will now have **Services**, **RCS**, **Pods**, and **kubectl** listed in the secondary menu.

Clicking on **kubectl** will take you to a page that allows you to run kubectl commands in your browser and also you will get an option to download a kubectl config file so that you can interact with Kubernetes from your local machine as well:

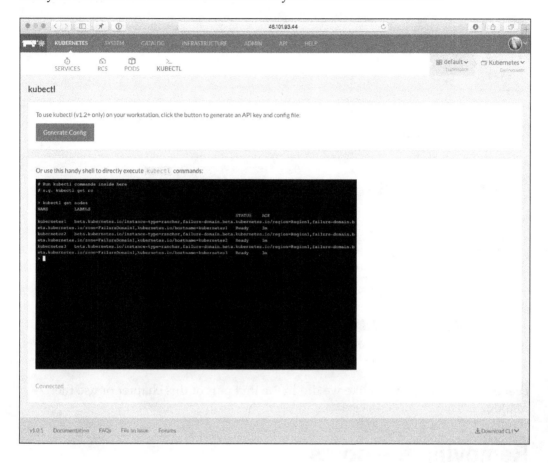

Another thing you will notice is that a different catalog has been loaded, this is because Docker and Rancher Compose files won't work with Kubernetes:

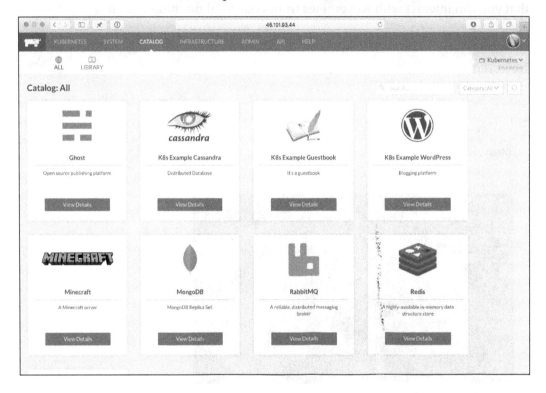

Feel free to launch services like we did in the first part of this chapter or use the catalog items to create a service.

Removing the hosts

At this point, you will have around seven instances launched in DigitalOcean. As we are coming to the end of this chapter, you should terminate all these machines so that you do not get charged for resources you are not using.

I would recommend doing this using the DigitalOcean control panel rather than through Rancher, that way you can be 100% sure that the Droplets have been successfully powered down and removed, meaning that you do not get billed for them.

Summing up Rancher

As you have seen, Rancher is not only an incredibly powerful piece of open source software, it is also extremely user-friendly and well-polished.

We have only touched on some of the features of Rancher here, for example, you can split your hosts between providers to create your own regions, there is a full API that allows you to interact with Rancher from your own applications and also there is a full command-line interface.

For a 1.0 release, it is incredibly feature-rich and stable. I don't think I saw it having any problems during my time using it.

If you want a tool that allows you launch your own clusters and then give end users, such as developers, access to an intuitive interface, then Rancher is going to be a match made in heaven.

Summary

The three tools that we have looked are not the only schedulers available, there are also tools such as the following to name a few:

- **Nomad**: `https://www.nomadproject.io/`
- **Fleet**: `https://coreos.com/using-coreos/clustering/`
- **Marathon**: `https://mesosphere.github.io/marathon/`

All these schedulers have their own requirements, complexities, and use cases.

If you had asked me a year ago which of the three schedulers that we have looked in this chapter would I recommend, I would have said Amazons EC2 Container Service. Kubernetes would have been second and I probably wouldn't have mentioned Rancher.

In the past 12 months, Kubernetes has vastly reduced its complexity when it comes to installing the service has removed its biggest barrier to people adopting it, and as we have demonstrated, Rancher reduces this complexity even further.

Unfortunately, this has left EC2 Container Service feeling like it is a lot more complex to both configure and operate when compared to the other tools, especially as both Kubernetes and Rancher support launching hosts in Amazon Web Services and can take advantage of the myriad of supporting services offer by Amazon's public cloud.

In our next and final chapter, we are going to be reviewing all the tools that we have looked at throughout the previous chapters, we will come up with some use cases as well, and talk about the security considerations that we will need to take when using them.

8
Security, Challenges, and Conclusions

In this, our final chapter, we are going to be looking at all of the tools we have covered in this book and answering the following questions:

- How the tools can affect the security of your Docker installation?
- How they can work together and when should they be used?
- What problems and challenges can the tools be used to resolve?

Securing your containers

So far, we have quite happily been pulling images from the Docker Hub without much thought as to who created them or what is actually installed. This hasn't been too much of a worry as we have been creating ad-hoc environments to launch the containers in.

As we move towards production and resolving the worked in dev problem, it starts to become important to know what it is that you are installing.

Throughout the previous chapters, we have been using the following container images:

- WordPress: `https://hub.docker.com/_/wordpress/`
- MySQL: `https://hub.docker.com/_/mysql/`
- MariaDB: `https://hub.docker.com/_/mariadb/`

All three of these images are classified as official images and have not only been built to a documented standard, they are also peer reviewed at each pull request.

There are then the three images from my own Docker Hub account:

- **Consul:** `https://hub.docker.com/r/russmckendrick/consul/`
- **NGINX:** `https://hub.docker.com/r/russmckendrick/nginx/`
- **Cluster Example:** `https://hub.docker.com/r/russmckendrick/cluster/`

Before we look at the official images, let's take a look at the Consul image from my own Docker Hub account and why it is safe to trust it.

Docker Hub

Here, we are going to look at the three types of images that can be downloaded from the Docker Hub.

I have chosen to concentrate on the Docker Hub rather than private registries as the tools we have been looking at the previous chapters all pull from the Docker Hub, and it is also more likely that you or your end users will use the Docker Hub as their primary resource for their image files.

Dockerfile

The Consul container image is built using a Dockerfile, which is publically accessibly on my GitHub account. Unlike images that are pushed, more on this later in the chapter, it means that you can exactly see action has been taken to build the image.

Firstly, we are using the `russmckendrick/base` image as our starting point. Again, the Dockerfile for this image is publicly available, so let's look at this now:

```
### Dockerfile
#
#    See https://github.com/russmckendrick/docker
#
FROM alpine:latest
MAINTAINER Russ McKendrick <russ@mckendrick.io>
RUN apk update && apk upgrade && \
    apk add ca-certificates bash && \
    rm -rf /var/cache/apk/*
```

As you can see, all this does is:

- Uses the latest version of the official Alpine Linux image
- Runs an `apk update` and then `apk upgrade` to ensure that all the packages are updated
- Installs the `ca-certificates` and `bash` packages
- Cleans up any artifacts left over from the upgrade and installation of the packages

So, now that we know what the base image looks like, let's move onto the Dockerfile for the Consul container:

```
### Dockerfile
#
#   See https://github.com/russmckendrick/docker
#
FROM russmckendrick/base:latest
MAINTAINER Russ McKendrick <russ@mckendrick.io>
ENV CONSUL_VERSION 0.6.4
ENV CONSUL_SHA256
abdf0e1856292468e2c9971420d73b805e93888e006c76324ae39416edcf0627
ENV CONSUL_UI_SHA256
5f8841b51e0e3e2eb1f1dc66a47310ae42b0448e77df14c83bb49e0e0d5fa4b7
RUN  apk add --update wget \
  && wget -O consul.zip https://releases.hashicorp.com/
consul/${CONSUL_VERSION}/consul_${CONSUL_VERSION}_linux_amd64.zip \
  && echo "$CONSUL_SHA256 *consul.zip" | sha256sum -c - \
  && unzip consul.zip \
  && mv consul /bin/ \
  && rm -rf consul.zip \
  && cd /tmp \
  && wget -O ui.zip https://releases.hashicorp.com/consul/${CONSUL_
VERSION}/consul_${CONSUL_VERSION}_web_ui.zip \
  && echo "$CONSUL_UI_SHA256 *ui.zip" | sha256sum -c - \
  && unzip ui.zip \
  && mkdir -p /ui \
  && mv * /ui \
  && rm -rf /tmp/* /var/cache/apk/*
EXPOSE 8300 8301 8301/udp 8302 8302/udp 8400 8500 8600 8600/udp
VOLUME [ "/data" ]
ENTRYPOINT [ "/bin/consul" ]
CMD [ "agent", "-data-dir", "/data", "-server", "-bootstrap-expect",
"1", "-ui-dir", "/ui", "-client=0.0.0.0"]
```

As you can see, there is a little more going on in this Dockerfile:

1. We will define that we are using the latest version of `russmckendrick/base` as our base image.
2. Then, we will set three environment variables. Firstly, the version of Consul we want to download, and then the checksum for the files, which we will grab from a third-party website.
3. We will then install the `wget` binary using the APK package manager.
4. Next up, we will download the Consul binaries from the HashiCorp website, notice that we are downloading over HTTPS and that we are running `sha256sum` against the downloaded file to check whether it is has been tampered with. If the file doesn't pass this test, then the build will fail.
5. Once the zip file is confirmed to be the correct one, we uncompress it and copy the binary in place.
6. We will then do the same actions again for the Consul web interface.
7. Finally, we will configure some default actions of when the container is launched by exposing the correct port, entry point, and default command.

All of this means that you can see exactly what is installed and how the image is configured before you make the decision to download a container using the image.

Official images

There are are just over 100 images that are flagged as official. You view these in the Docker Hub at `https://hub.docker.com/explore/`. Official images are easy to spot as they are not preceded by a username, for example, the following are the docker pull lines for the official NGINX image and also my own:

```
docker pull nginx
docker pull russmckendrick/nginx
```

As you can see, the top one is the official image.

A lot of the official images are maintained by the upstream providers, for example, the CentOS, Debian, and Jenkins images are maintained by members of the respective projects:

*   `https://github.com/docker-library/official-images/blob/master/library/centos`
*   `https://github.com/docker-library/official-images/blob/master/library/debian`
*   `https://github.com/docker-library/official-images/blob/master/library/jenkins`

Also, there is a review process for each pull request submitted. This helps in ensuring that each official image is both consistent and built with security in mind.

The other important thing to note about official images is that no official image can be derived from, or depend on, non-official images. This means that there should be no way a non-official image's content can find its way into an official image.

A full detailed explanation on the build standards for official images, as well details of what is expected of an official image maintainer can be found in the Docker Library GitHub page at `https://github.com/docker-library/official-images/`.

The downside of Docker Hub is that it can sometimes be slow, and I mean really slow. The situation has improved over the past 12 months, but there have been times when Docker's build system has had a big backlog, meaning that your build is queued.

This is only a problem if you need to trigger a build and want it immediately available, which could be a case if you need to quickly fix this application bug before anyone notices.

Pushed images

Finally, there is an elephant in the room, the complete images, which have been pushed from a user to their Docker Hub.

Personally, I try to avoid pushing complete images to my Docker Hub account, as they are something I would typically not recommend using, so why would I expect other users to use them?

As these images are not being built by a published Dockerfile, it is difficult to get an idea of the standard they have built to and exactly what they contain.

Docker has tried to address this by introducing content trust to the Docker Hub, what this does is sign the image before it is pushed to the Docker Hub with the publisher's private key. When you download the image, the Docker Engine uses the publisher's public key to verify that the content of the image is exactly how the publisher intended it to be.

This helps to ensure that the image has not been tampered with at any point of the image's journey from the publisher to you running the container.

More information on Content Trust can be found at `https://docs.docker.com/engine/security/trust/content_trust/`.

This is useful if you are using the Docker Hub to publish private images that contain propriety applications or code bases you do want to be publically available.

However, for publically available images, I would always question why the image had to be pushed to the Docker Hub rather than being built with a Dockerfile.

Docker Cloud

Since the time I started writing this book, Docker has introduced a commercial service called Docker Cloud. This service is described as a hosted service for Docker container management and deployment by Docker.

You can find details of the service at the following URLs:

- `https://www.docker.com/products/docker-cloud`
- `https://cloud.docker.com/`

So, why mention this service when we are talking about security? Well, in May 2016, Docker announced that they are adding a Security Scanning feature, which, at the time of writing this book, is free of charge.

This feature works with your Private Repositories hosted on the Docker Hub, meaning that any images you have pushed can be scanned.

The service performs a static analysis on your images, looking for known vulnerabilities in the binaries you have installed.

For example, in *Chapter 6*, *Extending Your Infrastructure*, we created an image using Packer, I still had an old build of this image on my local machine, so I pushed it to a private Docker Hub repository and took advantage of the free trial of both Docker Cloud and Docker Security Scanning.

As you can see from the following result, the service has found three critical vulnerabilities in the image:

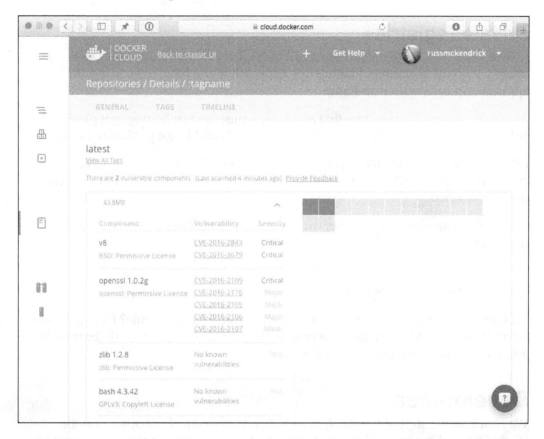

This means that it is time to update my base image and the version of NodeJS being used.

More details on the service and how it works can be found in the following announcement blog post:

`https://blog.docker.com/2016/05/docker-security-scanning/`

There are a few alternatives to this service, such as:

- **Clair**: `https://github.com/coreos/clair`
- **Banyan Collector**: `https://github.com/banyanops/collector`
- **The Docker Bench for Security**: `https://github.com/docker/docker-bench-security`

However, the newly launched Docker service is the simplest one to get started with, as it already has deep level of integration with other Docker services.

Private registries

Remember that it is possible to use a private registry to distribute your Docker images. I would recommend taking this approach if you have to bundle your application's code within an image.

A private registry is a resource that allows you push and pull images; typically, it is only available to trusted hosts within your network and is not publically available.

Private registries do not allow you to host automated builds and they do not currently support content trust, this is why they are deployed on private or locked down networks.

More information on hosting your own private registry can be found at the official documentation at `https://docs.docker.com/registry/`.

The challenges

So, why have we been looking at extending the core Docker Engine? Here are a few scenarios that the tools we have covered in the previous chapters could be used to add value or resolve a potential problem.

Development

Way back, at the start of *Chapter 1, Introduction to Extending Docker*, we saw the *Worked fine in dev, Ops problem now* meme and how it is worryingly still relevant today. Containers go a long way to resolve this issue; in fact, Docker is seen as a great unifier by a lot of people.

However, if developers do not have a way of easily introducing these tools into their day-to-day lives, then you are not resolving the issue raised by the meme.

The tools that could help developers start to use Docker locally as the first step of the development process are as follows:

- Docker Toolbox
- Docker Machine
- Vagrant

Along with the recently announced, but currently in private beta, native versions of Docker for OS X and Windows, more details on this can be found in the announcement blog post at `https://blog.docker.com/2016/03/docker-for-mac-windows-beta/`.

Additionally, depending on your existing workflows, you could also use the following tools to introduce containers to your existing workflows:

- Ansible
- Jenkins
- Packer
- Puppet

Staging

Depending on your requirements, you could use the following plugins in conjunction with Docker Compose to create a basic staging environment with multi-host networking and storage:

- Convoy
- Docker overlay network
- Docker Volumes
- Flocker
- REX-Ray
- Weave

You can also use these tools to give you a good level of control over where the containers are deployed within your staging environment:

- Ansible
- Docker Swarm
- Jenkins
- Puppet
- Rancher

Additionally, your developers could have some level of access in order to be able to deploy a test version using these tools either via continuous integration tools, web interfaces, or via command line.

Production

Again, you could use the following plugins to create a basic production-ready environment using Docker Compose:

- Convoy
- Docker Overlay Network
- Docker Volumes
- Flocker
- REX-Ray
- Weave

However, you will probably want your production environment to look more after itself in terms of reacting to failure, scaling events, and automatic registration of containers with services such as DNS and Load Balancers:

- Ansible
- Amazon ECS
- Docker Swarm
- Kubernetes
- Puppet
- Rancher

All these listed tools should be considered production-ready. However, as Puppet and Ansible offer little in the way of scheduling, you should only really consider them if you are introducing Docker into an existing Puppet or Ansible-managed environment.

If there is one thing I hope you have taken from this book, it is that there doesn't have to be one size fits all when it comes to using Docker.

As we discussed, there are tools supplied by both Docker and third parties that allow you scale your containers from a single host to potentially hundreds or thousands.

Summary

In the previous chapters, we experienced using combinations of the tools together.

For example, we have been using both Docker Storage and Network plugins to create a highly available WordPress installation using both the tools provided by Docker themselves, that is, Docker Compose and Docker Swarm, as well Kubernetes and Rancher.

We also deployed our underlying Docker infrastructure using Docker Machine, Ansible, as well as tools such as Kubernetes and Rancher.

Then, we deployed various first-party and third-party plugins to help with storage, networking, and features such as load balancing to take full advantage of the environment that we have been deploying to, such as Amazon Web Service and DigitalOcean.

All the tools that we have looked at compliment the core Docker Engine, and in most cases, there is little or no change needed to be made to your Docker images to start using the plugins or third-party tools.

All of this means that it is relatively easy to build a highly available, yet easy to use platform to deploy your applications into whether you are using a public cloud, your own virtual machines, bare metal servers, or just your local laptop, and tailor it to your developers, application, and your own needs, all while ensuring that if it worked in development, it will work in production.

Index

Etcd
  URL 111

F

Fig
  URL 52
Flocker
  about 90, 146, 147
  deploying 99-104
  features 90, 91
  installing 91
  setting up 91-98
  summing up 105, 106
  URL 59

G

Galera Cluster
  about 285
  URL 285
Gluster FS
  about 283
  URL 283
Go
  about 148
  URL 148
Grafana 240-242

H

Homebrew
  about 166
  URL 166

I

ImageLayers
  URL 194
images
  best practices, for building 196
  building, with application 185
  building, with Docker 185-188
  building, with Packer 188-191
  packaging 185

iptables
  about 276
  URL 276

J

JavaScript Object Notation (JSON) 189
Jenkins
  application, creating 203
  environment, preparing 197-202
  pipeline, creating 203-212
  URL 153
  using 213
  with Docker 196, 197
Jenkins 2.0
  URL 196

K

Kibana
  URL 243
Kubernetes
  about 215
  advantages 247
  application, launching 222-226
  cluster, destroying 246
  features 216
  installing 217-222
  principles 216
  supporting tools 237
  URL 215
  WordPress stack, launching 226
Kubernetes Dashboard 238-240
KVM
  URL 4

L

Learning VM
  URL 165
Logstash
  URL 243
Loopback Device
  about 74
  reference 74

M

MariaDB
    URL 297
Moby Counter
    URL 185
multi-host networking, with overlays
    about 110
    Consul 120, 121
    Discovery, launching 111-113
    multi-host networks, composing 121-125
    overlay network, adding 116, 117
    overlay network, using 117-119
    summing up 125
    Swarm, readying 113-115
MySQL
    URL 297

N

Network Driver Plugins
    URL 151
network, weaving
    about 125
    cluster, configuring 126-128
    Docker Compose, and Weave 131-133
    Swarm, calling off 135
    Weave, configuring 128-130
    Weave, installing 128-130
    Weavemesh Driver 135-144
    Weave Scope 133
NGINX
    URL 298

O

official images
    about 300, 301
    references 300
    URL 301
overlay network
    reference link 110

P

Packer
    about 188
    images, building 188-191
    URL 153, 189
    versus Docker Build 191-195
plugin
    about 148
    activation 150
    API calls, handling 150, 151
    discovering 148, 149
    starting 149
plugin service
    writing 151
power supply units (PSU) 15
private registries
    about 304
    URL 304
production environment
    creating 306
provisioner, Vagrant
    about 177-180
    Ansible 177
    Chef 177
    Docker 177
    File 177
    Puppet 177
    Shell 177
Puppet
    best practices 165
    Docker, using with 156-163
    example 164, 165
    URL 153
    using 154, 155
    versus Ansible 175, 176
Puppet Forge
    URL 164
Puppet Open Source Docs
    URL 165
pushed images 301

R

Rancher
about 262
advantages 295
catalog 281
Cattle cluster 269-271
Cluster application, deploying 271-275
Cluster application, executing 275-281
hosts, removing 294
installation, securing 265-269
installing 263, 264
Kubernetes cluster, launching 291-294
URL 262
Rancher compose file
about 289, 290
URL 291
REX-Ray
about 146
reference 59
URL 146

S

software-defined network (SDN) 15
staging environment
creating 305
supporting tools, Kubernetes
cluster tools 245
ELK 242-244
Grafana 240-242
Kubernetes Dashboard 238-240

T

third party plugins
about 145
commonalities 147
Convoy 145, 146
Flocker 146, 147
REX-Ray 146
Weave 147
third party volume drivers
about 72, 73

containers, launching with
    Convoy volume 75-77
Convoy backups, restoring 80, 81
Convoy, installing 74
Convoy snapshot, backing up 78-80
Convoy, summing up 82
REX-Ray, installing 83-87
REX-Ray, summing up 90
REX-Ray volume, moving 88, 89
snapshot, creating with Convoy 77, 78
volumes, blocking with REX-Ray 82
tools
need for 153, 154
used, at development process 304
used, for creating production
    environment 306
used, for creating staging environment 305
used, for resolving challenges 304

V

Vagrant
about 176
URL 153
with provisioner 177-180
Vagrant Docker provider 180-184
VirtualBox
URL 44
VMware vSphere
URL 4
Volume Driver Plugins
URL 151
Volume Hub token
URL 95

W

Weave
about 147
configuring 129, 130
installing 128
reference link 109, 144
summarizing 144